The
Good Line

Robert Young

The Good Line
Copyright © 2020 by Robert Young

All rights reserved. No part of this book, including icons and images, may be reproduced in any manner without prior written permission from the copyright holder, except where noted in the text and in the case of brief quotations embodied in critical articles and reviews.

Printed in the United States of America

I want to dedicate this book to my parents because they taught me the fundamentals of life: to work hard and treat people right.

My dad passed away from a long battle with cancer in 2017. The last time he stood on his two feet, he hugged me as tight as he could and said, "Son, I am so proud of you."

I'm certain he is smiling down on me, guiding me every day, and helping me tell my story.

The price we pay is well worth
holding on to our dignity.

- Frank Serpico

Letter to the Reader

The intention of this book is to shed light on an elite unit of detectives whose work fell victim to political interference within the Metro Nashville Police Department. In the face of adversity, my team was able to overcome roadblocks and excel to a level beyond our expectations, making irreplaceable memories along the way. But, just as in every profession, there are a few bad apples that can ruin the bunch.

I served as a police officer and detective with the Metro Nashville Police Department from September 2007 to March 2018. Each new position I took was a stepping stone to something greater. My journey began in the position of patrol like all officers, but soon enough I had joined a Crime Suppression Unit and then moved to the Specialized Investigations Division Narcotics Unit. My ultimate goal was to join the 20th Judicial District Drug Task Force so I could focus on large-scale drug trafficking organizations and Title III wiretaps. It took me six years to get on the Task Force, and this book spans some of that time period from March 2014 to September 2015. After getting my dream job, I never could have guessed that I would have spent more time climbing the ladder than I would in that spot.

These pages are filled with my personal knowledge, opinions, and recollections of the events described as I experienced them. Intercepted calls have been summarized and shortened, and any excerpts of documents are from my personal archives or can be found online as public media releases. Dialogue is not intended to represent a word-for-word transcription of what was said, but it accurately reflects my memory and fairly reconstructs the meaning and substance of what was said. The essential sentiments and timeline of events have remained intact. A Book Key has been included in the Appendix as a reference for coded words and speech used by both my team and our targets.

In the spirit of confidentiality, all identifying information for characters and places has been changed or shortened for both places and people to protect identities and preserve the integrity of the case.

As any individual within an institution may experience, sometimes telling the truth is discouraged and sometimes it is even dangerous. I was trained to obey a chain of command structured around closed-door political alliances, but I decided it would compromise my integrity to keep my mouth shut. It is in my identity and genetics to right what is wrong and to always uphold the truth. With all this in mind, I decided to write my story down and share the truth with others.

Thank you to those who taught, supported, and encouraged me every step of the way. To the public servants who give their all every single day, thank you.

Robert Young

MARCH 2014

1

"You hear back about the position, yet?"

"Not yet."

"Well, you'll get it," my dad said. "You've worked hard and have the right experience. You have as good a chance as anyone else."

I leaned against the patio table outside the windowless cinderblock building and shifted my phone to my other ear, tossing my newly cleaned Atlanta Braves jersey over my other shoulder. "Yeah, James says it's only a matter of time before the results come in. Paperwork just takes so much time. It's all paperwork and politics, you know."

"Oh, I know." My dad snorted. He wasn't bitter about his own experience, but he understood all too well the politics within the police department.

"Yeah." I kicked at the table leg and looked towards the gray door at the edge of the long gray building. It wasn't inspiring, but I loved the work I did. My whole life I'd watched my dad fight crime, and now I was actively getting drugs off the streets and bringing criminals to justice. As much as I wanted to get started on my current cases for the day, the dread of facing my boss Sergeant Richard Bagg kept me outside in the chilly morning wind.

As if reading my mind my dad asked, "So, how is Sergeant Dick holding up?"

I laughed at the nickname. Even after two years of working at the Specialized Investigations Division under Sgt. Bagg, my dad calling him "Dick" still hadn't gotten old. "Well, he snaps at me and everyone else constantly, and he's moping around the office saying he may as well just retire. He just can't get over the fact that James was promoted to the

Drug Task Force and not him, but Sgt. Cox has a spotless record and Bagg doesn't. What goes around—"

"Comes around," my dad finished. "That's right. Sgt. James Cox is a fine man and deserved the promotion. He'll do well in the 20th, and so will you."

I smiled. I hadn't been offered the job yet and couldn't get too hopeful, even if James had all but guaranteed I'd get the detective position. I'd spent the past six years climbing the ladder, working hard to become a detective, and now that my dream job of being on the 20th Judicial District Drug Task Force was almost within reach it felt too good to be true. But, James had been a mentor figure to me for most of my years as an officer, and I knew I could trust him. Sgt. Bagg, on the other hand, had a shifty way about him. Even if I got the position, I knew Sgt. Bagg would do everything in his power to make my transition as difficult as he could.

I said, "Well, I should probably head on in. Hopefully I can avoid Sgt. Bagg for most of the morning and get some real work done."

"Good luck, son. We'll be seeing you and Danielle at Sunday dinner, right?"

"Yeah, we'll see you then."

"Have a good day."

"You too, Dad. Talk to you tomorrow probably."

"Looking forward to it."

We hung up just as a car pulled into a parking space beside Sgt. Bagg's car. I always came early before most of the office, but sometimes Sgt. Bagg would beat me in. Then it was just the matter of getting to my office without him intercepting me.

I entered the kitchen and instead of walking straight down the main hall to my desk, which led me right past Sgt. Bagg's open office door, I weaved my way down the back hallway, around the back wall of Sgt. Bagg's office, and slipped into my shared office space. It was extra effort and time, but it was worth avoiding seeing him for as long as possible.

I hung my Braves jersey on the back of my chair and adjusted it so the number 10 and the name Jones was centered. Most guys had large t-shirts or button-down casual shirts on the backs of their chairs to put on when they needed to leave in a hurry to go undercover or for surveillance, but I always used Chipper Jones as my cover.

My desk was piled with papers and sticky notes about past and present cases. My coworker and friend Adam Bristol frequently joked that all the information exposed on my desk was also somehow encrypted by it being a mess. Adam also said I had a mind like a hard drive and would frequently ask me if I remembered details and names from cases many years back. It didn't bother me because I knew where everything was, both on my desk and in my head, and if someone asked me for information or a document I could find it within seconds. Adam's desk was right next to mine and was so spotless and meticulously organized that sometimes I would shift some of my papers or sticky notes to his desk just to see his reaction.

Right as I settled in at my desk, I received a text message from a confidential informant named Charlie asking me to give him a call. Like most informants, Charlie was working off charges by helping the police.

I had met Charlie a few years prior in 2011 when one of my pharmacist connections tipped me off to a patient paying cash for a few prescriptions. I followed the guy to West Nashville to a gas station where he did a hand-to-hand transaction, and then when he pulled away from the deal, he drove across the street to where I was sitting and he parked right next to my car. I knocked on his window, showed him my badge, and told him I was Metro Police and that I'd seen the whole deal go down. I had no idea what he'd received, but I told him to hand it over before I hauled him to jail. I was surprised when he pulled out an ounce of cocaine, and I told him so. "This is a lot of cocaine, dude. You can go to jail for a long time for twenty-eight grams. Now, I can bring you in for this, or you can help me bring that dealer in."

Charlie readily agreed to help, but I knew how flaky informants could be. Nine out of ten times the criminal will say they'll work and maybe one of them would actually end up being of any help. Being criminals, most informants can't really be trusted, but Charlie was different from most informants. He was reliable, provided consistently solid information, and he never tried to disappear on me. He ended up setting up the dealer, and the case was closed with a decent haul. He still owed me, though, and I had talked with him recently to see about bringing someone else in. I knew he was motivated by the fact that he had a family that he didn't want to disappoint by going back to jail.

I clicked through to call him. "Charlie, hey, sup man?"

"Hey, man, I got a guy. I think he's a big distributor, and I've known him for a long time, but I ain't never worked with him before."

"That's great. What do you know about him?"

"He's an old white guy out in Bellevue, a fishing guide named Nathaniel Richardson. I think he's a pretty big fish if you know what I mean, and he works for some even bigger fish."

I was skeptical as I didn't immediately recognize the name, but I said, "Okay, great. Let me get back to you on scheduling a deal."

After we hung up, I did some research. An old white guy who worked as a fishing guide did not fit the typical mold of a drug dealer. When I pulled up Richardson's criminal history report, though, my mind was changed. Nearly all his charges were cocaine related. I realized Charlie wasn't just full of shit, and he might actually have been on to something.

"Morning." Adam said as he sat down to his immaculate desk. "You hear about the 20th yet?"

"Not yet."

"Man, you're writing *another* sticky note?"

I swiveled my chair so Chipper faced him in reply, and Adam laughed. We'd been in the academy together, and we took to each other from the beginning because of our similar work ethics, morals, and values. Ever since we met, we had each other's backs and were a dynamite duo who could tackle anything. We'd literally tackled guys together to bring them in. Adam was simultaneously the most easygoing guy I knew but also the most obsessive compulsive, which probably had a lot to do with his being in the Air Force. He kept a pressed button-down on the back of his chair, and even the rug under his desk was spotless. The military's organized systems and lifestyle was ingrained in him, and I had a lot of respect for that. I just preferred my Braves jersey that harkened back to my childhood baseball days and my desk of chaos that only my brain could understand.

The only thing I couldn't understand about Adam's cleanliness and organization was why he kept the old, standard chair assigned to his desk when he joined the Specialized Investigations Division, or SID as we called it. The chair was in decent shape, but the fabric was darkened on the seat from many years of use. The first thing I did when I transferred to SID was order myself a new, pleather swivel chair. Many hours of police work are spent sitting at a desk doing paperwork, and I wanted to be comfortable. Plus, I didn't want a chair with mysterious stains or a long history of police asses.

"Hey," Adam said, and I turned back towards him. He lowered his voice so our office mates wouldn't hear him, "You seen Bagg today?"

"Hell no, thankfully."

"Well, he was acting normal when I went by his office. Could be a good sign."

"Could be. But 'normal' is not exactly a good thing either." We smiled at each other in a grim way. Even though the mopey Bagg was annoying, at least he stuck mostly to his office and communicated with cold scowls. Anytime someone talked to him he'd bring up how he may as well be retiring soon anyway now that the 20th chose "a guy like Cox," which, whenever I heard it, made me roll my eyes. Going back to "normal" Bagg meant we'd be seeing a lot more of the cocky, loud, domineering Bagg that took strolls through the office to hover and chat and allow officers to schmooze. The normal Bagg was insufferable.

Even though we'd kept our voices low, Derek from the across the room must have heard us as he walked by to his desk. He said, "Bobby, you better shut your mouth before Bagg hears what you say about him."

I grimaced. "Derek, you better sit down and mind your own damn business."

A couple guys in our shared office snickered. I heard Derek laugh, too and say, "Boy's got no respect," before sitting heavily into his squeaky chair, already having shrugged off my comment because of his easygoing nature. I eyed Adam and he grinned.

Derek had been in the Specialized Investigations Division for years, longer than even Bagg had been sergeant of the team, and he was the kind of officer that was going nowhere fast and fine with it. He was generally well-liked by everyone because he was always ready to make a joke or cut up with anyone else looking to take a break from the actual work. Adam said he was probably good for the team's culture and morale, and it was clear Sgt. Bagg liked him around, even if Derek wasn't exactly productive. For instance, after our exchange, he sat at his desk for only ten minutes before I heard the squeak and knew he had left the room again to roam the office. Some days I kept a mental tally of how much time Derek spent gossiping, wandering the building, making personal phone calls, and taking two-hour lunch breaks. Derek spent twice as much of his workday dicking around as he did the minimal required work to coast through life.

I'd noticed others worked like this, too, which was not how I pictured a job with Metro. I had wanted to be part of the Metro Nashville Police Department because I thought its size meant there would be more accountability and more rewards for doing the best job possible. From what I had seen, though, people wanted to work for Metro for the status and free food. They could be complacent like Derek and ride out their whole career with minimum work requirements. It didn't affect or change how I planned on working, though. I was there to get real work done.

On my first day on the SID team, Derek had walked me through the building to show me the other teams sharing the building: the gang units, prostitution and gambling unit, and security threats unit. He was older than everyone else on the SID team, but he walked with the swagger of a college frat boy and had his arm around my shoulder like he was my older brother. I was idealistic and starry-eyed to be joining the elite SID team because I knew this was where I could do some meaningful work getting drugs off the street. I thought Derek was about to take me under his wing and show me the ropes of this do-good department. Instead, Derek gave me the first taste of the reality of the job when he launched into a long-winded talk about the importance of sticking to the chain of command and how detectives and officers have silver badges and sergeants and above have gold. All of this had been drilled into me and every other recruit in the academy, so I didn't understand at first what he was really saying.

"Life's a lot easier for everyone if you keep the gold badges happy, you know what I mean? It's important to always pay your due respect in order to keep the peace."

I didn't ask the question going through my head: *Are you telling me to kiss gold badge ass?*

Derek had continued, smiling and waving to other teams we passed. "Some guys just have tempers, you know, and you have to learn to work around that because if you don't, these tempers can come back to haunt you down the road."

I remember looking at him, confused and disgusted at the political schmoozing he was describing as essential. He shook his head, disappointed, as he led me back to our office. "All I'm saying, Bobby, is that if you want to stick around here, you're going to have to keep your mouth shut and learn to kiss a man's ring."

I'd spent the next two years avoiding interacting with Derek as much as possible. We were on the same team, so we worked together often enough, but I kept a professional distance from him socially. I had since seen him walk every new guy that joined the team through the office giving each a similar pep talk of the importance of kissing rings. When Adam was transferred to our unit, he came back from the stroll with Derek and said, "Dude, you knew what he was going to say almost word for word."

I responded, "I'm a hard drive, aren't I? And Derek is a broken record."

Anytime someone pissed Sgt. Bagg off, though, and was moved off the SID team back to patrol, Derek would make a point to give me a knowing look that said, "This is what happens when you don't kiss his ring." Even though I saw how Sgt. Bagg was getting rid of everyone on the team except Derek and myself, I never gave Derek the satisfaction of a response to his knowing look. I was a hard worker who busted my tail on the hundreds of cases I worked on or led, and that's what earned me the respect from the team, not arbitrary political alliances. No one had anything on me because I showed my worth in my work as a team player. I didn't disrespect the chain of command, but I wasn't there to kiss any rings.

2

Sgt. Bagg strolled into the office later that morning. He was smiling and looking satisfied, meaning he'd just been on a round through the office. Since we worked in a building with six other teams of specialized units, he had about 100 people within reach that would potentially encourage his ego.

"Morning, all." His voice grated on my ears.

Everyone in our office turned to say "morning" back, and Derek made sure to speak the loudest, like a brown-nosing child.

"Hard at work, I see." Sgt. Bagg set his hands on his hips as he surveyed the room, his chest puffed up in mock pride. With his dark hair and beady eyes, a Glock hanging from his hip, and the top two buttons of his shirt left undone to reveal a spattering of chest hair, he was only missing the full mustache required in all bad 1970s cop dramas to land the leading role.

"How's the South Nashville case coming? You find your mark?" He asked Derek.

"Close. I've got some leads, Sergeant, that point towards a Misty's Barbeque joint out there, so me and Johnny will be checking it out this afternoon." I made a mental note to joke to Adam about Derek "checking out" a barbecue joint, which would definitely mean an extended lunch hour.

Sgt. Bagg was smiling but seemed to barely listen as he nodded his head, "Good. Good. And what are you working on, Young?"

Without flinching at the tone of his voice, I said, "Same case load, finishing up the last paperwork for an order, looking into a lead I got from an informant. Should be setting up a new deal next week some time with him."

Sgt. Bagg stood for a beat staring at me with that tense smile still on his face. I was grateful he rarely got involved in actual casework, but even his check-ins felt more like interrogations. It was like he was always trying to find something wrong with whatever I was working on. "Good to hear, Young. Keep working hard."

Sgt. Bagg moved on to check in with the rest of the team, and I relaxed in my seat. When Dave gave the update on the final count of his latest takedown totaling in at $26k, Sgt. Bagg crossed his arms and leaned against the doorway. I knew we'd be getting nothing done for at least a quarter of an hour more because Dave had reminded Sgt. Bagg of one of his glory stories. Derek looked way too excited about it considering we had all heard Bagg's stories dozens of times. Derek just loved to waste time.

"$26k is a good haul, Dave." Bagg said as he puffed up his chest even more, ready to wow us with his overtold tales. "Reminds me of the time back in '98 when I stopped a beat up Honda for swerving between lanes on the interstate. When he pulled onto the shoulder, he almost swerved into the goddamn grass." Bagg laughed loudly, and a few others laughed with him. Next was the description of the guys eyes.

"When I got up to that sonofabitch's window, his pupils were as dilated as a full moon and red as a fox." Two weeks prior, they were as red as a "tomato." "His hands were already shaking and he couldn't look me in the eye. Here I was figuring it was just a stoner needing to be brought in, but little did I know what this goddamn kid was hiding in the truck bed. I got him out and tried to cuff him, but he tripped and rolled into the grass. I thought he was trying to get away so I lunged for him, but turns out he was just high as a kite and dumb as a rock. Took me only a second to wrangle his hands into cuffs, but took forever to get him up and into the back of the car, the little shit. Called in support for the search, and what do we find but a brick of coke and a garbage bag of green. Found out later his dad was a big dealer over in Murfreesboro and the kid had gone and stolen a load of his shit and tried to make a run for it. He was just a goddamn dumbass and tried out his loot before escaping."

Derek and others were laughing and Sgt. Bagg's face was glowing with pride and sweat. "I tell you, that was the easiest $79k I ever brought in."

Derek wiped his eyes. Seriously.

For the first time in my career, I slipped up in front of Sgt. Bagg. I glanced at Adam and said under my breath, "Two weeks ago it was $70k."

"Hey," Sgt. Bagg said, holding his hands out to stop the team from laughing. "What did you just say, Young?"

"Nothing, Sergeant." I tried to smile like I didn't know what he was talking about. There was no way he heard what I said over the laughter.

Sgt. Bagg pointed his finger at me and said, "My office. Now, Bobby." He only ever said my first name when he wanted to show me who was boss. He then strutted from the silent room.

I took a deep breath and stood to follow.

Like a kid who's excited to see someone get into trouble, Derek let out a "Oooo." I said nothing and followed Bagg to his office.

"Close the goddamn door."

I did so and stood with my hands clasped in front of me and waited.

Sgt. Bagg paced behind his desk, his face reddening.

"Can't just keep your mouth shut, can you, Bobby?"

I considered answering with a "No, sir" but managed to do what he asked for the moment and said nothing.

He glared at me as he leaned on his hands on the desk. "Sit down."

I sat down. I'd only sat in front of his desk twice before: once on my first day with the team when Bagg acted chummy with me, and once the previous year when I saw Bagg's true colors. I'd worked on a pills case that required wiretapping, and I had actually gotten the sign-off to work temporarily with the 20th Judicial District Drug Task Force on the wiretap case. The first time I walked into the wiretap room and could actually listen in on the dealers' phone conversations, I was almost giddy with excitement. We weren't just focused on the drug peddlers or mules in a wiretap case. Recording key phone conversations was the way to bring down a whole drug dealer ring, including the suppliers! At the end of the case, we ended up seizing over $100k in pills and brought fifteen people in. It was the greatest month of my career to that point because I felt like we were actually getting real shit done.

When I came back to the team, though, Sgt. Bagg sat me down in his office first thing, pointed his finger into my face, and yelled at me, "That team is taking all the credit because of you, goddammit, and it's bullshit. How *dare* you go behind my back. You will never go work another wiretap under my supervision, you hear me?" Shocked and confused as to what could have possibly made him upset, especially because he had been the one to sign off on my working temporarily with the 20th, I had no idea how to respond. I hadn't done anything wrong and had no idea why he was yelling at me. Sgt. Bagg took his finger out of my face and pointed to the door. "Get out of here. I can't look at you anymore."

Sitting stiffly in the chair for the third time, I held my breath as Sgt. Bagg hovered over me like he was starring in *The Rockford Files*. At least he wasn't yelling. Yet.

"Don't look so smug, Bobby. Nothing's finalized for the 20th, yet, so you're not going anywhere any time soon. I know Cox will be playing favorites, but for right now you're under *my* supervision, and I expect a certain level of respect from you, got it?"

"Yes, sir." I managed to not roll my eyes at his comment about Sgt. Cox.

Sgt. Bagg stared at me a second before saying, "Also, we need to have a little chat about Karen Braden."

This was so out of left field it took a second for me to answer. "What?"

"She's transferring to the team next week."

"Okay. But, what does that have to do with me?"

Sgt. Bagg narrowed his eyes as he examined my face, trying to find the reaction he wanted. He sighed. "Goddammit, Young, I know how you gave her a hard time in Hermitage when you worked together. I've heard all about how you didn't get along with her and couldn't work together, and I won't put up with any of that shit happening on this team, you got it?"

I raised my hands, "Hold on, I did not give her a hard time. I just disagreed with her choosing to date a team member and then texting him during their constant domestic disputes while on the job."

"Hey!" Bagg spat. "Don't start spreading gossip, Young. I won't put up with that shit, so you need to check your goddamn ego before you start running your mouth." He leaned forward more, his voice raising at the same rate as his finger as he pointed it in my face. "If you can't get over your problem with her and learn how to work with her, goddammit, you better believe I will have you removed from this department immediately. No notice. You're gone." He snapped his fingers in front of my face.

I had always struggled with Bagg's character, his constant gloating, his one-upper personality, his disturbing chest hair pride, his tendency to talk fast and over everyone else, and his insecure power moves and vague threats. I could deal with all of those things, though, because he rarely meddled in our cases, and I barely had to interact with him in the day-to-day. I could take the moments of bullshit because, for the most part, I was doing the work I loved without his interference.

What I couldn't take was his finger pointing at my face.

What almost sent me over the edge was his fingers snapping in front of my nose.

I took a deep breath to steady myself, my fists clenching. "I don't have a problem with Karen. I only had a problem with her decision to date internally and text while on a job." I took another breath and said, "There will be no issues."

"Damn right there won't. I won't allow it, goddammit." Bagg then settled back in his chair, still watching me with his beady eyes. "I'll be watching you. Now, get out."

I stood and left immediately.

Back in the office, I told Adam, "I'm taking lunch." I wasn't even hungry, but I grabbed my jersey and pulled it on over my shirt to cover my gun and headed the long way back to the kitchen and back door. All the way to my car, I replayed the image of Sgt. Bagg's fingers snapping in front of my face. Of course he was bringing Karen on to the team.

She would fit right in with Derek, and they could be Bagg's personal cheerleaders together.

I clicked my dad's contact in my phone as I pulled onto the main road. I was heading to the mall to walk off the anger.

"Hey, son, you hear about the 20th?"

Dad's hopeful voice immediately broke through the image of Bagg. The 20th. I would be going to the 20th soon. I had to. Sgt. James Cox had all but guaranteed it was only a matter of time. I breathed deeply and felt my hands unclench slightly. Bagg couldn't stop me from leaving if I got the position.

"No, not yet. Just had a shit meeting and am heading to lunch."

"What'd he do this time?" Dad always knew it was Bagg.

"Well, do you remember me talking about Karen at Hermitage?"

"The girl with the work ethic of a house cat?"

I laughed out loud and the rest of the anger broke away for the moment.

"Yeah, that's her. Sgt. Dick just transferred her to the team."

"Well, that ain't a surprise. It's a good thing you'll be out of there soon."

I smiled. Dad was always on my side. Instead of bitching about the meeting and the finger snapping, I asked, "What are you and Mom up to today?"

"Ah, well, we are sitting in the waiting room for my checkup. I swear these doctor offices go slower than police paperwork. Your mom forgot her granola bar so if I don't have an arm on Sunday, you'll know why."

I laughed as I heard Mom in the background say lightly, "Watch it."

I said, "I forgot you had tests today. Keep me posted on the results."

"I'm sure they'll be fine. I didn't go and kick cancer's butt just to let it come back."

"Still, it's always nice to hear good news about it."

"Yeah. Oh, here we go. My turn. Bye, son."

"Good luck, Dad." I wasn't sure if he heard me. He had a bad habit of putting his phone in his pocket without ending calls, and since I was driving, I listened to his banter with the nurse until I could hang up at a light.

Dad said, "Your tests must be mighty prepped for the two hours I was sitting on my butt out there."

"Oh, hush," I heard my mom say.

"Maybe you could give me an extra test while we're at it." Dad continued, "Sitting so long made my butt go to sleep about an hour ago, and I'm worried it's done gone and left my body altogether."

I heard a rustle as Mom batted Dad's leg with her purse. The nurse laughed.

I hung up the phone and walked a lap around the mall before picking up some Wendy's and heading back to the office, calmed down and ready to face the rest of my day.

3

After verifying Richardson's arrest history and records that afternoon, Charlie and I set up a plan to meet one of Richardson's cocaine sources. I made sure Charlie knew that once we established the next level of supply, he would be phased out of the process. Detectives are always on the hunt for the "big fish" and Charlie, while fairly connected, was nowhere close to being a "big fish." He was just a regular construction worker who used and sold recreationally. He was the smallest fish in a drug line. After we collected the information needed from Charlie, he would be able to return to his normal life, and we could move on up the chain of dealers.

Since Charlie was proactive and motivated to finish his stint as an informant, he took it upon himself to set up a meeting at Richardson's house in Bellevue the following day. After wiring Charlie up for the meeting at a nearby Walmart, he drove to Richardson's house.

Richardson had made a few key investments: his house and his boat. His secluded yet suburban home allowed him to remain close to town and his connections, and no one could have guessed how valuable his boat and job as a fishing guide was. His boat created a perfect illusion of legitimacy for his life. If anyone were to ask, he was a fishing guide and having a nice boat made everyone believe he was good at his job. However, no avid fisherman took trips that required his type of boat, not in Middle Tennessee. Richardson loved to fish but it was only a supplement to his real income.

Richardson's home sat back far from the road in a nice neighborhood where the houses were separated by the surrounding woods. If it wasn't for the mailbox and paved driveway, no one would even know it was there due to the heavy shield of trees, which is just how Richardson liked it. He didn't want to draw any unwanted attention. He was connected in the drug world and had seen how being careless can get you sent to jail.

As Charlie parked in front of the house and headed to the porch, he found Richardson sitting in a rocking chair, sipping whiskey on the rocks, and telling war stories to a friend on the phone. As we listened to Richardson spout off jokes and stories on his phone call, I felt like he was trying to put on a show for Charlie as he stood there waiting. It felt like Richardson wanted to show off a certain persona, one that might remind Charlie of how connected and capable he was at introducing the right people to each other, but on his own clock. After Richardson hung up, he and Charlie got down to business.

"You know," Richardson began, "I took Braden Long out fishing last week."

The reference to the up and coming movie star felt forced. Charlie played it off by joking, "I figured you were still moving around the rich and famous on 'fishing trips.'" He emphasized the last words to land the joke. They had known each other for more than thirty years and Richardson's constant not-so-subtle name dropping irritated Charlie, but he never challenged it outright.

Richardson snorted and then spit loudly. "Yeah, they still call regularly. It keeps the lights on here."

"Oh, come on," Charlie said, "if you had to depend on your fishing trips to pay your bills, you would be homeless." Richardson laughed with Charlie.

"Well, what about you?" Richardson then asked, "You ready to meet some of my connections? Seems like you have been laying low recently."

"You know I almost got locked-up last year. I had to lay low for a while."

"A year's a long while. But, I've got a new guy you will have to get in with. We can set that up next week."

"How well do you know him? Is he moving good shit?"

"Man, you know I don't mess with anything but the best now! I'm too damn old to risk my neck. We're both too old for all that."

Charlie laughed. "Okay, big man, then are they moving decent weight? Have you upgraded from slinging the small shit?"

"Are you trying to piss me off?"

For a moment I got nervous for Charlie, but then Richardson continued, "You know I have legit connections. So, you want in or not? I don't have time to convince you to work with me. Besides, you came to me!"

"Yeah, yeah. Just set up the meeting."

We heard the front door swing open and closed. Richardson had gone inside, and we could hear his muffled talking.

Charlie, still on the porch, leaned back in his chair, thinking about his play. He later told me he was trying to decide how much he could order up without drawing too much attention while also proving he was legitimately back in the game. Richardson headed back outside and handed Charlie a glass of whiskey.

"Welp, today is our lucky day."

Charlie paused but said, "What are you talking about?"

"My man is already out here. He'll be here in fifteen minutes."

Charlie played it cool for this curveball, and I heard him take a sip of his drink. "That's fast. I hope he's not ready to make a deal today. I have to get my paper together."

"Naw, he has to meet you first. I said I know this guy, but nobody would just take my word on you being good. They gotta feel you out."

"Aight then."

"He's just gonna make some calls on the way over. Make sure no one has anything bad to say about you and your long time in this business."

They laughed and then settled in to wait. For the next ten minutes or so, the pair sat and continued to sip their whiskey, enjoying the fresh daytime air and chatting aimlessly. Charlie told me later that his mind was racing. He was surprised by the quick meeting, but he knew the faster he could finish this deal, the faster the charges would be worked off and he could return to life as normal.

We couldn't hear anything from the driveway on the microphone, but we knew someone had arrived when Charlie said in a low voice, "This your man? He looks awful young, like a kid."

"Naw, he's a grown ass man. These dealers just keep getting younger, but he's good."

Charlie told us later that he couldn't see the "kid" behind the wheel until he got out of the old green Toyota Corolla. It was a young man who climbed the porch stairs and shook Richardson's hand before being introduced to Charlie.

"Eddie, Charlie. Charlie, Eddie."

They nodded to each other, the tension seeming to grow as they sized each other up.

Charlie started, "So, how much can you get me?"

Eddie seemed to like Charlie's direct attitude. "I can get whatever you want."

He must have heard only good things about Charlie on his phone calls.

"What about a bird?" When Eddie didn't respond, Charlie prompted, "You know, a kilo?"

Eddie laughed. "No one calls it that anymore, but yeah, I can get you a 'car' if that's what you're looking for."

"How soon?"

"Few weeks."

"Aight. Get me a sample and we will talk. You have a number? I'll call when I have the paper all together."

"Give me your phone."

Eddie added his number to Charlie's phone and said, "But keep conversations to a minimum, okay?"

Eddie turned to leave but Charlie stopped him. "Hey, is this the business or family line? I heard you drop them fast."

Eddie said, "It's the good line." He then headed for his car and drove back down the driveway.

Charlie turned to Richardson, "You want me to keep you in the loop?"

"Hell yeah."

"Aight, I'll let you know when shit happens."

With that, Charlie headed down the porch and back to his car. Charlie was barely out of Richardson's driveway when he placed a call to me.

"Yo, I've got us a deal."

APRIL / MAY 2014

4

When I hadn't heard about the 20th by the end of the week, a few days into April, I called Sgt. James Cox to check in Friday afternoon. When we had worked together in Hermitage, we talked every day. Now I called him once a week or so to catch up on life and our families. Ever since putting in for the position with the 20th, though, I tried not to seem too eager or impatient, so I made sure to keep our conversations brief.

I told him about my conversation with Bagg about Karen and he was sympathetic. James, who never said a bad thing about anyone, had warned me before I was transferred to SID that Bagg was hard to work with and to "be careful." I now understood what he meant. He must have known that Bagg played political favorites all the time and was like a loose cannon when he got upset. James also probably knew that I wouldn't suck up to Bagg in order to stay on his good side.

"Sgt. Bagg is a strange man." James said. "Is he still pissed about not getting the job?"

"Oh, yeah. But, karma's a bitch. He shouldn't have taken that seized truck's plates to put on his car just to avoid renewing his tags. That shit is put on your record forever."

"That it is." We paused, probably both thinking about Sgt. Bagg's other antics earlier in his career. I usually didn't pay attention to the office rumors because they were untrue most of the time, but James had confirmed that Bagg used to take drug dealers' seized items like ATVs and boats home to "play." I didn't know how Bagg managed to work his way up to the rank of sergeant and not be fired, but I figured a lot of it had to do with the fact that he married up. His wife was a commander of a precinct, so she had a lot of influence and connections. They couldn't erase his record, though.

James sighed. "Well, I think Karen will do all right at SID with Bagg. And, off the record because it's not finalized and I can't make any guarantees, I think you would do all right with the 20th."

"Shit, I'd do more than all right!" I laughed.

"Well, maybe we will find out soon. Off the record, of course."

"Of course."

"I'll talk to you next week, Bobby. Be good. And try to keep your mouth shut a little longer, got it?"

"Will do my best. Thanks, James."

That evening, I met my wife Danielle at La Hacienda for an off-the-record celebratory margarita. She was working full time for the local police union as an editor for their newsletters and magazine, and she was in law school classes several nights a week. Friday nights were our date nights to decompress together because we usually spent Saturdays busy with work again.

Sunday nights were reserved for some work and then dinner at my parents' house. Ever since my dad was diagnosed with cancer in 2012, he wanted to start having me, my sisters Ashley and Angela, and our families over for a Sunday dinner each week to stay close and connected. As a kid, my dad's family always got together on Sundays for dinner, but when he moved to Nashville for a job he had missed the big family gatherings.

A few years prior, my parents had purchased plans for a large, open-concept log cabin while on a trip to Gatlinburg and, once it was built, they decorated it with pictures of wildlife, a black bear rug, and antlers surrounding the light fixtures. We sat on benches around their big wooden farm table, and my nieces always stood on the bench to sing a prayer before eating. After we finished eating, the girls would run around the house playing while the rest of us would sit and talk for an hour about our upcoming week and plans. I loved my work and didn't mind the long hours and stress, but the calm of being around family every Sunday always helped to energize me for the start of the week.

On this particular Sunday, after Ashley's girls finished their prayer but before we started in on the ribs and mashed potatoes, my dad gave a toast. We were not the types to make toasts other than at weddings, but my dad stood and held up his glass.

"To the off-the-record, newest member of the 20th Judicial District Drug Task Force. We are all so proud of you, Robert."

My family held up their glasses, even my nieces.

I held in my emotion as Danielle rubbed my back in support. We all took a drink and I thanked them.

It still felt too good to be true, and I was trying not to get my hopes up still. My dad's negative treatment by CSX after his decades-long career as a railroad policeman showed me that nothing was ever guaranteed. But, since Dad had still found work after leaving CSX, his experience also showed me that you could survive outside the system. One thing the police academy made you believe was that there was no future outside of the police department. Your worth was forever linked to being a policeman, and you couldn't have a career outside of the system. Dad wasn't super happy about being a hotel security guard supervisor in the latter years of his career, but it gave him purpose and something to do every day. He found that he *could* survive outside of the system.

I knew that if for some reason I didn't get the position with the 20th, my family would still have my back and be supportive. Ashley would hug me and be really sweet, my oldest sister Angela would be sarcastic and try to think up new career moves for me, my dad would relate it to his own war stories of systemic bullshit, and my mom would bake a cake.

When we set our glasses down after the toast, Angela asked, "So, I heard your boss was being an asshole again."

"Oh, Angela." Mom said, "Quit cursing around the girls." Ashley's girls were snickering behind their hands.

I grinned and said, "A bit."

I then spent a good part of dinner making my family laugh by doing impressions of Bagg, including unbuttoning the top two buttons of my shirt and strutting around like a peacock, which made my nieces shriek and hide under the table.

Chapter 4

Back in the office on Monday, we had an early team meeting so Sgt. Bagg could introduce Karen to the team. I hadn't seen her in two years, but I made sure to greet her at the coffee table afterwards.

"Hey, Karen, it's good to see you again."

"Yeah, hey." She said as she finished doctoring her coffee.

"Congratulations on the transfer. Welcome to our team."

She smiled in a strained way. "Thanks." She then looked around the room, clearly scouting out someone else to talk to.

I took the hint. "Well, if you need anything, let me know."

She nodded and walked away without responding.

When I walked to the doorway where Adam stood, he whispered, "Dude, you feeling chilly? Cause that was a real cold shoulder."

I laughed and tried to shake it off. "Yeah, that was weird. I guess I'm not forgiven for disagreeing with her work ethic."

We watched as Karen went to stand by Derek who was listening to Sgt. Bagg talk loudly about another story from his early days.

I turned to leave the room and said to Adam on my way out, "You know, it seems like all Bagg's glory stories are from twenty years ago. Makes you wonder if he's done anything since then."

Adam laughed and followed me out of the room back to the office. I didn't want to stick around and schmooze with the others, and I knew Derek would extend the post-meeting social for as long as he could. I didn't have time for that. I had cases to work on and a deal to figure out with Charlie to get to know this Eddie character better.

5

Charlie, still wanting to work off his charges as soon as he could, contacted me a few days later to let me know he set up a time to buy from Eddie that afternoon.

"Dude! I told you to wait until I gave the go ahead!"

"I know, man, but he's ready. It's been a week since we met, and I don't want him thinking I have cold feet now. Can we get it done?"

"Shit. Let me see what I can do."

I had to organize my team, find a tech to record the deal, and of course do some paperwork. This was sort of a test to figure out if this dealer, only known to us as Eddie, was worth pursuing. I knew that Eddie probably wasn't the biggest fish, but I was hoping he could lead us to the next level.

I filled out the mandatory voucher for the amount of money we'd need and then hurried to the lieutenant's office. If I had to get more than $10,000 I had to go to the captain's office, but since I only needed a thousand my options were Sgt. Bagg or Lieutenant Spine. It wasn't even a question; I always went to Lt. Spine. Thankfully, he wasn't in a meeting, so he signed the slip and handed me the cash from his safe. I thanked him and rushed back to the team to get them organized.

Because it was the first buy and relatively simple, everything fell into place quickly. The tech, who was just playing with camera molds when I requested his help, wasn't happy, but he showed up and that's what counted. I rallied three others to form the rest of our team, though not Derek because he must have been on one of his extended lunches. Adam rode with me to the Publix where we were meeting Charlie an hour before he was scheduled to meet with Eddie.

Charlie and his car were searched behind the Publix. I then handed Charlie $1,100 in $20 bills, and Charlie laughed.

"Man, these are way too crispy!" He proceeded to crinkle up all the bills, roughly smooth them out, and fold them into a wad. He then stuffed the cash into his pocket.

While the tech hooked the recording wire onto Charlie, I addressed the team and one of the tech's recorders to go over the situation on record. "Alright guys, Charlie set this deal up. It's for one ounce of coke and they're meeting at the bowling alley down the street. This is just a walk so let's follow the dealer off to get more intel on him. Don't get burned." Getting burned meant getting spotted by a dealer. It could immediately ruin both a case and an informant's connection. We would be performing a "buy-walk," giving Charlie money to buy the ounce and letting all parties go after the deal. Charlie would meet up with a couple of the detectives afterwards while the rest of us would follow the seller.

I passed around the radios so everyone could listen to the deal go down. "Now Eddie has been seen driving a green Toyota Corolla, but we will have to wait and see what he shows up in. Y'all know how these go. Any questions?"

Of course, no one had any questions; they had done hundreds of buys. The team collectively had over thirty years of experience between all of us.

We followed Charlie to the spot while the tech and a detective stayed behind at Publix. We watched from a distance and saw a white male, presumed to be Eddie, arriving in an old beat up green Toyota sedan. No one would ever think that the person behind the wheel of this hunk of junk was a large cocaine dealer, but Eddie parked next to Charlie, exited his car, and entered the passenger seat of Charlie's vehicle.

Eddie's voice sounded first on the recording, "Here is one and a quarter."

"One and a quarter?"

"Yeah."

"Hell, I thought you were only bringing one."

"Nah, it's one and a quarter. I don't like talking on the phone. I got some green if you want that too."

Charlie's voice sounded momentarily unsure, "Ah, I don't."

"Okay. Is there any way you can hold it, though?" Not only was Eddie trying to unload more coke than the original amount, he also wanted Charlie to move marijuana, which was definitely not part of the deal.

Charlie asked, "How much you got?"

"I got four pounds of it. They won't let me get any more of it."

"Four pounds?"

"At eleven hundred a piece."

Charlie knew he only had $1,100 in his pocket and no more. But, if he could work it out to move more product, his charges could be worked off faster. He said, "Let me call somebody about it."

"Good, good, it's mid-grade. I can get more of it, too."

"I bet I can get rid of it."

Eddie, keen to sell Charlie on moving the product, said quickly, "I've been selling them for thirteen, but I've been stuck with them because I have been shoving them down everybody else's throat. I can't get no goddamn more until this is gone."

"Ah, you can't get more of the—" Charlie paused, realizing Eddie was saying he needed to move the weed before he could get more cocaine to sell. "I got ya, I got ya."

"Yeah, till I clear up."

"Well, can you do the whole bird then when you clear up?"

"Yeah, yeah."

I grinned at Adam. Charlie was doing a perfect job at setting up a potential future kilo deal on record.

Charlie asked, "What is the ticket on that?"

"Let me talk to this guy. I met him last night. He bought a lawn mower from me. One of my buddies gets lawn mowers, brand new." This was more coded language, similar to his reference to a kilo being a "car" at Richardson's. A brand new lawn mower was just another way to talk about a high-quality kilo.

"Who's the guy?" Charlie asked, trying to get more information.

"A Mexican guy. Don't worry about it. I can get it for you."

"Okay. But, the green you said was eleven hundred a pound?"

Chapter 5

35

"Yep."

"Okay. I might be able to get rid of them for you."

"You can do them for twelve all day. I have been doing thirteen."

"I don't fuck with it that much. It's good, though?"

"Hell yeah. I can't get no damn more until I square them up. I'm on standstill."

"Aight, I'll hit you up later."

Once the deal was complete, Charlie was followed back to our meet-up location at the Publix, where he turned over approximately thirty-five grams of powder (one and a quarter ounce, as Eddie stated). The white powdery substance field-tested positive for cocaine, so we were good. Charlie and the vehicle were searched again, per protocol. We already knew there would be another deal based on the conversation, but we had no idea if Charlie would find a weed buyer. Regardless, we were getting some decent info about Eddie's abilities as a dealer.

In the meantime, the other detectives, Adam, and I followed Eddie as he drove like a bat out of hell through the parking lot. When Eddie pulled into Park East Condos, I told everyone not to follow him into the dead-end complex because I guessed he did not live there and was probably doing a "heat run." Sure enough, Eddie exited the front of the complex two minutes later. I noticed Eddie even went as far as changing his t-shirt. This guy thought he was smart. I terminated the surveillance based on Eddie's actions after he left the complex in case he felt he was being followed. We had his tag and I could take it from there; no need to take any unnecessary risks by following him further. I radioed and told everyone to pull off for the time being. I needed to complete the paperwork and get back to the property office.

The SID building was attached to the property office, but it had a separate entrance. It's called an office, but it acts more like a vault. After an arrest, any drugs or items seized go to storage in the property office to await court dates. Because the whole building lacked windows and shared a ventilation system, our offices always smelled faintly of marijuana, but that wasn't so bad compared to next door. The property office itself smelled like a hundred people just lit up or a closet full of spooked skunks. It was so strong it would saturate my clothes before I could get back outside. Perhaps unsurprisingly, everyone who worked there was really chill for being guards of a giant vault of seized drugs and items. You couldn't help but have a slight contact high after a few minutes in there. Before entering the office with the thirty-five grams Charlie had gotten from Eddie, I took a deep breath of fresh air.

When I got back to my desk, Adam said, "Dude, take a walk. I'm going to get buzzed sitting beside you."

I laughed and went back outside to walk a couple laps around the parking lot.

Only two days later, Eddie called Charlie asking for the money for the extra seven grams. Eddie saw the extra as being "fronted" and since Charlie couldn't exactly refuse it, we would have to find a way to pay up or risk the operation. Eddie wanted his money and was pressuring Charlie to move some of the weed, too. Our unit wasn't busy, so I set up a second deal with Eddie. This time it would be different. Eddie's green Toyota Corolla was registered under someone random, so I was still unsure of his name, so the next deal would focus on getting some identifying information on Eddie.

Same as the last deal, I met with Charlie to arrange it. Charlie called Eddie on speaker phone so I could hear, and just like a creature of habit, Eddie set up the deal for the exact same spot. I briefed the team, searched Charlie and the vehicle, gave Charlie the money, and the tech placed a listening device on Charlie. Drug deals are fluid and can never be predicted, but detectives' procedures are the same every time. We exchanged some vehicles, but everyone basically had the same roles and it didn't take long. Eddie arrived on schedule and in the same green beater. The marijuana deal went off without a hitch and Charlie again asked for the price of a "bird." Eddie said he would ask his source and they arranged another cocaine deal for a later date.

When Eddie left this time, I told the surveillance team to stick on him. He drove under the speed limit, took I-40 to Briley Parkway around to Clarksville Highway. I called a uniformed officer that I trusted and asked him to stop Eddie. I told the officer to make up a ruse for the stop, telling Eddie that his vehicle matched the description of a burglary suspect and then let him go.

That single traffic stop yielded Eddie's true identity as Edward Peterson of Mt. Juliet, TN. The officer did a hell of a job and even got Eddie to give him two phone numbers. This stop also solved the mystery of who the car was registered to: Eddie's uncle. Eddie was released and we continued to tail him. He headed into a rural area north of town. These rural areas were impossible for quick surveillance, so the team had to break off. No problem, it had already been a very successful day. I now had phone numbers and an address for Eddie, so it was time to set up the next stage.

After making two buys from Eddie's green Toyota, we had enough probable cause to order a GPS tracking device to place on the car. Getting a judge to sign an order with enough evidence was the easy part. Getting the device onto Eddie's car without being caught . . . that would take some creativity. But, I had time to figure that out. Moving forward with the tracking warrant meant we had to be caught up on the reports from the earlier buys, and then a tracking order and affidavit had to be drafted. Just to complicate things further, the operation would likely occur in Wilson County, which meant I had to arrange a date and time with a judge in that county to get the warrant granted.

In order to take the case to the next level and start a wiretap, we had to have evidence of at least 300 grams of cocaine. Tapping into and recording people's phone conversations was an incredibly expensive process, so we had to show proof that the high cost would be outweighed by the financial "gain" (a massive drug bust at the end of it). I had a feeling we'd have that 300 grams soon enough, and then I would just have to fight Bagg about letting me do another wiretap case. His words echoed in my head: *You will never go work another wiretap under my supervision.*

I prayed that I would be out from under his thumb soon, and God seemed to be listening.

6

"Dad, I just got the email."

Dad couldn't contain his excitement. "Yes! I knew it, I knew it was just a matter of time!" He then yelled to my mom, "Robert got the email!" I heard my mom yelling back her congrats in the background.

I couldn't stop grinning. There it was in black and white: Bobby Young had been accepted as the newest member of the 20th Judicial District Drug Task Force. There was nothing Sgt. Richard Bagg could do about it. It was official.

Adam and I took an early lunch, mostly so I could avoid seeing Bagg as long as possible to keep my good mood.

"You know he's going to make your life hell until you transfer." Adam said between bites of his burger.

I nodded and leaned back in my seat. The weather was cool and sunny, so we had gone to Sonic to sit in the car with the windows down.

"Don't I know it." I said. "He can't stop me forever, though."

"Who knows, maybe he'll just let you go. Maybe he won't fight it."

I glanced at him and we both laughed.

When we returned to the office, we walked the back hallway to our desks and settled in to work while everyone else seemed to have gone to lunch. After a few minutes, though, Sgt. Bagg appeared in the doorway.

He didn't even look at me as he said, "Young, my office."

I followed him and he said, "Shut the goddamn door."

I stood in front of the desk as Bagg paced behind it. "You may be transferring to the 20th, but you're still under my supervision until I give the go ahead, got it?"

"I understand, Sergeant."

Sgt. Bagg stopped and walked around the desk to face me, crossing his arms on his chest. "You think you're too good for SID, don't you?" The question was more like a statement, and his voice continued to raise as he talked faster. "Well, wipe that smug look off your face, Young. Don't be strutting around here like you're better than anyone else, goddammit, or I'll report you to Lieutenant Spine, and he doesn't take kindly to big egos like yours. You'll be back on patrol before you can count to three. Do you hear me?"

"Yes, sir." I kept my face blank and waited out the storm. Nothing he could say could make me react. I was still going to the 20th. The longer I didn't react, though, the more outrageous he got.

"You're green, Young. Young and green doesn't look good on a detective, does it? Especially with that ego of yours that makes you think you have the right to just run your mouth all the time." He began to frantically pace the room, gesturing with his hands as if he was angrily lecturing a child. "The best policeman is one who can keep his goddamn mouth shut and take care of his shit without parading it around like a goddamn peacock. And I hear you haven't given Karen the time of the goddamn day, which I can only assume is blatant disrespect of my orders, so you better get your act together while you're still under my supervision. Don't think I'm just going to forget about this, either. I've got a memory like an elephant; I never forget anything. Do you hear me, Young?"

"Yes, sir."

He continued on rambling, and I zoned out. I kept my face straight and looked at the wall behind him. Soon this would be over.

I tuned back in when what he said caught my attention: "That team is a waste of money and manpower, and if I have to take it down myself, I will, and I'll make sure you go down with it, goddammit, because if you can't learn to sit down and shut up then you have no future in this department. Look me in the eyes when I'm speaking to you. Goddammit, I'll make sure you come down off that high horse you're on . . ." He reverted back to talking about my ego, and I looked at his beady eyes without seeing much of anything. Had he just threatened the 20th? There was nothing a sergeant could do to meddle with the 20th. It was a joint force of police officers and district attorneys, and it existed under the DA's office. Bagg was just blowing smoke at this point.

Maybe he realized he was running his mouth because he finally pointed his finger in my face and said, "You are going nowhere until your cases are done, Young. You'll be sticking around for quite a while, so get comfortable. Got it?" He stared into my eyes an extra second and then said, "Get out."

I left the room and walked in a daze back to our office. Adam was still the only one in the room and he asked, "You okay?"

I took a deep breath and nodded. "I think Bagg just let out everything he's been holding in for two years."

Adam said, "So, it was gruesome."

I nodded.

"Man," Adam shook his head and looked back at his computer, "he's really got it in for you now, huh?"

A chill rushed up my spine as I reheard Bagg's words in my head: *If I have to take it down myself, I will, and I'll make sure you go down with it.* The momentary fear turned into anger at Bagg and his hypocritical bullshit and pathetic insecurities. He was always telling me to shut my mouth and do my work, and now he was basically threatening me and there wasn't a damn thing I could do about it. Because of the chain of command, I could only go to my immediate supervisor about my problems, but Sgt. Bagg was my supervisor. What was I supposed to do when Bagg was almost always the "problem"? Nothing, that's what. If I went above him to Lt. Spine, I'd be breaking the chain, and the lieutenant would let Bagg know I was stepping out of my station. The wrath of Bagg would be even worse.

So, I took a breath and tried to get back to work. The sooner I finished my shit the sooner I'd be out of SID and onto bigger and better things with the 20th. Until then I just needed to keep my mouth shut, like my friend James Cox said I should do. I just had to endure this a little longer and not get into trouble.

Over the next two weeks, I stayed busy with trying to close out all my open cases, assisting other detectives on their caseloads, and avoiding Bagg as much as possible. Every time I ran into Sgt. Bagg, including during his random check-ins, he'd hand me another case to work on or finish that he claimed he'd already assigned to me before the email. I recognized one as being the South Nashville case Derek had been "working on" that involved a barbeque restaurant. The arrests and searches had been done a week earlier, and the case was closed all except for the final filing of the paperwork. I rolled my eyes as Derek lolled by his desk, doing nothing and chatting with Karen, while I finished the formal paperwork and submitted it an hour later. It probably would have taken Derek a week to do that. He gave the team a bad name. The other detectives were diligent and hardworking, and we all worked together easily. The balance was tipped since Karen joined the team, and she and Derek spent a lot of time chatting, but I really respected the work my other teammates did, and I would always be grateful for their support and help on my cases over the past years.

I decided to withhold information about the Eddie case from Sgt. Bagg. He didn't need to know that I intended to take the Eddie case as far as I could go up the chain. As far as Bagg was concerned, my goal was to bring down some dealers using my informant Charlie. He wasn't letting me go until my cases were closed, and I didn't want to close this case. I wanted to bring it to the 20th.

Honestly, it didn't feel right to hide the case like that, but my goal was to get 300 grams of cocaine from Eddie so I could start up a wiretap when I was out from under Bagg's supervision. I didn't want Bagg to ruin this case for me, especially after all the hard work I'd done on it. I knew that he would try to sabotage or close the case if he heard I was trying to go beyond a simple dealer arrest. The worst case scenario was that Bagg would transfer the caseload to another teammate, possibly Derek, and I knew this wouldn't do the case justice. This was *my* case. I had a good feeling about it, and I was determined to not let him take it from me even if it meant living in the gray area between telling the truth and a lie.

When the tracking warrant was finally signed and the tracking device made available for me to place on Eddie's car, I made sure it was fully charged and set up alerts so I would know every time the green Toyota moved.

Putting a tracker on a vehicle is something that must be done very early in the morning when it is most likely the dealer is both home and asleep. It had been two weeks since Eddie and Charlie's last deal, but I knew that dealers don't stop the game once they start. I left the house at 3:45 am the next morning. As I neared our office building, I could see that Adam was already there waiting.

As soon as Adam got in my car, it started to pour. He glanced at me, "I knew we wouldn't beat the rain. Couldn't this have waited until tomorrow?"

"Sorry, man, but he is probably going to make a run this week, and we can't afford to miss it. I don't want to burn Charlie."

"Yeah, I get that." Adam yawned as he buckled up. "Plus, I know you're itching to get this case done so you can go on and leave us and Bagg behind. Unless he thinks of something else to stop you from moving to the 20th."

I laughed as I pulled out of the lot, "He can't stop me forever."

It was an uneventful drive to Eddie's house. We had already established a safe parking spot about 100 yards away. I felt confident that the rain would cover any noise, but it was going to be a mess. Adam took his position as lookout while I headed further into the woods towards the house and car, grateful for the cover of trees to hold off the rain. What I didn't know was that there would be a damn graveyard between me and the house. It was one of those small family graveyards, well-kept with many worn headstones. I'm not a superstitious man, but walking in a graveyard in the dead hours of the morning lent a new, creepy ambience to the mission.

I emerged from the woods to the paved driveway. I got on my hands and knees and crawled towards the target car. When I was within a foot or so of the tires, I paused when I heard something like a low growl. Two very loud, very close dogs began to bark, but I was not about to abort the mission. I held my breath and thought, *Please let them be tied up.* I waited, and they continued to bark, but they didn't attack. I said a quick prayer of gratitude.

For several seconds that felt like hours, I stayed still on the pavement within arms-length of the car, the rain pouring down on me. When the dogs settled, I shifted under the car and stuck the tracker into the underbody. I then crept back to the tree line as slowly and silently as possible, and then hurried back through the woods to Adam, my whole body humming with adrenaline.

I joined Adam in the car, shaking off as much rain water as I could, but I was soaked.

"You good? I heard the landsharks, but I figured you'd holler if they got too close."

"I guess they were tied up. We have got to find out about these dogs before we do this or someone's going to get bit."

"Or worse, bit and then shot by drug dealers."

"Would really ruin a case."

Adam laughed, "Or, you know, ruin your life?"

I laughed, and we headed back to the station. I dropped Adam off and headed home to shower and catch a couple hours of sleep, but I knew after that adrenaline rush, it was useless. I was doomed to be exhausted at work that day. But, what kept me going was the constant thought that all this work would lead me to a wiretap case, which I would hopefully be starting soon with the 20th. I just had to wait and tread water a little longer until Bagg released me.

I kept repeating to myself what I said to Adam, *He can't stop me forever.*

7

I touched base with Charlie a few times over the next several weeks, but we had trouble finding a time to set up another buy. It wasn't a big deal, though, because I could watch Eddie's Toyota move around town from the comfort of my laptop or cell phone. Every stop he made gave me a potential lead. I was plenty busy gathering data on the dozens of addresses we believed Eddie was selling to, but I was also wrapping up my last cases with SID.

When I finally submitted the last documentation needed for my last case with SID (not including the work I was doing with Charlie), I had to wait for the confirmation before officially transferring. I called Charlie, and he answered the phone on the first ring. Most CI's worked on their own time and communication was a problem, but Charlie was a good one. He always answered on the first ring. I guess he never forgot the reason he was talking to me in the first place: to avoid going to jail.

I asked Charlie to call Eddie and set up a buy. However, this time we were going to set the amount, and it was going to be bigger.

After the coke and weed buys, I decided that it was time to up the ante. I wanted to see if Eddie was all talk or if he could really produce. Charlie made the call and called me right back.

"His phone is off."

"Damnit! I bet he's changed his number. I need you to go visit Richardson again and get Eddie's new number."

"I'll call him now."

Sure enough, Charlie had Eddie's new number by the end of the day, and, even better, he had already set up a two-ounce cocaine deal with Eddie. The price was $850 per ounce, which is a damn good deal, and I knew that the quality wasn't going to be great. As long as it tested positive for cocaine, that was all that mattered to the judicial system. I got the team organized for the afternoon deal.

We had specific spots where we liked to meet our informants. On this day, we told Charlie to be behind a Lowes at 2 pm. As usual, we searched Charlie, his vehicle, and we wired him up. I handed Charlie $2,550 cash, and this time I gave Charlie mostly larger bills, to make it easy.

"I thought we were only getting two ounces."

"We were, but I just upped it, so ask for three." Three ounces was about eighty-five grams, which meant I'd be that much closer to the 300 needed for a wiretap.

Once everyone was in place and ready, I instructed Charlie to call Eddie and let him know he was on the way and that he wanted three ounces instead of the original two. Eddie said that he would have to call his "buddy" first, but he'd let him know. Fifteen minutes later, Eddie called Charlie back and told him they were still on.

This was working out perfect. The last-minute change forced Eddie to show his hand. We now knew he had the two ounces but also had the ability to get more easily. I felt confident he would eventually lead us to the next level of supply.

Eddie wanted to meet Charlie at a new location, though. He told Charlie to come to his uncle's tire shop on Clarksville Pike. I looked up the location and realized this would be tricky. The tire shop was a small brick building with a few stacks of old tires out front. Since it was in a rural area surrounded by open fields and a few residential lots, we would have nowhere to set up surveillance. I told the team to just hang around close, and we would have to be creative with driving by the shop while the deal was happening.

Charlie arrived first at the shop, which was normal because the buyer was usually early and waiting. I checked Eddie's tracker and saw he was nearby at another dealer's house, one known by both local dealers and officers as Squirrel. Eddie left Squirrel's house, and I was hoping he would take us to another location to pick up the third ounce, but Eddie headed straight to the tire shop, which meant he had all three on him.

Squirrel may have been his stop for the extra ounce, but we couldn't be sure.

Eddie arrived at his uncle's tire shop and parked his green Toyota in the gravel lot on the side of the building. Charlie was parked in front, and he called Eddie when he lost sight of his car. Eddie told Charlie to get out of his car and walk around to the back of the building. This was pretty smart on Eddie's part because there was no way that anyone could see a hand-to-hand transaction back there. At that point, we had to rely on Charlie to get the job done. It's nerve-wracking when you lose sight of an informant during a drug deal, but Charlie was wired, and we could hear everything.

Eddie said, "Here it is. Three of them."

"Cool."

"This shit ain't the best, though. I cooked some up last night and lost." What Eddie meant was that he converted the cocaine powder into crack cocaine and when he "cooked" it up, the total weight was less than the powder cocaine he had started with.

Eddie continued, "I wouldn't go cutting that shit with anything extra by the way. It's already cut to hell."

"I don't cut my shit, but I appreciate the honesty. I'll hit you up later."

Charlie returned to his vehicle and pulled out of the lot. I told the surveillance detectives not to follow Eddie away from the tire shop. The GPS tracker would take care of that for us. We made sure Eddie wasn't going to tail Charlie, and then I called Charlie and told him to follow me to a nearby church.

When I knew we were safe behind the church, we searched Charlie and the vehicle for any extra money or drugs. Charlie handed me a brown paper bag with three individual baggies containing a white powdery substance. I field tested a sample from one of the bags and it was positive for cocaine. I removed the wire from Charlie, debriefed him about the deal and that was it. Charlie left and I went back to the office to do paperwork.

The next day, a Friday, I had to work a mandated alternate shift in the afternoon and evening, which meant no date night or margaritas with my wife. The mandated alternate shift was a monthly assignment of specialized units to focus on "getting arrests" for a shift, which is a systemic formality to remind detectives that they are on the same pay scale and level as regular officers on paper. Spending a shift on patrol was an ineffective waste of time and money, but I used my hours to do some Eddie surveillance. I knew that any day now I would be working with the 20th and could make bigger strides on this case, so doing some extra research beforehand wouldn't hurt. Plus, being away from the office meant that I wouldn't come in contact with Bagg all day, which meant he couldn't give me any more "open" cases to finish.

I still did not know who was supplying Eddie with his cocaine, but the tracker showed me that he made multiple trips a day to a house off Brick Church Pike. I drove to the location Eddie frequented and set up a few houses down under the shade of a big tree. I checked on Eddie's tracker and saw he was only minutes away. Since it was already getting dark, I threw a t-shirt over my car radio to cover the light and slumped down in my seat, pulling my Braves cap lower on my forehead.

I watched as Eddie pulled in front of the house, exited the beater, and headed towards the front door. Eddie was inside for less than five minutes and then he was gone. I figured one of two things just happened: Eddie was either dropping off or picking up.

Shortly after Eddie left, two other cars pulled up one right after the other, and each person went inside for only a minute. My hunch was paying off. This trap house was looking like a candy shop! People were coming and going, getting their fixes. There was only one sure-fire way to figure out if the people coming and going from the residence were buying dope. We needed to stop them as they left. We had to be careful not to tip-off the source of supply, so the stops had to be made a good distance from the house. Since I was in my undercover car, though, I couldn't do it because it'd look too obvious.

When a black truck made a quick stop, I followed it for several minutes and called an officer who was on duty in the area. I told him what was going on and suggested he intercept the truck and make sure the driver stepped out of the vehicle to observe him for signs. The officer stopped the truck on the interstate. I hated traffic stops on the interstate, especially at night. More officers are killed in the line of duty because of traffic accidents than any other means.

I parked well behind the patrol car so the driver couldn't see my undercover car in the distance. While Officer Hill used his computer to check the driver's license, I told him I was going to talk to the driver for a minute.

When the guy stepped out of the car, he was visibly shaking and swaying back and forth. His face was lit up with sweat, and I asked for consent to search his person. He said yes, so I checked his pockets. I pulled out a folded dollar bill containing a white powdery substance, which the driver admitted was cocaine. The field test of the substance was positive and weighed approximately one gram.

The man stuttered, "I b-bought it from a guy named Jack. He walks the st-streets, the streets near my house in B-Bellevue."

Instead of pointing out his obvious lies, I placed the cocaine in a tamper-proof bag and handed the bag over to the officer to submit as evidence at the precinct. The driver was issued a misdemeanor state citation for cocaine possession. It was this guy's lucky day because the citation meant he wasn't going to jail.

The "pick-off" was complete. It was not a huge bust, but it showed probable cause that Eddie was delivering the cocaine that was trickling down the chain to this man in the truck.

I headed back to the office to make some notes, but when I pulled into the emptied lot, I spotted Sgt. Bagg's car. I considered turning around and leaving, but curiosity got the better of me. Bagg never stayed late at the office, especially not on a Friday evening. I went inside and walked the long way around the back of Bagg's office and straight to my shared office space and slumped down at my desk. Usually when I was one of the first in the building in the morning, the peace and quiet was calming. Without the chattering and distractions, I could really focus on tasks and get a lot more work done before Derek was around.

A second after sitting down at my desk, though, the hair stood up on the back of my neck. The quiet was not calming this time. It was an eerie silence. I tried to reason with myself that knowing Bagg was in the building had me on edge. But, when I had the sudden sure feeling I wasn't alone, I stood and turned around quickly. Sgt. Bagg was sitting at Derek's desk with an empty copy paper box in his lap.

I jumped. "Jesus, you trying to give me a heart attack?"

He stood up, his anger palpable in the way his beady eyes glared at me. He threw the box onto my desk, scattering papers and knocking over the picture frame of me and Danielle on our honeymoon.

Bagg may as well have been growling as he said, "Pack your shit. You're getting moved Monday."

He looked at me for an extra second, willing me to respond, but I remained silent. He turned and stormed from the room, stomping down the hall to the kitchen. The door to the outside slammed shut behind him.

I looked down at the box. I realized that Bagg had known for days that I was to be transferred Monday, but just out of spite he had kept the information from me. Because of his pettiness, Bagg had stayed late on a Friday to show me how angry he was by throwing an empty box at me.

I then doubled over and laughed so hard I felt tears form in my eyes. I was free.

JUNE 2014

8

"Welcome to the Batcave!" Sgt. James Cox grinned as he smacked me on the back. He had wanted to meet me in the parking lot of the 20th's building early Monday morning to give me a tour.

From my trunk, I hoisted the copy box full of my things from the SID office and said, "When do I get to drive the Batmobile?"

James laughed and led me to the door. "In your dreams."

Once inside, I watched in wonder as James scanned his finger at a biometric fingerprint scanner before the security door opened.

As we headed to the front desk, I said, "Well, that was the coolest shit I've ever seen."

James smiled and gestured to the secretary, "Melissa, this is Bobby Young. Bobby, Melissa Street. She is both our office supplies guru and the gatekeeper protecting us from the outside world. Nothing goes in or out of here without her knowing. She's our Alfred Pennyworth, if you will."

Melissa bantered back, "Sgt. Cox, I know you didn't just relate me to a butler again, right?"

James held up both hands, "What? No, of course not."

Melissa rolled her eyes. "You're lucky I let you in this morning. It's way too early for Batman references."

"It's never too early—"

"Go get to work." Melissa cut him off, but she was smiling. "It's nice to meet you, Bobby. Welcome to the team."

James adjusted his glasses and half-whispered to me "The *Bat*-team."

Melissa called a warning after us, "Sergeant!"

We laughed and James showed me to my desk before giving me a tour around the building, telling me who was in each office.

"These offices here have windows looking down into the warehouse. We can head down there from the kitchen, but there's a stairwell here, too."

As we descended, the clean office smell turned into the faint scent of gasoline and burnt oil. When we entered the warehouse space I was shocked.

"This place is enormous!" There were several cars parked along one wall near the big garage door, and I saw a small workout room in one corner. There were giant, three-tier metal shelves along three walls, packed with seized items and drugs. Everything was organized and labeled, and I said, "Amazing. It's like the property room, but it smells so much better."

We spent some time looking at the cars while James told me stories behind a couple of the hauls labeled and waiting for court dates, and then we headed upstairs.

James said, "Director Davis set up a welcome meeting, so we'll head there now. You've met most of the guys before, but you'll get to know the others pretty quick. We're a hard-working team here, and these guys take this job very seriously, something I know you've been looking forward to."

"That's an understatement," I said. "I can't wait to work with these guys and get some real shit done."

"Oh, it may happen sooner than you know." James grinned and gestured into the conference room where a group of guys were standing around talking. The tallest of the group broke off and came to me with his hand held out.

"TFO Young, it's been a while."

"Director Davis," I shook his hand, "I haven't seen you since your promotion, so congratulations."

He nodded, "Thanks, Young. It's been a wild ride since we worked together briefly in 2013 on that Dilaudid case. I've heard you've kept yourself busy since then."

I straightened up and still had to look up at his face as I grinned, "I hope you've heard only good things."

Director Davis patted James on the shoulder and said, "Sgt. Cox had nothing but positive reviews of your time with SID and at Hermitage. And, I know you know a couple of these guys," he gestured behind him, "because of your work on that Dilaudid case, and they've spoken highly of your work ethic since then as well. We can talk more details later, but welcome to the team."

"Thank you, Director. It's an honor to officially be a part of the 20th."

Director Davis said, "We're glad to have you." He smiled in a way that felt opposite of every brief smile I received from Sgt. Bagg. I realized he was being authentic and genuine in both his welcome and his supportive words, something I'd never gotten from Bagg. Even though I'd known him when he was still a sergeant with the 20th, I immediately felt that Director Davis was the kind of leader I could respect and trust, a leader like Sgt. James Cox. When Director Davis was promoted only a few months prior, it was his sergeant position that James and Bagg had put in for, and James had gotten it. Now, I understood why: Sgt. Cox and Director Davis seemed similar—both seemed to be fair, trustworthy guys who wanted to excel in honest work.

As Director Davis introduced me to the rest of the team, he was serious and direct, but the ease in his demeanor seemed to make everyone comfortable and confident. No one was competing for his attention, and Davis wasn't looking for schmoozing. Bagg's style would never have been taken seriously in the 20th. Davis wasn't putting on airs or hiding anything, and that was reflected in each of the guys I met or got reintroduced to. This was a very different boss than the kind I'd known for the last couple years, and the team seemed to be positively influenced by him.

"You remember Edgar Collins and Mike Hughes from 2013, and I know you've called them for some wiretap assistance and questions since then, too."

"Yes, I have, and you guys have always been patient with me. Nice to see you guys again." I shook both their hands.

"And this is your bunkmate, Thomas Wood." We shook hands and he joked about losing his private office. He didn't seem actually upset, though. He seemed like the easygoing kind of person who would let bullshit run off his shoulders.

Director Davis told him, "Don't you two get too comfortable, though. We have another guy in the pipeline who'll be joining your office, and I hear he's a bigger guy than I am." He then laughed with his head thrown up towards the ceiling. I couldn't help but smile because I had a guess at the future new addition. A guy I'd worked with at Hermitage and SID had put in for a spot at the same time as I did, but he came in second under me. He was a hard worker, definitely taller than Director Davis, and he grew a solid beard. I knew it was only a matter of time before my friend and one of the ushers at my wedding, Titus Price, would join me on the 20th.

Another guy came through the door a few minutes later and Director Davis introduced him. "And this is Jimmy Weakling. He shares an office with Hughes."

"Nice to meet you," I said as we shook hands.

"Nice to meet you, Young." Jimmy said with a small smile. In contrast to Director Davis' height and strong demeanor, Weakling was short and his features had a distinctly weasel-like quality to them. He seemed nice enough, though, so I tried to look past my negative first impression based on his looks.

"You can meet the main wiretap writer and tech guy another time." Director Davis said, "Let's get the meeting started." Director Davis told everyone to get some coffee and take a seat around the table.

I sat down beside my officemate Thomas with Sgt. Cox on my other side.

For the next hour, everyone shared the cases they were working on and what kind of assistance they'd need on it over the next week. Instead of sharing out of duty, like how it was done at SID, it seemed like everyone wanted to share where they were at, and the rest of the team, including Sgt. Cox and Director Davis, were just as interested and involved in the cases as the detectives.

Director Davis even asked if anyone would be available that night to help him assist another team with an investigation. "They have reason to believe this is a stash house, and they asked if we could help with carrying out the warrant this evening. So, let me know if you're available." I sat in my seat both stunned and feeling the adrenaline start. No leader I'd known had ever willingly worked overtime helping a different team make a huge bust, and Director Davis was here just asking if anyone wanted to come along for the ride. Before I could stop myself, my hand shot up.

"Yes, Bobby?"

"I'm in." I said.

Collins across the table laughed and said, "You look like you're ready to kick down doors."

"I am." I grinned, trying not to feel sheepish.

"Glad to have your help." Director Davis said, smiling.

The meeting wrapped up and I walked with Thomas Wood back to our shared office. I spent the next little bit unpacking my box and organizing my desk, and then I met with Director Davis in his office to go over protocols and details of the job. Now that I was a detective on the 20th, over-time was not only an option but a basic expectation of the job. Officers had to stick to strict shifts, so over-time was never an option before. I told Director Davis I had no problem at all with working long hours, and I assured him I would always be ready to work whenever I was needed.

He then briefed me on the evening's case and dismissed me saying I could always come to him if I had any questions. I left his office feeling on top of the world and ready for action, and I was not let down that evening.

When Director Davis and I arrived on the scene after dinner, the other team had attempted to enter the premises with a search warrant, but the suspect had immediately started yelling and becoming belligerent. They'd called the SWAT team in, and we stepped in to help with the plan as the house was surrounded. When the door was rammed in, we found the guy had disposed of a lot of cocaine down the garbage disposal, and his toilet was overflowing onto the bathroom tiles and into the hallway because he had tried to flush all his weed at once.

After he was restrained and secured in a squad car, we helped with the search of the house. The biggest find was a set of Porsche keys. After looking at some of the bills, we realized a lot of the guy's expenses were under his girlfriend, and we traced her to a house not far away. On a hunch, Director Davis and I drove by the residence after midnight. We walked up to the garage and peeked in the windows, and there was a car under a cover. He clicked the unlock button on the Porsche key and the garage lit up. We knew we had the right car.

We went to the door and knocked. A woman opened it as I made sure my recorder was turned on. For the next hour, we interviewed her and found out it wasn't her car, it was the suspect's, and she gladly opened the garage doors for us to seize the Porsche. The car was in mint condition when we uncovered it, and we walked around admiring it. Then we got to work doing a search to see if the suspect had left anything. When we opened the trunk, we found a duffel bag filled with over $100,000 in cash. Director Davis and I looked at each other and then back at the bag of cash sitting in the $75,000 car in front of us.

"Holy shit." I laughed. "This has been the best day ever."

Director Davis laughed, too, and patted my shoulder. "Thanks for your help tonight. Once we get this back to the warehouse, head on home and try to get some sleep before the morning."

"Fat chance." I said, still staring at the car and cash. It was like something from a movie, and I knew I would barely sleep that night from the excitement.

Only a few hours later, I was showered and heading back to the office. I wanted to get back to the office early since I couldn't sleep anyway. I had arrived home and left it again all while my wife was still soundly sleeping.

I texted my dad to see if he was awake and he called immediately.

"What are you doing up so early, son?"

"You mean, what am I doing up so late?"

"What? You never left work?"

"No, I did, but you won't believe this shit. I was out on this case till almost 3 am, and we seized 100 grand in cash and a Porsche by the end of it."

"Holy Hell!" my dad said. "And on your first day!"

"Exactly," I said. "It was only my first day, and this is just the beginning. This job is amazing!"

"Well, that's why they call it a 'dream job,' isn't it?"

I laughed. "I guess I just hadn't realized how amazing it would be. I feel like this is what I've been waiting for, and I'm about to get some real shit done now. I just can't wait to get back to the office and keep going."

I could tell Dad was smiling on the other end of the line as he said, "Yeah, but you can't get shit done if you never sleep, either, so take a nap." He laughed because he knew I hated naps. "Seriously, though, I'm real happy for you, son. You were made for this job. Just take care of yourself, too, okay?"

"I will. Thanks, Dad."

We hung up as I pulled back into the lot. Sgt. Cox had set me up with the biometric fingerprint scanner to enter the building, so I was itching to get inside and start back on my case with Charlie and Eddie. I also tried to take my dad's advice, though, so I leaned my car seat back and closed my eyes for fifteen minutes. It wasn't a nap, but I could say I at least tried.

9

A few days into my new position, I met with Charlie for the purpose of conducting a controlled call to Eddie to get a price on a kilogram of cocaine. This would be a major step up from the few ounces we'd been working with, but it would show Eddie that Charlie was ready to handle more product than he was getting.

Charlie placed calls to all three numbers utilized by Eddie, but he did not answer. It was common for dealers to carry two phones, but this guy thought he was extra slick and had three. One number was a local number and the other two had area codes from Utah and Florida. I monitored the GPS tracker which indicated the vehicle was parked at the local waterpark, so I let Charlie leave and told him to keep me posted.

That afternoon, Charlie called. "Hey, man. Eddie called me back. He was at the pool all day. I asked him for the ticket on a whole car. You know, a bird."

"Yeah, yeah, I know."

"Well, Eddie said he could get the car, but it would be an antique. Meaning expensive as fuck."

"Did he give you a price?"

"Well, he mentioned going in together and getting two whole ones for a better deal."

"Two? I don't know about that."

"Aight, well, he is going to see his 'buddy' sometime tomorrow and he'll get the ticket on them."

"Okay, just hit me up tomorrow then."

I was getting tired of playing Eddie's game. None of his deals had been straight forward, and, true to form, it ended up being two weeks before Eddie finally committed to a deal. We needed to move on from

Eddie's games and get to the high rollers who could move coke more quickly.

While I waited for Eddie to get his shit together, I helped out on my team's other cases and I began sending off subpoenas to the phone companies to collect phone tolls on Eddie's lines. There was one guy with Verizon who could get me my phone tolls back in less than an hour, so I knew it could be done, but this time around they took their sweet time and it was days before things were up and running. I continued to update my document of addresses Eddie frequented and pulled photos of the locations from Google Maps. It was not exciting, but every piece of information got us closer to the source.

I had started discussing the possibility of beginning a wiretap for this case with my team and Director Davis. We had to have everyone on board for this, and it would take dedication from the entire team to be successful. Thankfully, everyone agreed it was worth going up on Eddie's phone to follow him to his source and then on up the chain. I was so excited that when I left that day, late in the evening as always, I stopped at Melissa's desk by the front door to look at the three-ring binder where we logged all our cases. I had no idea what the hell would come of the case, but I went ahead and took the next number. I penciled my name next to control number "TF-1422." "TF" meant task force, and "1422" meant the year 2014 and the 22nd case started by the task force that year. Nothing fancy, but it was finally in the books. Whether it turned out good or not I had to wait and see.

The next morning, Charlie let me know a deal with Eddie was set for a couple hours later.

Eddie had told Charlie that four ounces of "good" coke was going to be $1,700 apiece and the other two ounces would only be $1,000 per ounce. As weird as this seemed, I was eager to make the deal and bring in the 168 grams. Now that the team was all in and ready to go, I was antsy to get started.

I met with Charlie behind a warehouse in West Nashville, and we talked for a bit about the six-ounce deal. This transaction was larger than any other, thus involving a lot more money. We were about to let $8,800 cash walk right into Eddie's pocket and then hopefully on to the main man, the source of supply.

Thomas Wood came with me to search Charlie's vehicle for money, weapons, and contraband. I searched Charlie as well. No contraband was found but Charlie did have some of his own cash.

"Damnit, Charlie, you know better than to bring your own cash."

"My bad. A guy's gotta buy lunch, though."

"Just making things complicated, aren't you?" I put his cash in a separate bag to hold until the deal was over.

I then handed Charlie $6,000 in 100-dollar bills, $800 in 50-dollar bills, and $2,000 in 20-dollar bills. Every bill had been copied before we left the office. We didn't have the luxury of a full-time tech at the Task Force, so Thomas and I equipped Charlie with an electronic listening device and a digital recorder ourselves.

As we finished preparing Charlie, Eddie called and told Charlie to be at the Big Lots off Lebanon Pike. Based on GPS surveillance, Eddie left his house and headed directly to the meeting spot. The rest of the team established a surveillance perimeter around Charlie and the location. Eddie arrived and parked on the far side of the lot from where Charlie was waiting. Charlie drove through the parking lot towards Eddie's green Toyota. It was go time!

Edgar Collins had his eye on Eddie and said over the radio, "Wait, he's getting out of the car."

"Wait, what?" I responded, wishing I was at the scene to keep an eye on Eddie. "He better not pull any stunts."

"He's heading into Big Lots."

I texted Charlie to wait in his car by Eddie's car until he came back.

Five minutes later Collins said, "Looks like he bought a pint of oil and is heading back to his car. He's opening the hood."

"He's going to do the deal under the hood." I replied.

"Charlie's out and looking under the hood with him. Yep. Happening on the sly."

Meanwhile I was listening to Charlie and Eddie talk about the engine and heard the rustling of the $8,800 cash being handed over.

Chapter 9

"I need to go pick up the six. I'll be back in an hour and a half." Eddie said.

Collins followed Eddie away from the site, and once a significant amount of time had passed I headed over to Charlie's vehicle.

"Well," Charlie said through his window, "that didn't go according to plan."

"No shit." Letting the money leave without the drugs was not ideal, but the tracker would do its job so Eddie wouldn't disappear on us.

"He just sent me a text." Charlie said and showed me his phone. Eddie had written, *This is my new num forgot 2 tell u.*

Why Eddie was using a number from Panama City Beach was beyond me. Maybe he wanted others to think that he was big time and had a condo down there. Charlie maintained contact with Eddie for the remainder of the deal by texting the new number.

An hour and a half went by, and Eddie had yet to return. Eddie had driven out of town to visit a residence, and Collins reported back that an Asian male in a black Yukon followed Eddie's car. Director Davis picked up surveillance on the two cars as they headed back towards Nashville, including a stop at McDonalds. By running the tag on the Yukon, we had identified the Asian male as Ken Phomvihan.

While they had lunch, I received a notification on my phone for a 615 number. We had set up an electronic GPS ping on multiple frequent numbers that Eddie contacted, and the alerts would show the location of a target phone every fifteen minutes. This particular 615 number had always stayed in and around Smyrna, outside of Nashville, and Eddie contacted the number almost daily. I was happy to see that the most recent ping showed the number at the McDonalds with Eddie, which meant the phone had to belong to Ken. He had to be the source of supply, and we were about to have proof of it.

Thomas and Collins followed Eddie back into Nashville and let Ken go.

Since it had been almost two hours since Eddie left Big Lots, I had Charlie call him and we recorded the conversation.

"Hey, man, you got it, yet?" Charlie asked.

"I just picked up the good stuff."

"So, you on your way back?"

"I got to get the other two."

"Damn, so you're going to be a minute."

"I got you. Call you in a few."

"Aight."

Charlie had no other choice but to continue to wait, and we stuck it out with him.

After the phone call, Eddie stopped at a rural wood shack north of Nashville. No way in hell we could successfully set up surveillance on the place, so Collins and Thomas did a few drive-bys, but they didn't see much detail.

Finally, Eddie called Charlie.

"I got the rest. We all good. Meet me at my uncle's tire shop again."

"On my way."

I followed Charlie to the tire shop and did a drive-by during the deal. Eddie and Charlie parked on the side of the building, though, so I couldn't see much. Thankfully, we had the recording device and Charlie's description of what happened.

Eddie entered Charlie's vehicle and handed over a purple crown royal bag.

Charlie asked, "Is it all in the bag?"

"All six of them."

"What's the difference in the two singles?"

Eddie laughed. "Shit, you will know the difference."

"Aight. Well, I'll hit you up later."

After the buy, Charlie left the tire shop and travelled to the church we used last time. Once we were behind the church, Charlie turned over the purple crown royal bag filled with six sandwich baggies of a white powdery substance, which all tested positive for cocaine. After the substance was recovered, I did a full search of Charlie, the vehicle, and conducted a debriefing. Before he left, I gave him back his small baggie of cash and Charlie took himself to lunch.

Thomas weighed each bag of cocaine and they totaled only 150.9 grams. Eddie was supposed to sell Charlie six ounces, which is 168 grams. I wasn't surprised we were shorted. This was par for the course when buying larger amounts from a mid-level dealer. I called Charlie right as he finished eating and told him to call Eddie and tell him that the cocaine was seventeen grams short and we would need to get that later. I left Charlie with the responsibility of calling Eddie about the shortage, and I headed back to the office to turn in property and begin paperwork.

10

A week later, I met with Charlie at a hotel parking lot downtown. Charlie jumped in the car with Thomas and I to have a chat. At this point we were close to the 300-gram threshold to get the wiretap up and going, but we had to "dirty" up the phone records with a little more dope talk. I had to rely on Charlie to pull as much information about the source out of Eddie as he could, even if it was in that cryptic, coded bullshit that all drug dealers use. I knew the language and could decipher it.

I explained to Charlie exactly what we were wanting to accomplish with the controlled phone call. Charlie understood, and I started the digital recorder as he dialed.

"What's up, buddy?"

"What you doin' boy? I just got back from hunting buffalo in Colorado."

"Oh, really?"

"Naw, I'm just fucking with you, man." Eddie laughed and then said, "But I am eating some buffalo. Well, it's really just summer sausage. What you up to?"

"Just checking in with you. What's your new boy doing?"

"He ain't new. He's just been outta town, but he's back and waiting on you."

"What'd you say that price was?"

"Fifteen and a half. It's a step under the $1,700 quality, but it's worthy."

"Would he do something about an antique car?"

"I'll have to talk to him in person. He wants me to finish this job first. There might be about, let me count here, probably about seventeen or eighteen, uh, half-cars left here." If a car was an ounce, this would be about nine ounces just sitting in front of him.

Charlie nodded, thinking, before asking, "So, what if I wanted a whole one, would it be the same price?" This would get Eddie to start talking in kilo terms.

"Shit, man. You want me to call him?"

"Yeah, call him, and then call me right back."

"You serious? I don't want to bullshit him."

"Yeah, I'm dead serious."

When Charlie hung up, I did a post-amble and turned off the recorder. I was pumped and high-fived Charlie and then Thomas. This was exactly what we wanted. Eddie was about to call his kilo dealer, and what Charlie didn't know was that we had a pen register going on Eddie's current phones. A pen register logs live calls, the numbers, and call duration. This way you don't have to subpoena the phone company for tolls and sit on your ass for three weeks waiting on the results. This was real-time evidence.

I stepped out of the car and away from Charlie to call our badass secretary back at the office.

"Melissa, hey, what number is showing up on the pen register."

"Nothing has shown up since the Charlie call."

"Damn. Okay."

We waited fifteen more minutes before I told Charlie to call Eddie again. Dope dealer time was always slow, but I was getting antsy. I started the recording as Charlie dialed again.

Eddie answered on the first ring and said, "Hey, I'm talking to him right now. I'll call you right back."

"Aight."

I stopped the recording and jumped out of the car again.

Melissa answered the phone, "Still nothing, Bobby."

I hung up before I started to curse. This meant that Eddie was using yet another phone, a fourth phone that we didn't have the number for to call his source. Eddie was playing it real safe. He probably used the fourth number just for this "new" guy back on the scene.

Eddie called back a minute later, and I jumped back in the car and fumbled with my recorder as Charlie's phone was ringing.

Charlie asked, "What's happening?"

"Nothing, man. I just got off the phone with him."

"What'd he say?"

"He wants me to finish up what I already got first."

I looked at Thomas and mouthed the word, "Damn."

Eddie continued, "But he said if you could clean me out he'd drop it down to $1,500."

"Okay, so he won't do a whole one or what?"

"No, he just won't give me that until I get off what I've got."

"Aight."

"I've got to get rid of the thirteen I have left first before he gives me more."

"So, they'll be $1,500 each, but I've got to get all of them?"

"Yeah, might as well get a deal."

"Hey, by the way, what about that half ounce you owe me?"

Eddie hurriedly said, "Yeah, yeah, I'm going to get that to you when we hook up."

"Aight. Also, is this the Mexican guy you mentioned a while ago who could do a whole one?"

"Yeah, yeah. That's him. I need to holler at you later, man."

"Aight."

When I stopped the recording I sat back in my seat with a headache. This was exactly why we needed to do a wiretap, to sift through all the bullshit that comes out of Eddie's mouth and get to the real dealers. Eddie was pretty bold, but much of what he had told Charlie was what we like to call "fluff." He had eighteen half-cars, and then he said he had thirteen. It felt like he didn't even know what all he had, or he wasn't willing to be straight about it. At this point, it seemed as if Eddie was full of shit, but if he was holding nearly half a kilo right now and he had access to more, we needed to pinpoint that supplier. I turned Charlie loose and told him I would touch base with him later. Back to the office, back to the drawing board.

Chapter 10

The next day around lunch, Charlie called to let me know he had seen Eddie with a large amount of money. Charlie believed Eddie was going to pay his supplier. We were back on! GPS surveillance on Eddie's car showed him driving around the Mt. Juliet area, and we recorded stops to places like the Providence shopping area and a hardware store. The vehicle tracker showed that it was stationary at the hardware store for an extended period of time.

Me and a few teammates headed for the hardware store, but when investigators arrived at the location, Eddie's vehicle could not be found. Several minutes later the GPS signal updated and showed the vehicle heading back towards Nashville, and we had to scramble back in his direction. Luckily, Director Davis was in the area and located Eddie's vehicle. Davis conducted loose surveillance as Eddie continued north of town until he arrived at the wooden shack he'd stopped at last time, which we had identified as the residence of Timothy Cook.

While the rest of the team went to Cook's house, Thomas split off to drive past the tire shop because it was located in the same general area where Eddie's car was seen. As he drove by, he observed a 1996 Mercedes parked at the tire shop, and a man standing outside the vehicle, talking on a cell phone. Thomas pulled over and ran the plate and pulled up the record of Hector Torres, someone we had also noted had been in frequent contact with Eddie. Ten years prior, Hector had been the subject of a wiretap investigation and had been arrested with forty kilos of cocaine. He had admitted to working for a large drug cartel based out of Mexico. He'd been released only recently, so spotting him at the tire shop moved him up on our suspect list and added a piece to the puzzle. Maybe he was Eddie's Hispanic source who had "been out of town" for a while? Thomas stuck around the area and then followed Hector back to his residence while we posted up at Cook's house.

With Hector's past, we were bound to land a massive bust but we had to keep an eye on him. Hector stayed at his house for an hour or so and then left. As if he was playing right into our hands, Thomas followed him directly to the residence of Timothy Cook. A black GMC Yukon, Hector's Mercedes, Eddie's Corolla, and a brand-new black Ford

F-150 stayed at the house for several hours. On one of Jimmy Weakling's drive-bys, he observed Ken standing outside next to his Yukon, talking on the phone.

Something big seemed to be in the works. It was nearing that 5:00 hour, and some of my team members were wanting to go home, but this felt too important. This was the first time that we had seen Eddie and Hector together, and they were all meeting at Cook's shack. The only car we couldn't identify was the new black Ford F-150.

The black GMC Yukon was the first to leave, and Collins followed alone as Ken travelled north. I had to make a swift decision on whether or not to continue following Ken because Collins was by himself. But, we would possibly need to follow Eddie or Hector also. I told Collins to let Ken go and we circled back.

Unfortunately, another hour went by and nothing was noted. Charlie called me again and said that he saw Eddie and Hector riding around in a black Ford F-150. I drove back by Cook's place in disbelief. The truck was gone.

"Who was supposed to be watching the north end of the road?" I asked over the radio channel. No one fessed up. I was pissed. Someone dropped the ball and missed the black Ford F-150 leaving Cook's house and the worst part was that no one even got the tag. We had no other choice than to terminate surveillance for the day. Everyone was already tired and cranky, even me.

The next day, Charlie came through for me again. He was turning out to be the best CI to ever exist. He must have been doing his own surveillance and putting pieces together, because he tipped me off that the black Ford F-150 was a rental and had a Tennessee commercial license plate. With that information, I submitted a subpoena to Enterprise Rent-a-Car requiring them to turn over information and documents pertaining to the rental of the truck.

When we got the rental agreement, it showed Eddie had rented the vehicle on 06/24/14 and paid for it through 07/01/2014. So, he was only keeping it a week. It was strange, though, that Eddie's Corolla had also been at Cook's the previous evening. It could mean he needed a rental car for some specific shady business, and we needed to track that truck.

I whipped up a tracking order and raced to the same Wilson County judge that signed the tracker for Eddie's Corolla. She was already familiar with the probable cause, so it didn't take long to read. After she granted the warrant I headed towards Eddie's home. It was late at night, but I wanted to see if the truck was there and make a game plan for applying the tracker. I didn't want it to be like the last time when I had almost shit my pants because of the landsharks!

The rental truck was parked at the house and close to the wood line. I called Thomas to assist on the application, and we agreed to meet up a little before 4 am.

When the alarm went off at 3 am, I realized I had barely slept at all. With such an important case in my head, I felt like I was wired from the constant adrenaline and focusing on all the details. I met Thomas at a warehouse close to Eddie's home, and he jumped into my car.

"What's up, man?" I said as I drove to the road.

Thomas said, "Tired as hell, but ready to go."

"Shit, at least it's not raining." I said, remembering the last time. As we drove to Eddie's, I made a mental note to text Adam to check in. I'd talked to him just two weeks prior, and he had offered to jump in to help on the case if I ever needed it. I knew I would need to take him up on that at some point, especially if we were going to bring in a lot of targets. But, it was hard to consider letting anyone on SID in on the case. I trusted Adam completely, but I didn't want Sgt. Bagg knowing what our team was doing. Not until this case was in the bag.

When we parked at the edge of the woods, I would be lying if I said I wasn't nervous. I moved slowly through the graveyard and woods, listening constantly for any signs of the dogs. The truck was in the same spot by the tree line and I thanked God. I shuffled next to it, and since it sat higher off the ground, it was easy to place the tracker underneath. I then scurried back through the woods to the car.

Thomas joked, "You looked spooked, like you just ran from a ghost."

I laughed. "Last time was a lot worse."

Later that day, as I scarfed down my daily "lunch" of a peanut butter and jelly Uncrustables, I got confirmation that the tracker was working. Eddie had left in the F-150 and went by Richardson's house in Bellevue first, then he drove to Cook's house out north. He then had a leisurely lunch at the Whiskey Kitchen downtown, and Thomas and I did a drive-by to check in. Eddie was sitting with an unidentified white male wearing blue jeans, a blue flannel button up, and a ball cap. After both had finished their meal, they left in Eddie's rental truck. We followed Eddie and the unidentified male to midtown where they went into a bar. After an hour of waiting for them to leave, Thomas and I decided to terminate surveillance. Eddie wasn't doing business; he was just out for happy hour.

JULY 2014

11

My team and I agreed that in our collective experience, drug dealers usually got a rental car or truck in order to make a haul. I guessed that dealers thought it was safer than using their personal vehicles, which would be linked to their names and addresses.

However, we had tracked that F-150 for a week, and the only helpful information we got was his visits to additional associates in the area. Mostly it seemed like Eddie was just running errands.

It was July 1st, though, which was the end of Eddie's rental contract. I was really hoping he would extend it, but instead he left his house early that morning and returned the truck with the tracker to Enterprise.

Thomas and I scrambled out of the office and across town to the Enterprise and arrived shortly after Eddie did. We watched from a distance as he returned the truck and then stood outside pacing and talking on the phone. Timothy Cook arrived in Eddie's Corolla, and I realized I hadn't gotten a recent alert for that car's tracker.

"Shit, why was I not alerted the Corolla was on the move?"

Thomas shrugged, "Technical error hopefully."

"It better be. If someone found it . . ."

"We'd be in deep shit." Thomas finished for me.

Since the device wasn't working, we decided to follow Cook and Eddie. Thankfully, Cook drove slowly and they returned to the shack up north. We sat nearby for an hour before giving up, and I tried not to be angry that one tracker had stopped working and the other was in the hands of Enterprise. The last thing we needed was for someone to rent that truck and drive it to California. We'd never see that tracker again, and those things weren't cheap.

We could have talked to the Enterprise employees to get their cooperation on returning the device, but it was hard to trust anyone when it came to this line of work. Instead, Thomas entered the office and acted as if he was going to rent a vehicle. When the employee's attentions were elsewhere, I casually walked onto the lot from an adjoining strip mall. Weaving between cars and ducking so as not to be seen, I found the truck and dove under it to get the tracker.

I texted Thomas and picked him up a few minutes later.

After pulling away from the building I asked him, "What did you tell them?"

"I said my wife just texted that she'd gone and gotten one already somewhere else."

"Brilliant."

Thomas shrugged and picked the tracker up from the center console. "So, who's next?"

"I'm thinking Hector's our next guy. He was there with Eddie and Ken at Cook's the other day, and he was at Eddie's uncle's shop. Maybe he's the missing link to the next level."

"Sounds like as good a lead as any."

We headed back to the Batcave to type up an affidavit so that we could stick a tracker on Hector's Mercedes.

Two days later, Thomas and I headed to Hector's residence in the morning. He typically hid his car behind the house, so we weren't sure he was home. We waited until the car came down the driveway with Hector driving and the owner of both the car and house riding shotgun, his elderly roommate named James Miller. The living arrangement was unusual, but we suspected it was all to benefit Hector and keep him nearly invisible while Miller got some kind of compensation.

We followed them to Rivergate Mall, and a couple others from the team joined us to help with surveillance. Malls were hectic and busy sites to follow a car, but they're ideal for dealers to do shady business. They were also ideal for detectives who needed to sneak under cars. Hector parked near the food court and they both entered the building.

While we quickly made a plan for a "tuck n' roll" to place the tracker under the car, Miller exited the mall and headed back to the car with a notebook in his hand. Then he returned to the mall. He repeated this twice more over the next fifteen minutes, Jimmy Weakling tracking him and reporting his movements. We had no idea what Miller was up to or if he would suddenly revisit the car again, but we had to get this done.

Thomas pulled his car right behind the Mercedes and barely came to a stop, just long enough for me to open my door, roll out onto the pavement and crawl under the Mercedes. I stuck the tracker, rolled out, and walked casually down the line of cars until Thomas circled back for me. I may have gotten a little road rash from this operation, but I did what I had to, and we all headed back to the office.

With the GPS device attached, we watched Hector for several days as he circled street blocks and pulled into parking lots for short periods of time before driving to his destinations. He drove below the posted speed limit while traveling on the interstate, too. These unusual driving patterns were consistent with those of someone who was conducting counter surveillance or heat runs. He was paranoid he might be followed, and rightfully so!

For a couple days, Hector made nighttime trips to rundown motels and trailer parks out of town in Buffalo Valley and then in Greenbrier. He would stop at each location only temporarily before moving on or heading home. We suspected he was picking up or dropping off cocaine.

When my phone buzzed early one morning after we'd been tracking Hector for almost two weeks, I had the gut feeling that something bigger was happening. Not once in the previous two weeks had Hector left his house at 4 am. Typically, dealers did their shadiest business under the cover of darkness when there were fewer police officers patrolling. This was probably something Hector believed too, but he didn't know I could track him from the comfort of my bed.

After making a couple stops on the edge of town, Hector headed west on the interstate. A few hours later, he was in Memphis. Then, just outside of Little Rock, AR, he stopped at a gas station only long enough to fill up. He then continued south and west from there, heading straight towards Texas. This was huge! Hector was traveling towards a border state.

That evening, as Hector entered the Houston area, I could have done a backflip I was so excited. When he finally stopped, I did a Google search of the location. The street view showed a short green metal building that was falling apart. Even though the building was barely standing, there was a well-kept 10-foot-tall fence topped with barbed wire enclosing the property. Nothing but junk filled the lot surrounding the building, but there was obviously something valuable in there. It looked like something out of a movie.

In the property photos, I could see a business sign: "SERVICOS A AMERICA." I wondered what "services" they provided. Must have been something quick because Hector was only there for an hour.

He then went to an apartment complex where he stayed the night.

Thank God for GPS trackers.

It was mid-July at this point, and we were working hard on the wiretap application to try and get it finished as soon as possible. I had a feeling Hector and Eddie could be connected, but there was no way to know until we could start wiretapping. Charlie had been a huge help so far, but he couldn't listen in on Eddie's conversations, which was the much-needed next step.

While Hector was still in Houston, I got an email that Friday morning that sent me back in time. Every two weeks there was an update to a department-wide spreadsheet that showed payroll status changes. Everyone checked it because at the bottom it listed who got fired or left the department. My name still hadn't shown up on the spreadsheet updating that I was with the 20th, and it was no different on this particular Friday.

However, after the updates were posted, I received an email reminder that I was scheduled for another mandated alternate shift the next day where I was supposed to patrol and make arrests. The kicker, though, was that the email stated I was still assigned to the old shift where Sgt. Bagg was the supervisor.

I stood up so fast, Thomas turned and asked, "What happened?"

I shook my head, not wanting to bring up the bullshit from my previous job or frustrations with the lagging system. "I need to find Davis." I left the room and hurried to his office, trying to hold the anger in. I already couldn't stand the alternate shifts because it got in the way of my work, and I was already planning on spending my Saturday working on the wiretap application and tracking Hector. The last thing I wanted to do was to submit to a pointless shift under Sgt. Bagg again.

I knocked on Director Davis' open door. "Davis, do you have a minute?"

"Of course, come on in. What's up, Bobby?"

I explained the situation to him.

He said, "Since you're now officially under the 20th, you should be on the Team 6 schedule."

"That's what I thought, too." I said. "It's been a month and half since I was transferred, but it's still not changed in the system."

Director Davis shook his head, but he didn't commiserate on the inefficient system. He still had to be a professional Director, which meant being tight-lipped about his opinions. He did say, "I will move you to the Team 6 'alternate shift' team, so you don't need to worry about Saturday."

"Thanks, Director."

I left the office feeling a little bit lighter. Maybe it was just a coincidence that the system lagged on changing my status, but seeing my name on the list under Bagg's gave me a sick feeling in my stomach.

The sick feeling returned when I received an email from Sgt. Bagg on Saturday afternoon. He had sent it to Captain Zander but copied me, Director Davis, and two other lieutenants.

I could hear his nasally voice through the email: "Bobby Young was the only one that failed to show up at work this evening. Had Det. Muze attempt to contact him to no avail."

I was working from home, so I found my wife and showed her the email. "Can you believe this? It's a fucking lie!"

Danielle's mouth dropped open as she read it. "Didn't Muze call you earlier?"

"Exactly! I talked to him and explained the situation, and he said he'd let Bagg know."

Danielle rolled her eyes, "You don't even see the guy for over a month and he's still trying to get you into trouble. So petty."

I agreed and texted Director Davis.

He replied all to the email and said, "I assumed he was on the Team 6 schedule now. My apologies for any inconvenience."

As much as I couldn't respect Sgt. Bagg, my respect for Davis grew exponentially with that email. He was honest, fair, straight-forward, and he didn't put up with Bagg's dramatic bullshit.

As soon as I was trying to relax into getting some more work done and putting Bagg out of my mind, I received another email from Director Davis.

I sat up at the subject line, "Verdict on Application."

I opened the attachment and reread the beginning:

> *This Application is being submitted to request an order authorizing the interception and recording of wire and electronic communications of Edward "Eddie" Peterson, Kensone "Ken" Phomvihan, Hector Torres, Nathaniel Richardson, and others as yet unidentified, concerning state felony offenses enumerated in T. C. A. §39-17-417(j); regarding the sale and distribution of 300 grams or more of cocaine, a schedule II controlled substance.*
>
> *This investigation is being conducted by 20th Judicial District Drug Task Force acting in conjunction with officers and employees of the Metro Nashville Police Department (MNPD), Agents and employees with the Tennessee Bureau of Investigation (TBI), Agents and employees with the Drug Enforcement Administration (DEA), and employees of the Office of the District Attorney General for the 20th Judicial District.*

All looked right.

I then scanned through the rest of the application and stopped at District Attorney General Peter Robert's determination.

This Application has been authorized by Peter Roberts, III, the duly elected District Attorney General for the 20th Judicial District, as evidenced by his written authorization of this Application, which is attached herewith.

"Woo!" I yelled.

From the other side of the house, Danielle called back, "Was that a good yell this time?"

I grinned and went to find her. "How would you feel about La Hacienda two nights in a row?"

She smiled as she stood up, "Was the wiretap approved?"

I nodded. "The switch has been flipped and we're on!"

12

We started tapping Eddie as fast as we could. We knew Eddie was using several phones to conduct his drug deals, so we just had to be strategic about which ones we went up on. We started with tapping Eddie's latest 615 phone number that Charlie had passed along to us. We had to have non-law enforcement civilians listening to the wires, so it took some time to get a schedule together and to make sure each monitor was trained on what to listen for. If a call was deemed unrelated to criminal activities, the interception needed to be suspended immediately. We also had to coordinate with contracted district attorneys to supervise the wiretapping.

Before anyone, officer or civilian, could assist with a wiretap case, they had to be "read in." The rules, regulations, and a copy of the order would be provided, and the individual had to read and sign that they understood the ramifications if any rules were broken. Confidentiality is paramount. Any unauthorized disclosure of intercepted conversations or of the progress of the investigation during the case would be treated as a felony charge under state law. In other words, if someone leaked any information about a wiretap case, they would be in deep shit!

Between running the over-time required for the team to work on the case, paying fees to the phone companies, compensating the civilians monitoring the calls, and paying a District Attorney to supervise the wire room, a wiretap operation could rack up bills quickly. We had to know there would be a successful take-down in the end . . . including a sizable seizure to make up the cost.

Three days after going up on Eddie's 615 number, we submitted a signed order granting the interception of Eddie's 850 number as well. Despite the focus on Eddie, I believed Hector was the key because he had all the characteristics of a "big fish" and we were ready to catch him. A successful high-level dealer knew that laying low would keep him in the game and out of jail. Most might have thought Hector's low-key lifestyle was a reason to overlook him, but I knew he was different, especially when he'd been in Houston for several days.

A week into the wiretap, the wire room intercepted an outgoing phone call on Eddie's 850 number to a Hispanic male. The monitors would not assume someone's identity until we had identified the participants, but our team recognized the male as Hector Torres. During the phone conversation, Hector told Eddie that he was in Houston dealing with the death of his cousin, and he would head back to Nashville the following day.

Hector ended the call with some cryptic information, though.

Eddie asked him, "You got good news?"

"My friend over there has been calling, and he told me he had good news."

"Is it the little bitty things?"

Hector replied, "My buddy sent it to someone else in North Carolina because they pay cash. I'll go see my friend when I get back tomorrow, though, and I'll let you know."

"Aight, don't forget about me!"

Hector was going to be driving back to Nashville and planned to meet a "friend" the next day, but the important point was him mentioning "over there." That phrase usually referred to Mexico. Although we couldn't confirm what specifically they were talking about in regards to North Carolina and the "little bitty things," we felt this was a good indicator of something larger getting moved.

Confirming what Hector had said, I got a tracker alert the next morning before sunrise, alerting me Hector was on the move. I had a geofence set up around his friend's apartment complex because I wanted to know exactly when Hector was coming back. I had to organize the team and alert them of the upcoming late-night surveillance work. A lot of detectives (and their wives) liked to know before a shift what time they would be finishing their day. I told them this could be a long one.

When I had woken up enough and sent off the texts, I realized I was more excited than at any other time thus far in the investigation. We were going to see what Hector was up to and hopefully confirm his involvement with Eddie's drug dealing!

Hector travelled I-45 to Texarkana, through Arkansas, hit Memphis, and then headed straight to Nashville. Thirteen hours after leaving Houston, Hector arrived in the Nashville area. Our team was ready, and we picked up surveillance as he moved down I-40 through West Nashville. We kept a close eye on him, hoping he would head to a stash house or storage unit, but we were way off. He drove straight home. A fear settled in my head: Could he have actually just gone to his cousin's funeral?

A few minutes after Hector arrived home, Hughes observed old man James Miller walking away from the home.

He radioed in, "What the hell is this old guy doing? He's just walking down the street."

While part of the team kept eyes on the house, Hughes and I watched as Miller walked a quarter mile and entered a Family Dollar.

"Bobby, you head in. I'll keep a distance." Hughes said.

I parked in the lot and jumped out, pulling my Braves Jersey on over my gun as I headed into the store. I wanted to see exactly what Miller was doing and if he was meeting anyone. I found Miller in aisle two. He had a basket filled with food and a whole, raw chicken.

As Miller proceeded to the checkout, and I got back into the car I radioed, "He just bought a chicken and TV dinners. I'm not even kidding."

We all laughed, hyped on adrenaline from waiting and planning all day for this moment of Hector returning to Nashville.

Hughes asked, "What kind did he get? Salisbury steak?"

I said over the radio, "Very funny. If he just goes straight back to the house, we'll give it thirty minutes and then we can pull off. I doubt Hector is going anywhere after that long drive, especially now that the fridge is restocked."

Hughes, still laughing, said, "You sure the old man didn't buy some powder . . . powdered gravy?"

Chapter 12

"Okay, I'm turning my radio off."

While Hector was laying low at home the next few days, the team shifted our focus back to Eddie and some key calls that came in. The wire room had calls coming in left and right. phones ringing off the hook and it was hard to keep up. One rule was that each intercepted call had to be listened to live as the call was occurring. Since we were up on three lines and sometimes only had two civilians working to listen to calls, we had to pick up the slack when they were slammed. It wasn't ideal because we preferred being out on the street, taking photos and watching deals go down, but sometimes it was a necessary to step in and listen in on the calls, too.

In one call, Eddie's uncle who owned the tire shop said, "I need you to get rid of something for me."

Eddie said, "That's fine."

"There is more stuff but you gotta come by my house to see it."

We knew something was up between the two, but we hadn't figured out what yet. Regardless, his uncle had just entered himself right into a conspiracy charge. He might not have anything big, but he was now clearly involved. They then talked about moving "materials" to Eddie's grandmother's house later in the day.

When they hung up, we then listened in on a conversation between Eddie and Ken.

Eddie asked, "You heard from A-Rod? I could really use anything right now."

"I been hollering at him," Ken said. "But, I'm gonna need 250. And if he can break me off some extra then I'll hook you up, bro."

I knew of one guy named A-Rod, but a professional athlete who lives in another state was probably not meddling with dope dealers like Eddie and Ken. Maybe this was the source of supply for Ken. We needed to identify A-Rod, but Eddie was also getting Ken in on his uncle's job.

Eddie told Ken about his uncle's proposal. Ken was interested in looking at the "product" so Eddie said he'd make his way to Ken's house. The two continued chatting like two school girls while Eddie drove to Smyrna.

"My homies are trying to tint some windows," Ken said.

"Cool. I can do that all day, every day."

"I have potential buyers to enter the tournament fee."

Eddie sounded excited. "I need two juices. How many windows are they going to tint?"

"Let me call you back."

Conversations like this required my full attention. Every word or phrase was street code, and as the lead detective, it was my job to translate. It was clear that a big deal was going down. The "tournament fee," meant how much cash would be needed upfront, and "windows" was slang for crystal meth. It wasn't our focus, but any type of deal would contribute to their charges later.

Ken called back and the two continued their conversation.

Eddie said, "Had to do some of the windows on consignment."

"They are only a dollar shy to be at fourteen. You need to figure it out, because he is leaving Saturday."

"What's the entry fee? I'm not doing no less than seventy-five."

"I'll tell them to make it worth your while. Don't be late."

Eddie was on it, "Aight. I am supposed to be picking up a load today because someone owes me some wop. There are about ten of them."

"I'm supposed to get with A-Rod today, too."

"If you did, then that would be perfect."

These two were pretty good at the code. Another monitor might get lost in the slang terms, but I kept on it. I knew Eddie and Ken were planning on moving a "load" of cocaine and maybe some pills, and on top of that they were still talking about crystal meth. They were also still talking about A-Rod, so I knew I needed to figure out who this guy was.

Ken continued, "We need to sit down together and do the math because I don't know where we are with owing each other."

Eddie immediately replied, "We are at 4750." They had run together for quite some time, so long it seemed that they were casual about owing each other money.

"Okay. Let me just get with A-Rod and I'll hit you back."

Chapter 12

"Hold up, you don't want to see what Willy has?" I wondered if this meant Eddie already had with him what his uncle wanted moved.

"Nah. I'm hitting up A-Rod. Just lemme know later."

"You motherfucker. I'm gonna charge you gas money." Eddie sounded pissed, but he took a breath and tried to cool off.

Ken didn't seem affected. "Alright, well do your thing, because they are ready."

"Is it gonna be one window or two?"

"I will have to see."

Ken was definitely looking like Eddie's main supplier. I watched as Eddie turned around and headed to the other side of town to his uncle's trailer.

We set up surveillance at the trailer to see what they were moving. Since it was getting late and it was so dark out, Eddie acted nervous and fidgety when he was hurrying to get inside.

After several minutes in the trailer, Eddie exited with a large blanket. He threw it on top of the Corolla and then backed the car close to the front door. Once he was satisfied with the distance, Eddie popped the trunk. Willy appeared and the two took the blanket, unfolded it and placed it in the trunk. They were acting like they were about to put a body in there. Hell, I wouldn't have been surprised, but we'd have to act on that. There was no letting a body walk like we do the drugs.

They made several trips back and forth to the trunk before they seemed to think the trunk was full. Since it was not a body, I assumed it must have been several pounds of marijuana, but I couldn't know for sure. I then followed as Willy drove Eddie's car and Eddie drove his uncle's truck five minutes away to Eddie's grandmother's. They both pulled under the carport and there was zero visibility, so I pulled off for the night.

13

The next morning, I swung by Eddie's grandmother's house and saw the two cars still in the carport. Even in the day time there was almost no visibility, but at least I knew there were things moving in and out of the house. This house was already high on my list for a search warrant when we took these guys down.

I called my dad on my way to the office and we talked about the Braves game the night before. Since I worked late I hadn't watched it, but Dad had and we commiserated over the Dodgers wiping the Braves off the field for the fourth game in a row.

"Things were pretty even till we stopped doing shit in the 5th and Kemp got that second two-run. I almost went to bed rather than see the end of it."

"Dodgers are first seed, though, so we kind of expected it."

"I expected we'd handle at least one game in the series. Four losses in a row, though? That's just shameful."

I laughed, "Yeah. A bit. If Jones had been there . . ."

"Oh," my dad started, "Chipper got in the hall of fame last year; he's doing fine for himself. You gotta find yourself a new favorite."

"Someday. Maybe. Chipper's always been my man, though."

My dad snorted. "Ain't that the truth. He was consistent, I'll hand him that. A fine player. A Brave all the way through."

"That's right. He's still my go-to cover on the job. Hey, do you remember my friend Titus?"

"Big guy who was an usher at your wedding?"

"Yeah, that's him. Big Chipper Jones fan, too. I got the official email last night that he's transferring to the team next month."

"That's great. Congratulations to him. I tell you what, he's the kind of guy I'd want on my side in a fight."

"No kidding. He could mess a guy up real good." I swiped my finger on the biometric scanner, which still made me feel like a badass, and waved to Melissa before heading to my office. "It'll be good to have Titus on the team."

I heard yelling coming from my office. "Oh, shit." I lowered my voice, "It sounds like Weakling is really laying into Thomas this morning."

"What's that guy's problem?" Dad asked. He had no patience for bullshit bullying. "It seems like that boy always has his panties in a wad."

I said quietly, "Thomas says it's 'little man syndrome.' Gotta make up for his size."

"Jesus, I can hear him from here. He must be *tiny*."

I laughed and said, "I'll talk to you later, Dad."

"Okay, have a good day."

I hung up and stepped into the doorway. Usually when anyone came to our office to touch base, they sat down in the chair beside the door next to Thomas' desk. The few times Weakling came to our office, though, he never sat down. He preferred to stand either in the middle of the room, pacing, or he would hover over Thomas' shoulder, looking down at him, shaking documents at his face when he thought Thomas had done something wrong. Thomas always stayed cool and low-voiced, and it always made Weakling crazier. It reminded me of how I dealt with Sgt. Bagg in our last "meeting" when I said nothing and he just spiraled into word vomiting. For a second, as I stood in the doorway, Weakling even looked like Bagg with his face growing red in anger and talking a mile a minute, cursing every couple of words.

Thomas turned to me and smiled. Regardless of Weakling's noise, Thomas said to me in a calm voice, "Good morning."

Weakling went silent as I said, "Morning, guys."

I sat down at my desk across the room and Weakling didn't even look at me, so I faced my computer.

Thomas then said to him in the most dad voice possible, "You don't need to worry about me or this case. Let's get back to work and do some good today, okay?"

Weakling shouted, "What the fuck, man? You never fucking listen when I talk to you! Did you hear a fucking word I said?"

"Thank you for bringing your feelings to my attention. Go on back to your office now and take some deep breaths, all right? You'll feel a lot better." Thomas said this quietly but firmly. I tried to keep a straight face as I stared at my computer screen.

"You piece of shit!" Weakling stomped out of the office, smacking the folder he was holding against the doorframe as he went.

I turned towards Thomas who had picked up his coffee to take a sip. I could tell he was on the verge of laughing, and I just shook my head in amazement. I asked, "How do you just let that roll off you?"

He shrugged and said, "Poor little guy."

I couldn't help but laugh and he joined in.

He then changed the subject, "Hey, I think Davis got a translator for Hector's calls."

"Thank God."

We were still up on Hector's phone and waiting to see if his trip to Texas was for business or pleasure. It had been nearly a week since he got back, and for the most part, Hector had been quiet, but when he did make a call he spoke in Spanish. I doubted he would hold on to a bunch of dope for this long if he had brought it back, but I had seen stranger things. I wasn't giving up on Hector. I still thought he was the right target, but it was difficult to get a Spanish-speaking civilian in to translate the calls.

Thomas told me that Director Davis had gotten in touch with the newly promoted Sgt. Franco Lazaro to see if he knew of anyone we could use. Sgt. Lazaro recommended his wife and his niece for the job saying it would be good for his niece because she was starting to head down the wrong path. Sgt. Lazaro had taken her in to get her on the right track.

Thomas said, "I guess his wife and niece are coming in later today to help translate. Hopefully, we get something good."

I nodded. We really needed a good call to come in from Hector or we'd need to drop him altogether.

Unfortunately, once Lazaro's wife and niece had been trained and sworn to confidentiality, the records ended up being personal conversations and no business. I was starting to get nervous that Hector wasn't dealing after all. The following day, though, we finally got a good conversation between Hector and his buddy Kingston Thompson.

Kingston said, "What's up? Just got back."

"Alright, cool."

"You got something for me?"

"I'll tell you when I see you."

"Alright, meet me at Maxwell House Hotel. I'll be there in fifteen minutes. I'll let you know."

We scrambled to our cars to get to the hotel before them. I was feeling good about this one, but it was partially just relief that *something* was happening at all for Hector. We needed a deal to go down to make the wiretap worthwhile. Part of our team followed Hector as he drove straight to a law office downtown.

Hughes radioed in, "I don't know where this guy's going, but it's not to the hotel."

I started to get nervous. Did this mean he wasn't meeting with Kingston? Maybe he was just paying a bill from his old court case. Our wire room recorded that Hector tried to make several calls to Kingston with no answer while he meandered around downtown, even stopping at the farmer's market. Finally Kingston picked up. It'd been thirty minutes since they'd last talked.

Hector asked, "Man, where you at? I'm downtown and I'll be at the hotel soon."

"Alright, I'm about to leave the east side. I'll be there in a minute."

Hector went to the hotel and sat in the parking lot in his Mercedes. A half hour went by and there was still no sign of Kingston.

Hughes had his eye on him and radioed in, "He just got out of his car, oh, slammed the door. He just stomped his way into the hotel. He's pissed."

I laughed. "Man, they can't wait thirty minutes, but that's what we do all day, every day."

While Hector waited at the bar with a drink, he texted Kingston, "How far are you from Maxwell?"

When Kingston didn't respond immediately, Hector called him.

He seemed like he was on the verge of yelling as he asked, "Man, where the hell are you?"

Kingston answered nonchalantly, "I'm here."

"Where?"

"I'm the black truck, about to pull in."

"I'm in the lobby. Do you want me to come outside or what?"

"I can come in there and go by the bar real quick. It ain't going to be long. I still gotta make a run."

"Alright. Just meet me at the bar."

They hung up and Hughes and I joked over the radio that there was no black truck in sight. I said, "I love when they say 'I'm here' or 'About to pull in.' They are *never* where they say they are."

"Almost feel bad for old Hector here. He's been twiddling his thumbs for an hour, and who knows when this guy's actually going to show up."

Sure enough, fifteen minutes went by before the black truck arrived. Kingston parked and exited the truck on the passenger side, which meant someone else was driving. Right after he went inside, a red Volvo with an out of county tag pulled up next to the driver's side of the black truck. The driver of the truck exited and got inside the red Volvo.

Hughes called over the radio, "Dope deal!"

I said, "No surprise. I still got my eyes on the lobby. It looks like that was a quick conversation. They're coming out now."

The red Volvo drove away after the truck driver got back into his car. I had other TFOs follow the red Volvo across the street to the Exxon, and we alerted an unmarked patrol car in the area of what we'd seen. We asked that they assist us in stopping the Volvo once it left.

Just as Hector in his Mercedes and Kingston in his truck departed, Kingston sent a message to Hector: "Half Moon 262."

The civilian monitors had no idea what this was, but I did. I had a knack for pills ever since my 2013 Dilaudid case I'd done with the 20th. I found pill cases intriguing. Kingston was talking about a 15mg Opana pill that had the markings of a crescent moon and the number 262 stamped on it. Opana is oxymorphone, a powerful Schedule II narcotic meant for someone in severe pain. These pills were central contributors to the opioid crisis because of their addictive nature, and it would often lead people to heroin when they couldn't get the pills. This category of narcotics was the root of so many other issues, and it brought in a pretty penny for dealers.

Kingston and his driver headed across the street where they met up with the Volvo again. This time Kingston got in the Volvo, but just for a second. He was in and out, really quick, and then Kingston got back in the truck. Several of us followed the truck.

A flex car followed the red Volvo away from Exxon. Once they were a good distance from the Exxon, the officer initiated a traffic stop. We used uniformed officers to make it look normal. The driver and passenger, a male and female from Cheatham County were identified. A search was done, but nothing was found. We knew they were most likely buying pills, but shit, those things were so small that they could be hidden *anywhere*.

Even though the stop didn't pan out, the night had just begun for Kingston. He rode shotgun all around town, making stops along Jefferson Street, meeting with people in parking lots, hands meeting hands, quick trips behind buildings, this almost seemed too routine. Plus, as much as I didn't want to admit it, he was just dealing pills. Yes, it was still illegal and we could have arrested him, but this wiretap case was focusing on cocaine. He was off the hook for this case, but I knew we would see Kingston again someday.

Later that evening, a conversation was intercepted between Eddie and Ken. During this conversation, Ken told Eddie that he had gone out of town.

"Where you at?" Eddie asked, clearly surprised to hear Ken had left.

"You know where I'm at. Dancing with the wolves."

"Did you talk to your boy?"

"We all had shit to do. They landed at the same time. I'll be back next week."

"What about the windows?"

"I haven't talked to him yet either. Damn, man!" Ken sounded impatient, "I'm out of town trying to get something together. If this hits, then we will all win."

"Okay, okay," Eddie said. "Just let me know!"

After the insightful calls between Ken and Eddie over the previous few days, we were able to add Ken's number to the wire and it quickly paid off. Ken made calls every few minutes, and he didn't hide anything. He went so far as to brag about visiting his marijuana grower in California as he took his customer's orders. Eddie wasn't interested in marijuana, though.

Since he was out of town and working with his marijuana business, Ken gave an unidentified male Eddie's phone number to contact. At first, the unidentified male was unsuccessful in contacting Eddie at the number Ken provided. This was crucial and we thought Eddie may have picked up another line. Eddie finally answered, though, which was a load off our minds.

"Where do you want to meet?" Eddie asked. "Do you want me to bring back the window I was unable to install?"

"Yeah, sure, if you want to. Meet me at King Market in Antioch."

"Alright, I'll be in a silver Camry."

"I have a white Altima."

Shortly after I arrived at King's Market and established surveillance in the parking lot, the Altima pulled up and I saw he was Asian like Ken.

Of course, Eddie was running late and he was driving a Toyota Camry registered to his grandmother. What a sweet grandson! It didn't take long for the two to make their exchange and head in opposite directions. The exchange lasted only two minutes. Surveillance was terminated on Eddie, and I followed the Altima.

The unidentified Asian male left King Market and turned onto Antioch Pike. The license plate registration revealed an address off of Rocky Parkway in Antioch, and that is exactly where he parked the car. I drove past the residence and observed him retrieve a green bag from his trunk. Yet another person added to the list. Since it was "windows"

Eddie was returning, I knew it had to be crystal meth in the bag, but these dealers seemed to deal in everything at the same time: marijuana, pills, cocaine, and now crystal meth. It was frustrating and hard to track since our focus was cocaine, but I had no idea just how frustrating things were about to get.

AUGUST 2014

14

In the first week of August, we commissioned Officer Bouasan Thammavong ("Vong") to translate intercepted phone calls on Ken's line. For some reason, Ken had stopped talking about drugs on his number a few days prior, and he was making more calls speaking in Vietnamese. He must have gotten a new dope phone while in the middle of planning a marijuana shipment from California because suddenly all drug-related calls just stopped. So, while it was slow, Thomas had called up Officer Vong to help with translating some of Ken's most recent calls. Officer Vong was eager to help and had a lot of questions about the wiretap targets, and he and Thomas got along well.

Prior to listening to intercepted phone calls, Collins supplied a copy of all paperwork to Officer Vong. He said that Vong read the wiretap monitor instructions and asked, "Where do I sign?"

Apparently, the conversations Officer Vong translated were uneventful. Ken did talk about his trip to California, but he didn't say anything about the drugs or activity. It sounded mostly like calls to home to update on a vacation. I figured maybe he had just taken all his orders and was now taking care of business. Officer Vong wasn't there long, and he was frustrated he'd even had to come in just to listen to Ken's vacation chat. I was thankful for the work he put in to help, but I also felt like this case was starting to come loose at the seams.

With Ken focusing on marijuana and his phone going silent, Eddie waiting around for a big "windows" pill deal and his phones going silent, and the assumption that perhaps Hector really had gone to Houston for a funeral, team morale was low. Plus, we'd removed the trackers from both Eddie's and Hector's vehicles because they were spent, and I didn't even know whether or not to put new ones on them since Eddie used several cars and Hector didn't seem to be going anywhere ever. It felt like we were reaching a dead end.

Several of my team members suggested I should cut my losses and drop the case. The expenses couldn't be recouped, but it would avoid additional costs of going up on more phones and possibly spinning into a rabbit hole that wouldn't produce a major cocaine haul, the whole point of the case.

I asked my teammates' opinions and listened to what they said, but this case meant too much to me and I still had a strong feeling that Eddie would lead somewhere. There was no way in hell I could give up. With Eddie picking up new numbers nearly every week, I contacted Charlie and asked him to place a call to Eddie on both of the numbers we had. It had been a while since the two had spoken, and we needed a solid update to keep the case moving forward. Every phone number we had seemed to be going dark.

"Hey boy." Charlie said.

"Let me holler back at you."

"Is this—"

"BYE." Eddie hung up immediately.

Clearly Eddie didn't want to talk to Charlie on the 615 number that we were up on. Later, Charlie called me back and said Eddie had just called from a new phone, a new 615 number. No surprise there. We knew he had many, and this would be the third number we could go up on for Eddie.

I thanked Charlie and then had to make a choice: Ignore this new lead and pull the plug, like some of my teammates suggested, or get an order to go up on the new number.

I'd already made up my mind, though. I had to beg Collins to get this new number up and going quickly. He was about to go out of town for a few days, and I needed it done. Since it was Eddie's third phone, Collins could reference the previous orders, which made it easier to get the order finished and accepted. We were up within three hours, which was a serious record, so I definitely owed Collins!

There wasn't a lot of activity on Eddie's new phone immediately, but I remained hopeful. The next evening, the wire room intercepted a call between Eddie and an unidentified male. New numbers with new voices were always a good sign!

The unidentified male asked, "You ready for me?"

"I'm about to get in the shower." Always leave it to Eddie to be frank. "I'll be ready in fifteen minutes."

"It's gonna take me longer than that because I got to go get it."

"Aight."

After hanging up, and allegedly taking a shower, Eddie called the male back. "Hey, can you do the Foreman Grill like they ate last time but like Pop's or better?"

"The what grill?"

"The Foreman Grill. I stopped by Pop's place yesterday and his was A-1."

Eddie's associate didn't seem too certain with his next question. "Like, his?"

"Yeah. Pops said that you stopped by and dropped off a Foreman Grill and I tried it out. The hamburgers were a lot better than I had last time, but the burgers were a little burnt. You understand what I'm saying?"

"I gotcha buddy. You want two?"

"Yep."

Holy shit this is some coded language! I think the unidentified male was even lost at one point. I know I was. What I figured out, though, was that a Foreman Grill was white and guess what else is white? Cocaine. That's how these people think. I've heard it all. Even the dealer, who was obviously another source of supply for Eddie, seemed to give up and just ask straight, "You want two?"

Thanks for making it easier on us Mr. Dope Dealer!

Eddie said yes but then his phone went dark for the evening, so we had no idea if he met up with this unidentified dealer or not.

In the meantime, it was time to shake the tree. I asked Charlie to meet with me in the same hotel parking lot as before. When Charlie arrived, I told him exactly what I needed him to say. He had to record a talk with Eddie about getting a kilo of cocaine. It would justify the case and ramp it back up.

As we listened to the phone ring, I started the recording.

"What up, bud?" Eddie seemed happy to hear from Charlie again. I hoped that meant he had some product to move.

"What you doing?" Charlie asked.

"Not much. On my lunch break."

"You taking an all-day lunch break?"

"Yeah, something like that. Started a job this week."

"Yeah? Where you working?"

"Downtown doing construction shit."

"Ah, I hear ya. Well," Charlie said, getting to business, "I just wanted to check with you on a price."

"Alright, what size car you want."

"A nine or a whole one." Nine ounces was a quarter-kilo, so this was a big ask, but Charlie went a step further and was asking the price on a whole kilo, too. Charlie continued, "I know it's been a while, so I just wanna get a price from you so I can get my money straight."

The call suddenly dropped. I froze. Thankfully, Eddie called right back.

Charlie said, "What happened?"

"Hell if I know. It just cuts off whenever it wants to. So, you're interested in a whole car or something like that?"

"Yeah, if you got it. What would a whole one be?"

"Fourteen for each."

"Like fourteen for a half?"

"No, Fourteen dollars for, you know, each one."

"One for fourteen?" One ounce for $1,400 seemed steep, but dealers knew quality was part of the game.

"Yeah, I could try to get him to do a little better. I got one the other day and it was a piece." I nodded my head in understanding. It was good quality, which meant it'd be more expensive.

Charlie said, "Yeah, call him and see what he would do if I got a whole one. Can you call me back?"

"I'll call you back in a minute."

Charlie and I waited in my car, hoping it wouldn't take long. Eddie called back only four minutes later.

"I talked to him." Eddie said. "He can do them for $1,350 a piece."

"What does that add up to? I can't do the damn math."

"Uh, let me get a calculator. Hold on one second." There was a clicking of a calculator on Eddie's end. "It'd be forty-eight, six."

"$48,000?"

"Yeah. $48,600. Wait, that's wrong. No, no it's right."

"I just did the math on my phone. I got $43,600."

"$1,350 times 36 is $48,600." Thirty-six ounces added up to just over a kilogram. Eddie was confident about his math and said, "Yeah, that's right. So, you want the whole thing?"

"Yeah. But, I'm assuming I gotta give you the money and you gotta go get it?"

"You wouldn't have to wait as long as you did last time. He'd come to me for something like that."

"Aight. Well, hell." Charlie was playing it off cool.

Eddie was now sounding more excited with the chance of a big deal. "Tell me what you wanna do and he'll come off it and come wherever you want him to, bud."

"Is this your boy you were talking about when we were over at Richardson's?"

"Yeah, he knows where I live, and I know where he lives."

"The guy from Mexico right?"

"Don't worry about it."

"Well, if it's from Mexico, is it going to be good?" I mentally thanked Charlie for the save on this one. No need to make Eddie suspicious.

"Hell yeah. It's gonna be good." Eddie said. "I hit some of it last night. You got my word."

"Okay, I just want to make sure because that last shit wasn't no good. Real shaky. On something big like this, you know, I need to know it's good."

"Naw, buddy it's gonna be A-1."

"You need a day heads-up or what?"

"Yeah, with my new job and all, try to give me at least a two-day notice."

"Aight." Charlie said. "Let me holla back at you."

I gave Charlie a high-five once the call and recording ended. Before I could begin debriefing him, Charlie's phone rang again and I got the recording restarted.

"I was going to tell you," Eddie said, "if you pick up the pace a little bit then he could do better than that."

"What could he do?"

"I don't know, but he just said if you didn't take so long then he could do better."

"I thought that dude was going to take care of that other one, but he didn't, so I had to get it off slow myself. I had to cut it to make any money."

"If you wanna look at it later this evening, I promise you'll give it your seal of approval."

Charlie paused and looked at me, and he said, "Is it nice and shiny?"

"Oh, hell yeah."

"Aight. Well, I'll take your word on it. I'll hit you back later."

When I finished debriefing with Charlie and was heading back to the office I called Melissa. She had the records of Charlie's call with Eddie, but when Eddie called his guy, we had no record of it. He had yet another phone. We knew Eddie had recently moved into his grandma's house, so now we would shift our attention back to him and figure out a way to get that other number. Things were moving back in the right direction, though, and I was grateful to have had Charlie to fall back on yet again to get the ball rolling. He was definitely earning his informant status, but I knew he'd be glad when I didn't need him for the case anymore, which I hoped would be very soon.

15

The next morning, August 12th, Thomas was standing in the middle of our shared office when I arrived. The first thing he said was, "There's been a leak."

"What?" I responded, feeling the four words chill me to the bone.

"I received a call from a citizen informant last night."

"Yeah?" A citizen informant was different from our standard confidential informant who was working off charges. A citizen informant came to us voluntarily, and we didn't always know their motive for giving us information.

Thomas nodded slightly and said, "He said, 'Y'all have a leak.'"

I stared at Thomas, almost unable to believe what he was saying. "How is that possible? What happened?" I had to sit down.

"Well, he's someone close to Eddie, but he has to stay anonymous. I'll call him Chance. He heard Eddie moved his guns and called me."

"Shit. How do you know this CI?"

Thomas said, "Chance has been a citizen informant for us before so he had my number. I didn't reach out to him when we started tracking Eddie this go-round, but he reached out to me."

I tried to wrap my mind around this. "Wait, so Eddie just moved his guns? That could mean anything."

Thomas shook his head. "No, Chance also said that Eddie had gotten a tip-off to move his shit because he was being watched. Chance said Ken is who warned Eddie and that Ken has someone on the inside who let him know."

"Someone on the inside, like an officer?"

"Yeah. Apparently Ken was told that his picture is on the wall."

My brain was spinning processing this information as my anger started growing. Ken had someone on the inside, and I hated a dirty cop. I asked, "Did you ask when this all happened?"

"Chance said Eddie started moving his shit like the first day of August or last day of July. He wasn't totally sure, though."

"That was when the lines started going dead. Wait, that was also when Officer Vong was in here translating calls, right?"

Thomas nodded, and he seemed to be trying to stay calm.

I, on the other hand, stood and started to pace the room, the anger exploding. "That motherfucking dirty cop! If he leaked something to ruin this case, I'm gonna kill him. I can't believe this!"

Thomas said, "I called Director Davis immediately to let him know." He shook his head. "I just can't believe it either."

Director Davis showed up in the doorway a few moments later while I was still pacing, pissed and yelling about how a leak would ruin my case and how I'd take Vong down myself.

Director Davis had me sit down and take a breath, and he then told us he had called the police chief, Chief Smalls, to talk over the next steps. Davis said, "I told Chief Smalls everything, told him there was smoke, and we agreed the best course of action would be to place a tracker on Officer Thammavong's car. He's the only officer we've had in on the case who may be running in the same circles as Ken and who may even be going to see him."

"You told him about Vong's involvement in the wire room?" I asked.

Davis nodded and then gave me an order, "The Chief has already authorized it, so write up an affidavit as soon as possible and get a tracker placed on his car." He looked at Thomas, "I also want you two to interview the informant face-to-face today and get it recorded. We need more details. Report back after you do that."

When Davis left the room, I worked on keeping my mouth shut and refraining from yelling again about this betrayal by one of our own, but it was hard to keep quiet. This case was like my baby, and I would do anything to protect it, especially if it meant taking down a fellow cop who was dirty. After months of work and surveillance, the long hours and never-ending focus, the idea that it could be over with just one call, one threat, seemed terrifyingly possible. I resolved to do everything in my power to make sure the case wouldn't fail. I'd put too much of myself into it, and I wasn't going to let anything stop it. It was the longest affidavit for a tracking order I had ever written, but I put every detail imaginable in it to justify the possible suspicion of Officer Thammavong. We needed to monitor him and see if the connection became clear. If it didn't, then we'd have a much bigger problem on our hands; we wouldn't know where to even start with pinpointing the leak.

When we met with Chance behind a church, he looked calm and at ease, leaning against an old beat-up sedan.

Thomas greeted him before starting the interview. "Thanks for meeting with us. I know you told me everything last night, but we need to get it on recording if you don't mind."

"That's fine with me. I'll tell you as much as I know."

After briefing Chance on his rights, the interview was short as he only knew the basics of the situation. Ken told Eddie they were targeted, Eddie was moving his shit and was furious about having to drop his lines again, Ken had found out from someone on the inside, etc.

"It must be an Asian." Chance concluded with a shrug of his shoulders. "They're real tight in that community, know what I mean?"

"Is there anything else you can add to the timeline?"

Chance thought a moment and said, "Eddie said it was less than a week ago when Ken found out. Thursday or Friday. It was before the weekend, I know that."

"So, would that be July 31st or August 1st?"

"I don't remember exactly. It's one of those, though."

"Thanks for the information."

Chance nodded. "I'll keep you posted if I find out anything else. Hope it helps." Chance then got into his car and drove out of the lot.

Thomas and I headed back to the office, both circling around the idea that Officer Vong may be involved with Ken. Officer Vong had come in to the office on August 1st to translate calls, so it was critical to know if Ken had found out that day or the day before. If it was the day before, the information couldn't have come from Officer Vong. I had to hope the tracker would shed some light on the possible connection.

After I submitted the tracker order that afternoon, the wire room intercepted a call between Eddie and the unidentified male who'd talked with Eddie about Foreman Grills on his new number. What seemed like a simple phone call turned out to be a pivotal part of the investigation. I had already instructed the monitors to mark the number as a source for Eddie and to let me know ASAP when there was any contact. Despite my instructions, the call wasn't even marked important or "drug pertinent," as we called it. The conversation content didn't sound drug related to a civilian, but that was for me to decide. It was just a short discussion about a house way out in the boonies, near a rock quarry, which I marked in my maps for later. That short conversation set the stage for a meet-up later that evening.

A bit after 9 pm, after everyone in the office had left for the day other than me, James, and Melissa, the "meet" call came into the wire room.

Eddie asked, "You in the area?"

"Yep."

"How long will you be?"

"Two minutes."

After hearing this call, James and I left the office and sped to the area near Eddie's grandmother's house. I had a feeling this was going to be important, and the smell of my engine burning was worth it. I saw Eddie's green Toyota Corolla and a maroon Chrysler PT Cruiser under the carport. This was a good sign because we had not seen the maroon car before.

Only five minutes after we arrived on the scene, the PT Cruiser pulled out of the driveway and on to Clarksville Highway. The car traveled several miles and turned into Kroger. Not sure why the suspected supplier parked under a street light, but I really appreciated it. I got sweet pictures of him getting in and out of the car.

Melissa was still in the office to help me, so I had her run the tag and she even got me a photo of the suspected driver within minutes.

"His name is Daniel Harding." Melissa told me over the phone. "He was stopped in that same car last month and is on parole for selling cocaine."

"You are a badass!"

"A badass who is heading home now."

"Okay, thank you for staying late for this, Melissa. Have a good rest of your night."

"You too. Be safe."

So, the unidentified male who was Eddie's supplier might have been this guy named Daniel Harding. Daniel stayed in the Kroger for over an hour, and James and I speculated on how much groceries this guy needed. When he finally reemerged, he had only a single bag and was on his phone. I wished we were already tapping his phone, but I knew we would be soon now that he was identified.

We followed him only five minutes away to his home address, and we pulled off.

"I got a feeling," I told James as we pulled back into the office parking lot. "I think this guy's going to be our ticket to the big leagues."

James laughed and said, "I hope you're right, Bobby. With this leak scare, we need to make this case a good haul."

"We will. I'll make sure of it."

"Are you heading to Vong's tonight?"

"Yeah, I got the tracker this afternoon. I'll probably head there real early tomorrow."

"Need back up?"

I took a breath and shook my head. This was my case, and I was who had written the affidavit, so I felt it my duty to place the tracker on my own. "Vong's not expecting us to track him. If he's got landsharks or some complicated security I can't get by, I'll let you know."

"Good luck then, Bobby." James patted my shoulder and we went our separate ways.

Thankfully, my 4 am placement of the tracker went over smoothly. I was still angry about the possibility that a leak could completely shut down the case, especially if it was a fellow officer. The one thing good cops hate the most, above criminals and crime, are bad cops. If Vong had thrown us to the wolves, he'd find very little mercy with me.

Over the next week while we set up the wiretap on Daniel's phone and started listening in on calls, I monitored Officer Vong's movements. Not once did he go to Antioch, much less to Ken's house. I still had pings on Ken's phone, too, and the locations never crossed paths. It still wasn't proving anyone's innocence, but it wasn't getting us any closer to pinpointing his guilt.

We finally got a good call on Daniel's phone that distracted me from the leak stress for a while. Daniel and a new unidentified male talked in code, of course.

The unidentified male said, "Hey, I ain't gonna have time to grab that from the house, can you come up here?"

Daniel asked, "Where you at?"

"Work. It's Space Park South off Antioch Pike. I'll text you the shit."

"I'm about to hit the slab."

"I got three bands on me."

"Bet."

They hung up and we waited for the text before heading to the address. The unidentified male's "bands" meant he had $3,000 on him in cash to pay Daniel. We watched them do the deal and noted the green Ford Fusion with dark tinted windows. We got the tag and sent it in for identification of the buyer. Drew Turner was now another guy to add to the conspiracy list.

I could barely sleep that night, and I got to the office extra early the next morning hoping for another good call on Daniel's line. The wire room had intercepted a series of phone calls between Daniel and another unidentified male. Drug dealers had lots of contacts, especially Daniel, but this one talked big and seemed like he could be a source of supply.

This unidentified male told Daniel that he still had four or five of "them" left, and then he went on a rant about how he let someone borrow thirty to forty bands and how he couldn't keep doing that. Dealing in that many bands meant we were talking kilo deals now! Street price on one kilo in Nashville was roughly $32,000. When I heard these calls, I nearly had tears of joy. Daniel was definitely a kilo-level dealer, but he was still a small fish. We had to get to his source.

When the two talked again, the unidentified male still wouldn't shut up, which was great for us.

The unidentified male asked, "Does it look good? Like glass?"

Daniel said, "All the way through."

"Does it look like it's been hit?"

"Nope."

"Shit. Big D said that the panties were taken off." I almost laughed out loud at this. Dealers will figure out the craziest code for things. "Panties" meant the plastic wrapping taped or vacuum sealed around the kilo bricks.

"They still on." Daniel said, "But it's open."

"Aight. Imma pull up on ya and look."

I made sure to get GPS alerts on this guy's cell phone. Some of my teammates called me the "Ping King" because my cell phone was pinging constantly with the whereabouts of all the guys I was tracking. I liked knowing where all the players were every fifteen minutes.

A couple days later, we decided to track the ping from this unidentified male who talked about moving kilos like it was nothing. We followed the pings to a Kroger in North Nashville, and Sgt. Cox spotted a gold Chevy Malibu he recognized. A Malibu had been at one of Daniel's recent deals, but we hadn't been able to get the tag. This time, though, we knew the cell phone was pinging from inside the Kroger, and no one was in the Malibu, so we waited. About half an hour later, a black male wearing green shorts and a black t-shirt got in the Malibu and took off. I had just received a ping only a minute before, so it was a guessing game as to if this guy was our mark. We took a chance and followed. About fifteen minutes later when we approached the corner of Charlotte and 51st Avenue, I got another alert on the number. The ping showed the phone at that exact corner. Bingo! We'd made the right guess.

Collins had stayed back at the office, working on the wiretap affidavit for this unknown male source. It didn't matter that we didn't know his name yet. You don't have to have the target of the wiretap identified before you go up on their phone. There were a lot of detectives who didn't want to identify the target until they were arrested because it could be easier that way. Personally, I liked knowing everything about my targets before kicking down their doors.

We sent in the car's tag for identification just as Collins submitted the wiretap application to the District Attorney for his signature. We were working fast because we knew that the current District Attorney was retiring in only three days, at the end of August. A former defense attorney, Chad Ball, had won the race and was about to take over, and I didn't feel confident he would be as easy to work with.

By the end of the night, after the order was signed and sent off to the cell phone company, we knew the name of Daniel's supplier: Lewis McDonald. I spent an hour reviewing his mile-long rap sheet and saw he was on parole for selling coke. The 20th had been the last team to arrest him, too, just as he crossed into Davidson County with some kilos that he had brought back from Atlanta. Lewis had clearly not given up the game, so here we were again.

I spent the next day on surveillance at Lewis' mother's house in North Nashville. The pings showed Lewis laying his head in Franklin, TN which is thirty minutes south of Nashville, but I knew he wouldn't be doing deals from that bachelor pad. Lewis had told more than one dealer to stop by "his mom's house," and I shook my head thinking about how disrespectful a son Lewis was for dealing dope out of his mom's nice house in a quiet neighborhood. I'd gotten to his mom's house early and set up a camera facing the house to record the comings and goings of Lewis' frequent shoppers.

Some of the team met up with me late in the afternoon to watch a deal go down with yet another unidentified male that we planned to track afterwards.

He had called Lewis earlier and said, "I'm coming from the hotel on Demonbreun. I want two. You know it's my birthday, and I'm getting fucked up tonight."

Lewis had replied, "Catch them sales and I'll see you later. Come to my mom's."

A little after 10 pm, a gray Chevy Silverado truck with a Florida tag arrived at the house. Lewis greeted his birthday buddy outside and they went inside. Two minutes later, Lewis walked him back to the truck, and they talked for a few more minutes. *Take all the time you need*, I thought to myself. The lighting was just right, and I was snapping all the pictures. The guy then left, presumably with the two ounces of cocaine in his pocket.

When he left in the Silverado and turned onto Whites Creek Pike, I got right behind him. The truck went straight to a housing project, but that ended up being his first stop. When he headed towards Demonbreun where he said he was staying, Thomas pulled ahead of him and got to the hotel first. The Silverado pulled in seconds behind Thomas, and he watched a slender male, wearing a white t-shirt and black jeans, get out of the truck and walk towards the breezeway. Thomas got out on foot to see which room he went into, and I texted him to tell the guy Happy Birthday. Once we knew his room, we made up a ruse with the front desk clerk to get the room roster. Little did this guy know that this was a birthday he'd never forget.

Chapter 15

16

"Titus, welcome to the team!"

Titus shook my hand, smiling. I was the first to arrive in the meeting room to welcome Titus to the team, and I nodded to James who had just given him a tour.

Titus said, "It'll be good to work with you again Bobby. This place is legit!"

"Right? You already do the tour?"

"The fingerprint scanner—"

"Right?"

"And the warehouse—"

"Dude."

"Sgt. Cox is right." Titus said, gesturing to him. "This shit *is* the Batcave. But, where do I get my mask and cape?"

We laughed and joked with James about the Bat-team some more.

Titus then asked about my dad because they'd gotten on well at my wedding.

"He's good. Talk to him every day and see him every Sunday for dinner."

"Nice. His health still okay?"

Dad had been vocal at our wedding about his battle with cancer because he'd gotten the all-clear only a couple months before.

"Yeah." I said. "He gets regular checks and things seem to be stable."

Titus nodded. "Good, good."

"He's really excited actually, well, we all are, because my sister Ashley just had a baby boy last week."

"Congrats!" He said, patting my back. "Her fourth right?"

"Yeah. Three girls and now a boy. I'm going over this weekend to meet him since I couldn't make it to the hospital."

"You and Danielle need to catch up, now, huh?"

I laughed. "We've only been married eight months! Jesus."

Hughes arrived to the meeting room and Director Davis and Thomas came in a minute later. Collins was a few minutes late because of traffic, and Jimmy Weakling strolled in a quarter past our team's meeting time. I could tell he had puffed up his chest to try and look as big as possible, but next to Titus he looked like a little kid. No one made fun of him, but Thomas and I must have had the same thought because, as we sat down to the meeting, he whispered, "He's just a little guy."

It took everything in me not to laugh. Weakling had a habit of coming to our office at least once a week to pick a fight with Thomas. Thomas always laughed it off since Weakling just had "little man syndrome." Since Thomas wasn't the biggest guy on the team, Weakling must have felt he had to challenge him rather than anyone more threatening.

Director Davis had us go over our current situations with our cases and then he dropped some big news on us.

"Good work guys. Before you get back to work on your cases, though, I need to give an update on the leak issue. Titus, have you been briefed on the situation?"

"Not yet, sir."

"Good, I'm glad to hear it isn't becoming a rumor and running rampant. It's best if this doesn't get out because it's a very delicate situation that could compromise case TF-1422, the one under Bobby's lead. In addition, it could affect a fellow officer's career, something that shouldn't be taken lightly. Thomas and Bobby can give you more details after this, but the summary is that Thomas received a tip-off from a citizen informant two weeks ago that some key players in the case found out they were targets from someone on the inside. We've managed to continue monitoring them, and we are monitoring a suspect who shares an ethnic community with one of the targets, an officer who helped with translating some calls. Even though we've only been tracking the officer for two weeks and we've not seen any suspicious activity, I received notice this morning from the Office of Professional Accountability (OPA) that we need to set up an interview with Officer Thammavong for today, if possible."

"Today?" Thomas said. He realized he'd said it out loud and then apologized. "It just seems too soon for that, sir. We just don't have a case against him."

Davis nodded. "I agree with you. Unfortunately, it's not my call to make. OPA makes the call, and they want a recorded interview with Officer Thammavong today, if possible. Thomas, I'll need you to ask him to do more translation work and set up a time for as soon as he is available. Tell him it's urgent. Let me know when you do, and I'll alert OPA Investigator Sgt. Korbin."

I used to play softball with Korbin and knew him to be a nice but overly competitive guy. I hadn't seen him in a long time, though, so I looked forward to catching up with him.

After the meeting, Titus walked with me and Thomas back to our shared office space and he started to set up his desk.

"Wait, Bobby, is that the chair you had at SID?"

"Why should I buy another? This one's perfect."

He shook his head, laughing. "Well, at least you're still repping Chipper, even if you are weird about where your ass sits."

"Okay, don't start sounding like Adam Bristol."

"How's that guy doing anyway? I don't know when I last saw him. Shit, probably was at your wedding."

"He's good. I talked to him last week. He may be shipping out of here in a couple months again."

Titus nodded as he set up a picture frame of his wife by his computer. "The military is a respectable path, but, man, I'm glad to not have to deal with deployments."

Thomas chimed in, "Same. I couldn't be away from my family that long." I saw his face change briefly and remembered the difficult situation he dealt with at home. He snapped out of it though and said, "And the hours. You have to be *on* literally every waking moment."

"Shit, and every non-waking moment." Titus laughed.

I said, "I wouldn't mind the hours I don't think."

"Because you're a working machine, Bobby." Titus said, still grinning.

I shrugged and looked back to my computer. "Maybe you can learn how to get shit done while you're here, Titus. Ain't no sitting around or gossiping on this team."

"Hey, I'm ready for some action!"

"Well, you'll get it soon enough."

Thomas called Officer Vong and then went to report to Director Davis the schedule.

Sgt. Korbin, a tech, and an Assistant District Attorney arrived at the office after lunch. The meeting room was bugged and the speakers set up in my office for the rest of us to listen in. Sgt. Korbin greeted me warmly, but then he kept conversation minimal and distant the rest of the time he was in the office. I didn't take it personal because I understood he was on the job, but he was very different from years back when we played softball.

Thomas went to pick up Officer Vong and led him to the meeting room where Sgt. Cox greeted him and asked if he could ask some questions.

As Sgt. Cox asked questions, Vong sounded both hesitant and confused, denying revealing any information about the case after his translating services.

Sgt. Cox asked him specifically if he knew of Ken, but Vong didn't know the name. "We see here on Facebook, though," Sgt. Cox said, "that you have a mutual friend, a Mookie Villavong."

"I went to high school with Mookie, but I haven't talked to him in years. It's one of those Facebook things where we just added each other because we're still around town. I don't have any idea what he's doing these days. We were never even friends."

"He's lying." Sgt. Korbin said, standing next to me and gripping the desk as he listened. "He rushed through that last part. He's getting nervous, which makes a guy sloppy."

Sgt. Cox asked him a few more questions about Mookie, showing examples of Mookie's posts on Ken's walls and some shared pictures, but Vong continued to deny knowing Ken. He did say to one photo,

"That looks like the brother of a friend of mine, but I don't even know his name."

Sgt. Korbin jumped up from the desk and yelled, "He is a liar! I got him—he's lying! We're gonna take this lying sonofabitch down!"

I didn't know how to react other than point out Vong had denied everything and seemed authentic in all that he said. Sgt. Korbin waved me off and hushed me to keep listening.

I was more than ready to take Vong down if he was the leak, but the facts weren't lining up.

Before I knew it, the interview was over and Sgt. Korbin had left the office to head back to OPA while his tech and the Assistant DA wrapped up at our office.

I went by Sgt. Cox's office after Thomas left with Vong and asked how he was doing.

He shook his head. "I couldn't detect anything off. If he wasn't telling the truth, he was hiding it extremely well."

His phone buzzed in his pocket and when he looked at the screen he said, "It's Captain Zander."

I started to stand and said, "I'll leave."

"Nah, stay," he said before answering the call. "Good afternoon, Captain."

I sat back down and listened to James' side of the conversation.

"Yes, we just finished the recorded interview . . . Ah, you talked to Korbin, then?" He looked at me, his eyebrows drawing in with concern. A few seconds later, his face changed to surprise and he stood suddenly, saying, "Sir, we can't do anything, yet. Do not decommission him until we know for sure. We don't have near enough evidence to prove anyth—"

He had been pacing the office but he stopped, staring out of his window for a long time.

He then said, "Understood, Captain."

After hanging up he tossed his phone onto his desk as he sat back down. "Shit."

I said, "So, they want to decommission him already?"

He nodded.

Chapter 16

"Shit. I mean, we don't have any other leads, though. This is the only thing that makes sense."

"He'll be put on the green mile." Sgt. Cox said, shaking his head and looking at his hands. "If he did do it, that's not punishment enough. If he didn't do it . . . well, there's no bigger shame than the green mile."

Going on the green mile was when an officer was stripped of his badge and forced to report to work every day at headquarters where he had to sit full shifts in the lobby. No one would talk to the officer unless they, too, wanted to be ostracized. It was a form of punishment that encouraged the officer to quit out of shame. It was basically a grown man's timeout.

There wasn't much we could do about it, though.

Later that day, we got the notice to go ahead and take the tracker off Vong's car, so I did late that night.

As I drove home with the tracker, I reflected on the emotional rollercoaster of the past few weeks. Things had been going well with Eddie and Hector, and then suddenly their phones went dark. Things began to pick back up with Eddie, and then we heard we had a leak and the case would have been closed down completely if I hadn't fought for it. We watched Vong's tracker as he drove everywhere except to Ken's house, and he was still being pinned with responsibility for the leak. Titus was officially on the team, though, so that was awesome. And, things had picked back up in the case, and we were targeting someone up the chain that the 20th had brought in before, which was a good sign that we were on the right track.

It'd been a rough month, but I had a feeling we were in the fast lane going in the right direction. If we could just keep our heads down and bring down the leak at the same time, I would ride this case all the way to the top.

SEPTEMBER 2014

17

Coming in like a wrecking ball, the newly elected District Attorney, Chad Ball fired five Assistant District Attorneys immediately for not setting up "interviews" with him. As in, they didn't schmooze. There was a lot of talk about it being political retribution. Four of the five that were fired had publicly supported the opposition during the race, and it seemed Chad Ball had taken note. I guessed he had to make some moves to fit his personal picks in certain positions within the office and courthouse.

It sounded like some petty bullshit to me, but he ran the race and won so he was now basically the boss of the 20th, though the DA rarely got involved in the day-to-day. Some of the guys told me they'd heard rumors that Ball had even gone to Chief Smalls and ordered that several officers he didn't like be fired. Apparently, Chief Smalls told him to run his own office and not to worry about the police department. I knew this would be bad for tensions between the two entities. Since both the District Attorney and Chief of Police were on the board of directors for the 20th, I dreaded the possibility that future tensions might affect the team's work.

But, I couldn't think too much about that because just as fast as the DA's office was changing, so was our investigation. On up the ladder we went, gathering names and making more and more connections. We'd dropped the small-timers like Charlie, Eddie, and Hector, and we had moved up to Ken and Daniel. Now we were moving up the ladder to Lewis and a new piece to the puzzle: Slick. Before we put Daniel on the sidelines to wait for judgment day, I had noticed that he had a second source using a 513 area code number. I linked this same number to Lewis who, when he was running low on stock for people like Daniel, reached out to the 513 number for more supply.

Nashville is a growing city, but it ain't that damn big. When a kilo dealer ran out of dope and was waiting for a new shipment to come into town, he always had a backup plug to keep the dope rolling. This 513 number was the backup plug for Lewis and Daniel, and they both only referred to him as "Slick."

I went ahead and set up a ping on the 513 phone number as soon as I made the connection that Lewis and Daniel were using him as a source. Hell, I was pinging ten phones at this point, so why not add another? I wanted to identify Slick, so I drove to the area of the ping. I saw a bronze colored Buick Lacrosse with a TN specialty tag pulling away from Couch Drive. Again, I was solo, and I didn't want to follow Slick all alone, especially because I was sure he had gotten that name for a reason. An hour later the ping was showing up at an apartment complex in Murfreesboro, forty minutes outside of Nashville. The phone stayed there all night, which was a good sign that Slick was laying his head in an apartment there.

Early the next morning, I got Jimmy Weakling on board to set up at the apartment in Murfreesboro to identify Slick. Slick emerged in the late morning and headed for the bronze Buick. He retrieved something and then went back to the breezeway. Weakling didn't see what the number was on the apartment door but could tell it was the one on the top left. Good enough for me.

The car tag was registered to a female (of course) named Lawanna. Drug dealers were careful on the phone, rarely used real names, and registered their vehicles in other people's names if they could. Slick was no different, but I was a little slicker. It took some serious digging in my best database to track down all of Lawanna's information. I found an old address that she used and then a list of other individuals that used the same address. All I could do was start at the top, pull up each and every driver's license photo until I found him: James Glover, aka Slick.

Shortly after pulling his record, I discovered I had arrested Slick during a search warrant execution years before, and we'd seized over

$7,000 cash from him. I remembered very well how he acted like his cash getting seized was no big deal. Now I knew why. He probably had plenty more stashed away elsewhere.

Collins had worked quickly to get the wiretap affidavit complete to submit for a signature from DA Ball, his first one. Without hesitation, DA Ball gave his stamp of approval, and I let out a sigh of relief. Maybe working with Ball wouldn't be so bad after all.

By the next morning, we were up on Slick's phone and already taking calls. It was looking like Slick was the go-to guy and his phone was blowing up.

A series of phone calls had been intercepted between Slick and an unknown male. During the intercepted calls, Slick agreed to sell the unknown male nine ounces of cocaine or a "nina." I had so much work to catch up on, I couldn't afford to get out and do surveillance for this deal. I had to hope I'd get other valuable intel soon enough. These dealers never stopped, so something was bound to come up. Sure enough, on my way home later, I got word from the wire room that Slick was about to head to his stash. Now, I had a general idea of where this was, but I wasn't certain.

I headed to Antioch around 11 pm. When I got to Lawanna's address, I identified Slick's white Impala in the driveway. I knew I had the right spot, so I hunkered down and waited to see if Slick came out of the house. Fifteen minutes before midnight, the garage opened. Slick and Lawanna came out and got in the Impala and headed to Murfreesboro.

I let the tracker do the work from there and headed home.

I thought about all the addresses that we were going to have search warrants on, including Lawanna's house. At that point, we were already up to twenty-seven locations, which meant I needed to get to typing all those warrants.

While working our asses off on the case, we were also working to either clear or hammer Officer Thammavong for the leak. A few days after our interview with him, Hughes came by our office and said, "My buddy just texted me that Vong's on the green mile."

I immediately thought of the conversation Sgt. Cox had with the captain only a few days earlier. Even though the tracker on his car revealed nothing, our interview produced no results, and Sgt. Cox had specifically said, "Do not decommission him yet," the administration had stripped Vong of his gun and badge and made him sit on display at headquarters while he was being investigated.

"So," I said, "they must have found some evidence?"

Hughes shrugged. "I guess so."

I hoped so. Either they'd somehow actually proven he'd done it or they were just barreling ahead with punishment based on Sgt. Korbin's word.

We got the official email in the weekly stats alert of department employment changes. Vong was listed as decommissioned. I couldn't imagine what Vong must be feeling sitting at headquarters in silence all day every day. If he leaked the info then he needed to pay, but if not then we needed to figure out who the hell had so we could bury them and release Vong.

Since Weakling wasn't leading a strong case at the time we found out about the leak, Sgt. Cox had appointed him as the point person on the leak. We needed someone in the office who could spend more time on identifying the leak, and Weakling was a great detective who could gather evidence and focus on putting the pieces together. It had been a couple weeks, though, and he seemed to have done nothing on the leak case. Anytime someone asked about it, Weakling was getting increasingly defensive and unresponsive about details. It was a lot of pressure to put on a person, so I didn't give it much thought, but then he started complaining frequently about not wanting to work on the leak project. Sgt. Cox didn't know what to say because the rest of us had heavier workloads, and it didn't make sense why Weakling was so angry about being the leak point person.

Arguments were frequent in our office, but this level of tension and uncertainty felt like the drama back in SID. Weakling had never acted hostile towards me when he came into our office and badgered Thomas, but he was starting to snap at everyone. He had always shown due respect for Sgt. Cox, but now there was an air of resentment in his manner towards him.

It got worse one morning when Sgt. Cox told me that Weakling had gotten drunk and called him the night before. "He just kept yelling that he didn't want to work on the leak. He's always been a little theatrical, but this is going too far."

When Weakling appeared in the office that morning, he brooded and avoided interacting with anyone. I asked Sgt. Cox that afternoon if Weakling had spoken to him or apologized. James answered, "You know, I don't know if he even remembers."

A few days later, Weakling didn't show up to the office at all. While we were working on my case and trying to coordinate with him, he left all communication unanswered. The next day, he told us a pretty blatant lie about taking care of some "personal business."

Soon after this, I guessed at the extent of his "business." Our team was sent an alert that the Office of Professional Accountability (OPA) department was beginning a team-wide investigation. They would hold isolated interviews of each person in the office to get more information on the leak issue. We knew there was bullshit in the works, but there wasn't much we could do about it.

In the interviews, OPA did not focus on our current efforts to pinpoint the leak. Instead, I learned that our guys were being grilled about the conversations and details surrounding the surfacing of the leak two months prior. Because Thomas had brought Vong in for the translating services and had also been the initial contact for the citizen informant, his interview was first and lasted the longest. He must have had a huge target on his back at OPA, and the interview was brutal.

The morning after Thomas' interview, he closed our office door when I got there and said, "So, other than spending five hours blasting me with questions about every fucking detail about my life two months ago, OPA accused me of sleeping with a CI."

I looked at him in shock. Thomas was a dedicated family man who left the office early many days to pick up his kid and take care of his wife with a mental illness. His wife had gone so far as to shoot herself in the leg in a fit of depression, and she'd spent a brief stint hospitalized afterwards while Thomas took care of their kid. I knew that every moment he wasn't at work, Thomas was at home taking care of his family, and I could bet my life on it. There was no way he would sleep with an informant.

"You're kidding." I said.

He shook his head and sat down heavily, placing his head in his hands. "This is just too much. A guy called me up from my old unit last night to let me know the rumor was already making its rounds. I don't know where OPA even got it, but this kind of thing could ruin me. I went off on them when they accused me of it. I just couldn't stand that kind of bullshit." He gripped his hair with his fingers like he might rip it out. "But now I'm nervous they're going to come back at me since I blew up on them."

Thomas, who always stayed cool and collected, who could reduce Weakling to a child with just one rational turn of phrase, who let anything roll off him as he shouldered the weight of life stoically and confidently, looked to be on the verge of a breakdown.

I didn't know how to react, but I had a suspicion of the source of the rumor. It seemed a little too tidy that Weakling inexplicably disappeared for a day and then just a day later we were suddenly under investigation by OPA. Now, there was a rumor running rampant about Weakling's least favorite coworker . . . I kept my mouth shut about it, though, because Thomas didn't need anything else to piss him off.

I tried to be helpful and said that the rumor was unfounded and wouldn't ruin him, but I didn't say that I *had* seen it happen many times before. It could follow him for years. Only people like Sgt. Bagg somehow weaseled their way to the top despite the rumors. If I knew of a rumor being spread about me cheating on my wife, I would stop at nothing to find the culprit and deliver a serious ass-whooping.

Thomas, though, looked worn out and almost resigned as he said, "These interviews are bullshit."

I nodded. "I know."

"It's like they already have formed their judgment on it, and they're just waiting for me to say something to prove it." He looked up at me and he looked years older than the previous day. He continued, "The way they form their questions is manipulative. They ask me about the smallest details in conversations that happened a month ago to find holes in my memory, and then they bring in allegations against my personal life? It's bullshit! It feels like they're trying to take me down. You know that I reported the CI call immediately after it happened, and I haven't once tried to hide anything. I can't help that Eddie and Ken dropped their phones right around when I got Vong in to translate. I mean, does OPA think I was trying to sabotage our own case?"

Thomas looked almost panicked, and I couldn't blame him. Things looked bad.

"Look," I said, "remember that Chief Smalls is who suggested the tracker and to start the investigation. The administration is who decommissioned Vong with or without evidence. We're just doing what we can to find the leak while we work on this badass wiretap case. They have no evidence against you, dude, and that rumor is just fucking ridiculous. OPA's job is to interrogate and intimidate to get the information they want. Our job is to focus on busting huge drug rings, and we're doing a damn good job of it."

Thomas smiled and nodded, seeming to calm down again. I still felt uneasy, though, as we got back to work. Because Chief Smalls had given the order against Vong without clear evidence, I knew OPA was looking for someone else to blame to allow the chief to save face. They would pick apart the case, looking for any violation that could be pinned with responsibility. That was the purpose of an investigation: to find the culprit. Or, at least a scapegoat.

18

As the OPA interviews began to randomly cut in to our daily routine, a call was intercepted between Lewis and Slick one afternoon that gave us a reprieve from the internal bullshit and got us refocused on the case.

Lewis asked, "You want a dime?"

Slick replied, "All he could do was a dime? Did almost nothing come through?"

"Yeah." Lewis said with a sigh. "So, nobody got nothing still while he's recovering. I got one right here I want to snatch, though." I assumed the "he" was Lewis' supplier, and something must have put a hitch in the supply line.

"What you gonna do?" Slick asked.

"I'm about to cut 'em open now."

"For real?"

"I knew you probably were just fixing Daniel's four."

"Nah, he cool." Slick said. "He's out of town right now anyway. So, really, man, you only got a little bit that came through?"

"That's all he can do. You feel me? I think he said he got fourteen altogether. He only got ten more, so give some of these little dudes half of it. He wants to get it off right quick, and I'm about to go home and make the call."

"Let me see what I can come up with," Slick said. "I'll call you in twenty. If I can't, I'll just keep working with what I got and just get rid of it, and then next time he come through, I'll just try to get the bus load."

Lewis and Slick spoke to each other several more times throughout the day about the cocaine purchase. Slick wanted to get three of the kilos the supplier had, two for his boys Dell and Harry. Lewis told Slick that he should charge his buyers $38,500 each so he could make some money off the deal.

Lewis finally said, "How about this: I'll just tell them to have three of them ready in the morning." They made a plan then for Slick to bring the money for all three kilos to Lewis' mom's house and the kilo exchange would happen later on. This was going to be a huge leap in the case to see such a big deal go down!

That night, though, Lewis had a problem. His source of supply wasn't answering his phone. Lewis told Slick that his source was in the hospital after a motorcycle wreck, and since he couldn't reach him, they'd have to wait until the morning to see what happened. Meanwhile, though, Lewis had counted the money from Slick and something was off.

Slick said, "It was $68,000 and then I gave you a fifty to kill the seventy-three."

"Not sure it's straight little buddy."

"Fuck that, I know it's straight. I used the machine."

"Aight," Lewis said, trying to keep his customer happy. "Well, I'm gonna go meet him at the hospital. Something just tells me this number is off. You feel me? But, I'll recount."

"I feel ya, bro. I assure you it's all straight."

The important thing we learned from this was that the supplier had been in a motorcycle accident, so the deal would have to be postponed. We had a way to narrow it down, but we had to figure out who of Lewis' associates rode a motorcycle. Lewis was popular though, as we'd learned, so I might've had more luck finding that out by knocking on Lewis' mom's door and just asking.

The next day, after listening to more conversations, we found that Lewis had gotten the fourteen kilos from his supplier and the deal was on. For a moment I was frustrated because I didn't know how we had missed Lewis' meet-up with his supplier. I let it go, though, because, we had a lot of deals to watch now.

Lewis made the calls one-by-one to each of his buyers and we took down all the information and numbers. We'd recently planted a camera across the street from Lewis' mom's house on a tree, so we had a great view of the front door. Our goal was not to take down every dealer leaving the house, but to gather the intel to make a huge bust at a later date. We still had to keep Lewis comfortable so we could move up the ladder. Knowing that all that dope would hit the streets was tough to swallow but imagining what could come with patience was more appealing to me.

We were set up by 8 am and were in position to see the first buy. Buyer #1 was going to bring $33,000 cash to get one kilo of cocaine, and we were pumped to see a kilo deal go down in front of our eyes.

Buyer #1 arrived in a bright red Dodge Ram. A short, black male hoped out of the truck and headed for the front door. Lewis opened the door, looked left and right, and then let him in. I realized I recognized the guy, and Slick's mentioning of Dell had me realizing I was seeing Cordell Sims again. Dell had popped up on a previous wiretap case I worked, but it was a federal bust and they hadn't wrapped up as many people as I thought they would, including Cordell Sims. Clearly, since his last supplier had got busted by the feds, he had found a new one. As I looked at his record later, though, I remembered years before when I had arrested Dell and Slick at the same house. It was all coming together perfectly, and I wasn't surprised to see the circle hadn't changed much.

Dell, now officially identified as Buyer #1, was grinning ear to ear when he came out the front door. A bright orange bag with a white "swoosh" was in his right hand and contained his product; it looked heavy! I thought he only had enough money for one kilo, but it looked like he was walking out with two. Maybe he had been fronted a "whole one" and that was why he was so happy. Dell left and we let him roll. Dell was known to run from police so there was no point in trying to make that stop.

Shortly after the first deal, a call was intercepted between Lewis and Buyer #2. This male kept the lingo to a minimum, asking for "one" and Lewis knew exactly what he wanted. The price for Buyer #2 was a little higher than the first. Lewis was going to make some money off of this sale. Lewis told Buyer #2 that the price was going to be $37,500 and the second deal was set. Buyer #2 was on his way.

At 10 am, Lewis was right in the middle of his second kilo deal. Collins immediately recognized Buyer #2 as Kendrick Mills. Kendrick was a large man, weighing in at over 350 pounds with a bald, pointy head. When Kendrick got out of his Excursion, the whole damn car shook back and forth. He went inside, came out wearing a big smile, and tossed a bag into his car. Kendrick never went anywhere fast, but he did the deal quick.

Only twenty minutes later, a silver Toyota Camry pulled into the driveway. The new car had a barcode on the driver's side window, which meant it was a rental. We had a direct connection to Hertz rental cars, so we would find out in due time who was driving. There was a small problem, though: this arrival was not prompted by an intercepted call. That meant Lewis had a second phone he was making deals on. No one just showed up at a dealer's mom's house to "hang."

Since no one immediately knew who Buyer #3 was, I wanted to follow this one away. We got great pictures of him coming out holding a white plastic bag, and after Lewis stepped outside for a moment to glance around for anything suspicious, a few of our team followed the buyer to the Antioch area. When he got into a neighborhood, though, we had to terminate surveillance so we wouldn't get burned, and we headed back towards Lewis' mom's house with the car's tag in our back pocket. The name of the game is to identify as many people as possible, to add them to the conspiracy, and add their address to the list for takedown day.

Meanwhile, Hughes reported that Lewis was walking to his car carrying two large bags, most likely containing cash. If Lewis sold three kilos of cocaine that morning, then he had over $100,000 cash in those bags. It was hard to let that walk! But, in the spirit of seeing it all the way through, we did nothing. He left his residence and surveillance officers followed his Chevy Malibu to see where that money was going. This wasn't going to be easy since we didn't have a tracker on him, yet. We did have a phone ping set up, so we hung back and hoped the pings would be enough to keep up with him.

Sure enough, a ping sat right on top of a house on Brooketrace Drive, so we headed that direction. This old duplex had been updated and converted into a single-family, all brick home with a 10-foot brick wall going all the way around the property. It was definitely the nicest house in the area, which is what a detective would call a major clue.

I radioed to the others that I had been here before. I'd served a search warrant on this very house two years prior when I was using a confidential informant to buy cocaine from the person living there at the time, and, well, that dealer went to prison.

Lewis wasn't there long, and we watched as he headed straight back to his mom's house, and Hughes noted he was on his phone. We had another address and suspect added to the list, but I wanted to know who he was talking to and on what line. I called Melissa and she said no call had come through on the lines we had wired. Either he just had an extra line, or he had dropped his old lines after the deal and got new ones, something I knew dealers would do. I hoped for the former because finding new lines would be a pain in my ass.

Buyer #4 came by after lunch, and he added an interesting twist to the situation. The guy arrived in a Ford F-150 and had long dreadlocks. After Melissa did some digging, she found our guy: Tony Yates, aka Big Mack, who worked for Slick. Since Slick was sending Big Mack over to Lewis' house, could it mean that he didn't really trust him?

Equally interesting was that Lewis exited his house with a big white bag and got into the truck. He returned to the house a few minutes later without the bag, but Hughes noticed a significant bulge in his right pocket area. He radioed to us, "I imagine $30k would make quite a bulge."

Weakling chimed in, "Or he's just excited to see Big Mack."

We couldn't help but laugh and shake the thought out of our heads.

I followed the F-150 to Slick's part of town but lost him near Slick's stash house, which he passed by.

Shortly after I got back to Lewis' mom's house, a series of phone calls began to be intercepted between Lewis and Dell. I breathed a sigh of relief: Lewis was still using the phone we were up on. During the intercepted phone calls, Dell expressed to Lewis how he was not happy with the quality of the cocaine he had purchased. Between the calls, we learned that Dell had busted one kilo open and in addition to lumps being visible, the cocaine was "not getting hard and not proper."

After going back and forth over the tampered cocaine, Lewis offered to give Dell his money back if he returned the cocaine he had already bought. However, Dell was not yet biting and needed some time to think. This was big. Lewis was seen as a credible supplier to some of these kilo-level dealers. Being told that your cocaine was not "proper" could lose you all kinds of street credibility.

After the call with Dell, Lewis left his residence in the Chevy Malibu. None of us were available to follow Lewis so we let the GPS phone tracking do the work. We were up on him, watching his every move.

Lewis called Big Mack to make sure he got home safe, and he confirmed that he did. That was the funny thing about these dealers. They were so hard in the streets, but on the phone, they were coddling each other, making sure everyone was okay. It truly amazed me how some of these dope dealers juggled their personal lives with their dope dealing life. Even big-time Lewis spent time talking to dealers about taking his son to football practice and the necessities of being a father. These guys would talk about their lives with each other in a way that sounded like friends or brothers rather than business associates. I guess with taking the huge risk of dealing drugs, dealers end up bonding over daily life struggles, too.

After confirming Big Mack was home safe, Lewis wanted Big Mack to inspect his "one" to ensure it was "proper." Big Mack confirmed that the product was not glass quality.

Lewis had to think fast. At this point, he had two buyers who were not happy with their product. Lewis headed straight over to Brooketrace Drive again and entered the large brick walls. Based on what we had seen earlier in the day, that had to be where Lewis was getting kilos and dropping off money.

We soon learned just how pissed Big Mack was. He called Slick to bitch about the product. This made a wiretap case so much better when everyone openly talked about the quality of cocaine. When things were good, there was not much to talk about, but when things were bad, they wanted to tell everyone. Customer service industry: what can you do?

"This looks like garbage!" Big Mack yelled at Slick.

"Damnit! Aight, let's try to whip it into something good. I'll call Lewis to see what I can do."

Big Mack told Slick that he could cook up something and make it work. Slick agreed and Big Mack headed over to Slick's house to start cooking since his oven was broken.

Judgement day seemed to be coming for Lewis, who was sitting behind the brick walls, probably planning what to do next. After hanging up with Big Mack, Slick called Lewis immediately. Slick told Lewis that he and Big Mack discussed the quality of the cocaine, and that both Big Mack and Dell were dissatisfied with their buy. After several minutes of heated discussions, Lewis folded and told Slick to give his "boys" his phone number. At the end of the day, this was a business, and customer service was important. If Lewis didn't treat his people right, they wouldn't come back. Or, even worse, they might decide to come after him.

Luckily for Lewis, Slick had good news a couple hours later. Big Mack cooked some product and it came out right, so they were good. For now.

I was glad that these guys were telling me everything about their cocaine and how it wasn't right, but I was still focused on the source of supply for Lewis, the person inside the brick walls. I found in our database that a couple North Precinct officers conducted a knock and talk at the home last month. I called the sergeant that was working that night and asked him to come over to the task force and tell me what happened. Sgt. Sweat arrived and came into my office. He explained that one of his officers got a tip that the person at the residence was selling drugs. So, several officers attempted to knock on the door.

A black male came barreling out the front door, stopping officers from coming onto the property. The irate male was identified as Marlon Cummings. He had whipped out his cell phone and was yelling that he was calling his lawyer. Sgt. Sweat encouraged it, telling Marlon that they were not breaking any laws. Either way, the officers were not getting anywhere close to that front door. Marlon's attorney, who I guess he had on retainer and was in the area, showed up soon after.

"It was crazy," said Sgt. Sweat, "The attorney was there within minutes and told us to get off the property." I assured Sgt. Sweat that the day would come when we hit that place with a search warrant and when we did, I promised his guys would be on the battering ram.

Late that night I looked for Marlon Cummings on Facebook and found his account was public. Someone had posted on his wall only an hour before asking, "how r u man???"

Marlon had replied, "Broke bone in ankle is all, crutches suck but I'm going to be stronger than a mf. Bike good ordering fairing now."

Home run! Marlon had the bike accident and was very likely Lewis' source. Thank God for social media!

19

It was only nine days into September, and things were really taking off with the case, even if things were getting more complicated and tense at the office.

I had tracked Dell's Dodge Ram to Hermitage, TN, and decided to spend my morning surveilling the area and noting the cars parked at his house. I identified them as his girlfriend's and his daughter's, so I felt sure this was where Dell laid his head.

After leaving the Hermitage area, I went straight to the courthouse to get a tracker warrant signed so I could attach a GPS tracker to Lewis' Malibu. We were sure Lewis was a big player, which meant he would lead us to the next level. I got the warrant signed and then checked the pings on Lewis' phone location. I was shocked to see he was at the courthouse, too! My immediate fear was, *Is Lewis following me?* I called Thomas to check if Lewis had any recent citations and was relieved to find out he did. Lewis had to book himself.

"Shit, Thomas. Bring me a tracker as fast as possible. I got the warrant signed, and if I can place it while I'm here that's one less trip to make at 4 am."

Thomas hurried over and we found the car parked in broad daylight on the street. It was risky, but I rolled under the car and placed the tracker in just a few seconds, then we hauled ass out of there.

I found out later that Lewis would have to turn himself in because he missed a couple court dates. It was almost a relief because I could get caught up on some of the endless paperwork piling up on my desk. Every time something pertinent happened or we covered a deal, it had to be documented not only in reports but in the later search warrants. The warrants always had to be up-to-date and ready to go because we never knew when a big load would come in that we would decide to take. If the paperwork wasn't ready, we could lose it all.

That evening, Dell had money on his mind. He wanted to play middle man to make a couple dollars, so he called Slick and set up a meeting. They had to arrange dropping off their kids and finding a middle location, and they decided on the Maxwell House Hotel near downtown Nashville.

At 7:15 pm, Director Davis observed Dell in his Dodge Ram at the gas station across from the hotel. Dell grabbed some smokes and then headed across the street to the Maxwell House Hotel parking lot. I was ready in the backseat of my car. Dope dealers were always on lookout, too, but luckily if they saw a car sitting with no one in the front seat, they wouldn't pay any attention to it. Slick texted Dell that he was leaving his spot, but Dell couldn't wait.

Slick called him and said, "I'm in the process of coming that way but there is a wreck, where are you?"

Dell replied, "He and his momma wanted Popeye's, so that's where I'm at."

"What Popeye's you at?"

"On Jefferson."

"Hell no, that's a flame torch! As soon as I fight this traffic, I'll call you and let you know how far, how long."

It was almost 8 pm when I observed Slick's Chevy Impala pull into the Maxwell House Hotel parking lot. The vehicle circled and then parked on the passenger side of the Dodge Ram. I observed Slick exit the passenger side of the Impala and walk around and get in the passenger seat of the Dodge Ram. When Slick was walking to the Ram, it appeared that there was an object in his shirt. *Wonder what that could be.*

Slick got out of the truck and walked back to his Chevy Impala with only a phone in his hand. Shortly after, the Dodge Ram left the parking lot and turned onto Rosa Parks. Slick and Lawanna in the Impala jumped on the interstate and she punched the gas. I was trying to follow, but it was hard to keep up and I eventually lost them. Maybe his girlfriend was a professional racecar driver in another life.

The next time Slick and Dell talked, though, the subject wasn't just about business. Only a couple days after their deal, Dell called Slick to let him know about a mutual friend's death.

Dell said, "My luck ain't no good, man."

"What's up?"

"My boy, Bird, the one that owed me a fridge, he dead. He swallowed his drugs and died."

"What? Why did he do that?"

"Guess he got stopped. I don't know. Got pulled over and had to get rid of shit, so he put it in his drink, drank it, and died."

"Shit, man."

Dell had just sold coke to this guy, and suddenly he was dead. The news seemed to hit him hard. Dell sounded actually upset, but I didn't know if it was over the death or the lost business and money.

The thing about dealing cocaine is that it's dangerous and you have to assume your day may come. Most dealers think that their worst day is when they get caught, and everyone does eventually get caught one way or another. But what happens when the "drug life" takes your life? I guess some people just live in the moment, worried about money and daily issues and don't think about the larger consequences.

After hearing their heartfelt call, I contacted my friend at the 18th Judicial District Drug Task Force, which covered Sumner County, where a dealer named Bird made his rounds.

I asked, "Did y'all stop a guy that drank some cocaine and died?"

"Yep. How the hell did you know that?"

"Let's just say I heard from a little birdie. What happened?"

"Well, when we pulled him over and got him out of the car, he was just standing on the side of New Island Lane, wobbling, swaying back and forth. And then, suddenly, bam! He hit the ground hard. Police rendered immediate aid and called for an ambulance, but it didn't take long for that stimulant to hit the bloodstream and run its course. He died before the ambulance loaded him up."

"Damn."

Chapter 19

"His wife was in the passenger seat. Saw the whole thing and told the officers what happened. At first, she tried to lie, but once there was no bringing him back, she admitted the truth. When he saw the blue lights, he pulled the baggie out of his pocket and dumped all twenty-eight grams into his drink. Then he downed it."

"He must have had no idea what would happen to him."

"I hope he didn't. That's not a good way to go."

I thanked the detective for the info and hung up.

This incident didn't affect our case much, but Dell was awfully worried about the police having Bird's cell phones. They could have potentially tracked the number to his supplier, so soon after his call with Slick, Dell's line went dead.

Slick's didn't, though, and he spent the rest of the day calling and telling everyone the same story about a guy eating his cocaine.

He told his fellow kilo-dealer friend Daniel Harding about it, and Daniel asked, "Who, the guy down in Columbia?"

"No, up through here out east. Dude got pulled over, put the work in the cold drink and tried to drink it and died."

"Shit. I ain't doing that. I'd just have to go back to jail."

Slick boasted, "I would let them come up on me, and then when they are close, I smash out."

"Man, I tell you, do anything but that." Daniel seemed to have more sense than Slick.

"I hear that dude owed money and couldn't catch a break."

"That isn't an excuse."

"When a man is down money, his mind is on stupid shit."

Bird was just a local drug dealer who was dealing with Dell, and he was going to his grave owing people money. He hadn't popped up on our radar for this case, but he had still chosen that life and it had cost him. He pulled over, panicked, and took a stupid risk. If he had just given up the coke and took the charges like a man, like Daniel said he'd do, he would have gotten out of jail sometime. Maybe he knew drinking it would kill him, but maybe he was just reacting in the moment. Now, his wife and kids would have to visit him at the graveyard instead of in jail. Dealing drugs always had consequences and sometimes they were fatal.

While Dell, Slick, and the higher-ups were dealing with this issue, we were rounding up the first batch of search warrants. It was time to drop the lines for Eddie, Ken, Hector, and other players that were just too small, but before we did so, we wanted to try and get some intel from them. We planned on executing search warrants and doing interviews to see if they'd speak up about the leak, but we wouldn't make any arrests. If we arrested them, the affidavit could disclose key facts of the case and reveal that we were doing a wiretap on their ring. The whole drug circle could find out what we were doing. Search warrants were risky on their own because the big guns would probably drop their numbers again, but at least we wouldn't have to reveal anything about our business. We wanted to see if Ken and Eddie would offer hard evidence about their connection on the inside. Plus, these guys had to be held accountable for dealing drugs, even if cocaine wasn't their main deal, and I was ready to bash in some doors and seize some drugs off my city's streets.

On September 18th starting at 6 am, fifteen search warrants were executed across several counties in Tennessee. I started at Eddie's house, a one-story red brick ranch house on three acres of land. He was asleep when we arrived and his grandmother, who owned the house, was surprised by our early arrival. I spent two hours interviewing him, trying to become his friend and build a rapport. When I couldn't get any relevant intel out of him, OPA Investigator Sgt. Korbin came to the house to try. He went round and round with Eddie, but the only thing we could get out of him was: "Ken just said our faces were on a wall. I don't know who told him."

It was late morning by the time I reached Hector's place. Miller, his older roommate, lived in a loft area while Hector lived in a tiny downstairs apartment. The house was more like a barn, and it smelled like garbage and dirty laundry. Both had been interviewed after the search, and neither gave any information and were hostile.

I'd only been there for fifteen minutes when Thomas leaned in and said, "So, we just found out this place is crawling with bed bugs."

I high-tailed it out of there and radioed Sgt. Cox to ask about Ken. "James, please tell me he's talking."

"Not a word." James replied.

"Shit." It was already almost lunch and it sounded like a drive out to Antioch would be a waste of time. "I can't wait to indict these assholes later."

James agreed. "Well, it's not a complete waste of time. We've got a bunch of their guns at least."

"And it's only the beginning."

I headed back to the office. Hopefully soon we could arrest these guys, but we still had a lot of work to do to take down the big guys also.

That afternoon we compiled the numbers and found our warrants had brought in 8 ounces of cocaine, 3.5 pounds of marijuana, a significant amount of meth, several hundred pills, 48 guns, and $10,615 cash. Eddie and Ken were brought to the OPA building to be interviewed again, but neither budged on a "source" for the leak, but they admitted that there had been a tip-off. So, the leak *was* real, but we were no closer to knowing who had done it.

The next morning, my time had come with OPA. I got an email from them with a scheduled appointment time for my interview. When I arrived at the OPA building the following day, they put me into a padded room and left me there for over an hour, wasting my time. I still had paperwork to complete for the arrests and warrants, and it was hard to not get pissed off sitting around with nothing to do. The dealers never stopped calling, and I was missing it!

When it was my turn to get into the hot seat, I told the truth to the investigator. I had no control over how they would skew the information I gave them. All I could do was tell them exactly what happened and when. Vong came in on August 1st, a couple days later Chance called Thomas, and Ken got the tip-off either on July 31st or August 1st but we didn't know which date for sure. I could tell they didn't like what I said, and a part of me knew there was a possibility that my story wouldn't be relayed in full in the summary. Thankfully, they didn't try to pull any tricks with my personal life like they had with Thomas, so I kept my cool.

At the end of the interview, Sgt. Korbin came into the room. I knew he must have been behind the mirror listening in, and I wondered if he had jumped up and down yelling, "I got him! He's lying!" like he had done to Officer Vong.

He seemed calm though as he stayed standing and muttered to me, "Pull the plug on this case, Young."

"Excuse me, Sergeant?"

"Look, just shut it down. You have done enough, and this case isn't going anywhere. Continuing the case puts your team in jeopardy and it's a waste of everyone's time and money. All it's done is create trouble for everyone, so pull the plug."

I stared up at him, the anger coming on suddenly. He didn't know about Daniel, Slick, Dell and Lewis. He didn't know I was on the trail of Lewis' source, Marlon Cummings, whose arrest could bring in a huge haul of drugs and contraband. The last thing I was going to do was let anyone tell me what to do with this case. When things were looking bad with Eddie and Hector and the team encouraged me to quit, I kept on it and now we'd moved farther up the chain in less than a month. I wasn't going to let Korbin put a guilt trip on me.

Sgt. Korbin began to leave the room, but I couldn't let him walk away like that, so I said, "Thanks for your perspective, Korbin, but it's something I'll decide with Director Davis."

He glared at me for a second, and I almost expected a wrath like Sgt. Bagg's. Instead, he said in almost a whisper, "That's *Sergeant* to you, TFO Young."

He then slammed the door behind him.

When we played softball together, Korbin was a solid dope cop. He was respectable and hardworking, and he was also an honest team player. He didn't seem like the kind of person who'd drink a full glass of the political Kool-Aid. As I left OPA that day, I realized that Korbin wasn't the same Korbin I used to know. It seemed like he was under pressure to make someone pay for this leak and *fast*, so he was trying to wrap it up and push it under the rug. I wondered if that meant they didn't have evidence against Vong even though they had gone ahead and decommissioned him. Now, maybe they were realizing their mistake. I had the sinking feeling that even if we found evidence of the real culprit soon, it might be too late.

OCTOBER 2014

20

Like most other mornings, on the first of October, Director Davis came into our office to greet us and check in.

"How's it going?" He asked before sipping his coffee.

"Trying to figure out how we are going to get Marlon's number since we can't figure out Lewis' secret number." I said. "I have subpoenas out for phone tolls on two of Marlon's old numbers and his ex-wife's number. I got that shit from my 2012 search warrant from the Brooketrace address."

Davis nodded, thinking. "Well, didn't Sgt. Sweat tell you they did a knock and talk? And Marlon called his attorney . . ."

"Shit, if I have the attorney's number, I can get the tolls on his phone for that date and time! Pretty damn clever. Good idea, Davis."

"Well, get typing! I'll get you the attorney's number."

We knew Marlon was the source of supply for Daniel, Slick, Lewis, and maybe Dell, but proving it was a very different thing. After getting his attorney's number, I drafted and submitted the order to the phone company. As soon as I got Marlon's number, I would get a GPS ping order on his phone so we could start tracking him and seeing his deals go down.

Titus was out doing surveillance on a case Hughes was leading, but he radioed the office before lunch and said, "Anyone who's available, I'm at the corner of Cherry and 29th and just heard some gun shots. Oh, shit, there's a black male running from the direction of the shots, he's getting in a car, blue Altima, old. I'm in my car so I'll follow, but I could use some backup."

Thomas and I were already running from the office to the parking lot. Sgt. Cox was already in the lot getting into his car, and we three headed in the direction of Titus as he continued naming cross streets. He said the guy pulled into the Burgundy Inn Motel but had continued back out of the lot heading east. We were almost on the motel, so I turned off and cut over that direction, heading east.

Titus said, "I have to turn around. Stay on him."

"Got my eye on him." I said.

Sgt. Cox radioed in to go ahead and activate my lights and siren, so I turned them on and sped up to ride the guy's tail. He didn't even slow down, and instead he turned into an apartment complex and weaved through the snaking parking lots, riding hard over the speedbumps.

We were approaching a dead end, and I watched as the driver's side door opened while the car was still moving, and a guy rolled out onto the pavement.

I heard Titus yell into the radio, "Gun, gun, gun!" I stopped the car and hurried to get out.

As I ran after Titus and the suspect, I watched as they leapt through bushes to a fence.

I yelled, "Police! Stop!"

I had my gun out and pointed at the suspect, but Titus was right on his heels. Both went over the fence, one after the other, with such ease.

"Shit!"

I couldn't holster my gun because my holster was one that tucked inside my waistband, and it had flown off when I jumped out of the car. I stuffed the Glock 40 in my pants and made it over the fence. It wasn't graceful, but I knew I had to get over fast in order to keep up with the foot chase. I sprinted across a backyard and around a house, and I saw the suspect fly into the front bushes of a house across the street. Titus was behind him and running to the far side of the bushes.

I radioed back to the others to let them know and then yelled for the suspect to lay down on the ground as I approached. The bushes were moving, though, and he popped out on the other side of the front porch.

Thankfully, Titus was ready and waiting, and Thomas and Sgt. Cox were closing in on the scene. All were yelling for him to get down, and the suspect realized he had four guns pointed at him. I didn't see anything in his hand, so as he slowly made his way to the ground I ran up behind him and grabbed his arm. Titus grabbed his other arm, Thomas latched the cuffs to his wrist, and Titus began to recite his rights.

We heard sirens approach as we searched his person. When the officers arrived, we put the suspect in the back of a car and then searched the lot for the missing handgun, finding it in a flower bed by the fence we'd scaled. Titus identified the gun as being the same that the suspect had been holding, and two other cars arrived to take statements and retrieve the gun from the flower bed.

When we finally headed back towards our cars, it was early afternoon and Sgt. Cox patted Titus on the back. "Good work today, Price. I didn't know a guy as big as you could climb a fence that fast."

Titus laughed and said, "I thought the fence might buckle."

"It was shaking like crazy when you let go." Thomas said. "I think James and I here made the wise decision of just going around the fence and letting you two do the adrenaline work."

We all laughed and Titus said, "The real adrenaline, though, was seeing Bobby here grab that guy's arm like nothing. He could have still had his gun on him."

"Nah," I said, "I saw his hands were empty and knew he'd dropped it."

"Still, though, all this adrenaline works up an appetite, huh?" Sgt. Cox said as we came up to our cars. "How about I swing by the gyro place and bring some food back to the office? My wife won't eat it, and I've been craving it for weeks. My treat."

"Hell yeah!" Thomas said and I agreed.

"Thanks, Sarge." Titus said.

"You boys earned it. I'll see you back at the office in forty-five minutes. Try not to eat your arm off in the meantime."

After an afternoon of paperwork, gyros, and cutting up about our foot chase, I spent the evening drafting the GPS tracking order for Marlon's number and let the team know it would be up by morning.

I texted the whole office, "Anyone up for some surveillance on this mf tomorrow?" Everyone answered they were in and, surprisingly, Weakling answered first and the most enthusiastically. Maybe he was ready to start pulling his weight in this case more if he wasn't going to do much about the leak investigation.

We began the next morning by monitoring Marlon's phone pings and going towards those areas. We knew Marlon drove a big ass truck, so it should have been easy to spot, but it was never where the ping was marking. It seemed like the pings were coming from a general area rather than his specific phone, but we searched and finally found the truck outside of a brick compound very similar to the one on Brooketrace Drive. Clearly, Marlon had a particular design aesthetic he stuck to with his properties.

According to the property records, this new residence was owned by a "Jade" Cummings. The property was claimed in 2013 for $7,000 and was now worth an estimated $200,000. As we looked into "Jade's" records, we found he had two other residences in his name, neither of which were homes but were only empty pieces of land.

Hughes, who had brought up the information, let me know that all of Marlon's assets were under the name of Jade Cummings, but it wasn't a middle or given name, it was the name of his 4-year-old son! We were all both shocked and disgusted by this. Out of curiosity, I looked at the deed and whose name did I see signed on the dotted line but Jack Moorehead, Marlon's personal attorney.

"That dirty little shit." I said to Hughes.

He nodded. "Putting a child's name on multiple properties so daddy dope dealer wouldn't have anything in his name. Fucking ridiculous."

"How does this guy sleep at night?"

"Which one?" Hughes laughed.

"I was meaning Moorehead, but yeah, they're both trash." I shook my head. "Man, that poor kid."

We headed back to the office for the afternoon because it seemed like Marlon wasn't moving.

While we waited on Marlon, an afternoon call between Dell and Slick alerted us of another supplier who seemed to roll just as high as Marlon. It didn't seem possible to have another heavy-hitter in the city because cartels usually stake a claim on a city as their turf, but the way Dell talked sounded like this other supplier was going to be a game-changer.

Dell asked Slick, "How many you want, boy?"

Slick said, "First I got to look at it though, you feel me? See how they look."

"They are pretty, man. I can get 'em in my hands, but I gotta get another phone. He ain't gonna talk over that phone for shit." This was when we were clued into a supplier, "he" who clearly had rules for what phones to use to contact him.

Slick said, "Well, grab one and holla at me."

"Aight. He just gave me a number. How many you think you want, though? He said he gonna be right back with 'em next week, but I gotta know about how many."

Slick wouldn't budge and said, "I don't push like that though. You feel me? Just go grab one, let me look at it."

They hung up, and we waited in anticipation for the next call, but they must have used other phones for their next conversations. An hour later, though, we picked up a call between Slick and Big Mack.

"Yo," Slick said, "I just talked to Dell and he's got somebody that's got some for $37,500, but it's coming from this other cat . . . a dude named Creep who be way out west."

"Yeah? But I heard they been hittin' that shit when it comes over."

"Man, Dell says it's glass."

"Let's just look at it before, you know."

"I know, man. I'll hit you up when I see it. If it's that good, you can get as many as you want."

This was the type of call a dope detective dreams about. You have two kilo-level dealers talking to each other about another dealer who has access to "as many as you want." They even go into detail as to the quality of the cocaine and how Big Mack had heard the kilos from Creep were being cut and wasn't as pure as when it came across the border.

As excited as I was, I also had to think about my next play. If this guy named Creep was as big as Dell was making him out to be, then it might mean he had a different source of supply than Marlon. One source coming across the border might not pin two high-rolling dealers like Marlon and Creep against each other in one city. So, if Creep was rolling as high as Marlon, it could mean there was a different source, a different cartel working the city. And, thanks to Dell, it looked like we had a connection to both of those sources.

That night, I barely slept with anticipation. Thinking about all the different avenues this investigation could go made it hard to get any rest. I tried my best to remain calm, acting like I'd been there before with the several wire cases I'd both worked and led. But, nothing was as complex as this. We were looking at the highest level of city supply, and it was turning into *two* of them!

The following day Dell called Slick back and said, "Man, this was some good stuff. And they were crazy about it. Hit Harry with a whole one yesterday. Got that motherfucker off in an hour."

It was clear that this was some good quality cocaine, so good that Dell's buyer, Harry, was able to resell a whole kilo, all thirty-six ounces, within an hour. The guy must have made one hell of a payday.

Dell was certainly a busy guy. He wanted to show his supplier Creep that he had the connections and could get shit off quick. That way, Creep would trust him with more and more each time. Dell was getting calls all over the place. Sometimes there were multiple conversations going on at once, like when Dell was talking to both Lewis and on the other line with Creep.

Dell said to Lewis, "That's my guy right here calling me. He got four waiting. Just a second, hold on."

We could still hear him on speaker phone in the background.

Creep said, "I'm comin' out."

"What I need to do, homie?"

"Just hit me up later. Heading to my PO. I'm gonna call you back in about an hour or so."

"Okay."

Dell ended the call with Creep and was back to Lewis.

"His PO just called, so he got to go see him."

"Who was that just calling you?" Lewis asked.

"Creep. He was just telling me his PO called him, the PO. he was fixin' to meet."

"Oh, man. His PO."

"Hell yeah, man. Damn."

We learned a lot through this interaction. We had a pretty good idea that this Creep guy was the main man, the guy with all the kilos. He had at least four of them right now according to Dell, and Creep had a record. The one problem, though, was that we still hadn't tracked who he was. All we knew was he had a probation officer, but that wouldn't narrow down the suspects. One way to identify him would be to follow Dell around town, but, shit, we would need 24/7 access to the helicopter or the state's plane because Dell drove like a fucking maniac. We'd never be able to follow him on the roads.

21

While the calls were coming in, solidifying my hunch that Creep was just as big a dealer as Marlon, something miraculous happened later that same afternoon. I got a call out of nowhere from a confidential informant I hadn't heard from in years who'd been a huge help in a previous case.

"Is this Bobby?"

"Yep, who's this?"

"You don't recognize my voice?"

"Nope!"

"It's Chuck."

"Oh, shit! How the hell are ya?"

"Good, good. I actually just got out and wanted to link up with you. I figured I owed you since you helped me out on that trial, so I got something to tell you."

"What's that?"

"There's one guy running this whole damn city."

"Oh yeah?" I was skeptical because Chuck had been behind bars for two years, so I didn't know how much he really knew of the outside game anymore. He was very familiar with all drugs, though, and he had been candid about his involvement in the dope game for decades.

"Trust me," he said. "This guy's slinging weight. Let's meet up and I'll rap with you."

I got Sgt. Cox to come with me that evening to meet up with Chuck. I didn't want to waste any time because this felt like information that could be coming at the perfect time. Chuck promised that he had done his homework and the information was on point. I tried to maintain good relationships with my CI's because everyone deserved to be treated like a human being. This was something that so many dope cops had a hard time doing. Yes, these people had messed up, but they didn't deserve to be treated like dog shit. Now, if they were messing up while working for you, then you had to handle it, even if that meant they went to jail. But when they were doing good by you, then they deserved some respect. And, sometimes they deserved a new phone.

"So, why are you getting the golden ticket?" James asked as we headed to the meeting.

"Good question. I mean, all informants are motivated by either money or avoiding jail time, right?"

"And he just got out of jail."

"So, money. I promised him I'd buy him a phone in exchange for some solid intel."

We met at a Walmart and Chuck jumped into the car. After greetings and a briefing on recording the conversation, Chuck readily offered a list of names with their nicknames, phone numbers, and back stories. Chuck even provided buyers names and a hot location called Donkey's where many deals were going down every day.

According to Chuck, Shawn Perry was the man we needed to watch. I almost laughed when Chuck said, "He's got the whole city on lockdown and goes by 'Creep.'" That was the fastest I'd ever deciphered a code name, and it was just handed to me! This was the best information I'd ever gotten from a CI.

"So, why are you giving us all this? Don't get me wrong, it's amazing, but what's the motivation?"

Chuck sat back against the seat. "One of Shawn's guys crossed me, which is why I had to waste the last two years of my life behind bars."

I looked at James. Chuck was motivated by both money and revenge.

Chuck talked for so long that my recorder ran out of space. I told him to call the next day.

As James and I headed back to the office, we were stunned by the information Chuck had just dumped on us. It had only been the previous day when Dell had told Lewis about his source, Creep, and now we had confirmation of the source's identity. We were already wiring head honcho Marlon's phone, and soon we'd be wiring an equally big but separate head honcho named Shawn Perry.

"Man, my head hurts," I said, laughing.

"This was a damn good coincidence," James said.

Back at the office, I stayed late into the night looking up the information and criminal history for all the names. These were some good targets with extensive rap sheets. I created a folder on my desktop for each of these dealers and decided to just put it all in my back pocket.

Shawn Perry was still on federal probation from a large-scale drug case stemming out of Texas, which was why he had a PO. My research showed he was on federal supervised release and his probation officer was Brittany Helton. I contacted Helton the following day and told her I might be looking into one of her "clients" named Shawn Perry. She was very familiar with Shawn. I learned he was released from federal custody in 2011, and he had a conviction for possessing 500 grams or more of cocaine. In March of 2009 Shawn was sentenced to a term of sixty-eight months incarceration and four years of parole. He was released in December 2011 to begin his supervised parole.

I hinted around about a home visit and Helton told me her team had done one on Shawn the day before at his residence located at 424 Irwin Lane in Nashville. Helton stated that Shawn was supposed to be driving a truck for a company called "On Point Produce" from 4:30 am to 1 pm and that he worked for a company called "King Janitor" in the evening. I didn't mention Chuck's information that Shawn was also running a barbershop on Clarksville Highway. It was something I would need to look into. I also didn't mention he might be back dealing kilos of cocaine since I didn't know anything for sure, yet.

Helton said that Shawn said he was driving a Chrysler 300, but when she arrived for the home visit neither the car nor Shawn was on the property. His son had to call him, and he showed up driving a Nissan Altima with a temp tag. She also gave me his current cell phone number. I thanked her for the info and let Helton go.

I wondered why she hadn't nailed him for a violation of driving a different car and not being home when she arrived, but I wasn't going to say anything. I didn't want to tip her off to anything I held in my hand just yet.

The next morning with Shawn's GPS phone tracking order in my hand, I went directly to Judge Abbott who had signed all the previous orders. I got there before 8 am, but he was already in his office as usual. He and his staff were getting used to me during this case because he signed all the ping orders and wiretaps. Judge Abbott was a good judge and I considered him a friend. He was police friendly but also liberal. He was the kind of judge who would read every word of whatever was brought to him to give it his fair judgment. Sometimes he would deny a warrant but also provide his reasoning and suggestions for possibly making it work later.

I handed him the GPS ping order, and he read it and signed it with his fancy blue ink pen. It helped that he was already so familiar with the whole case up until this point.

I headed back to the office and got to typing. I sent the ping order to the phone company and had a shit ton of work to catch up on. All I could hope was that all five of the phones we were up on right now would stay quiet for a couple hours.

My wish halfway came true. These guys must have had a late night because the chatter on the phones was slow all day. We didn't get a good call until almost 6 pm when some of the office had already gone home.

I was in the wire room talking to the monitors as this call came in, so I took it myself.

"Boy, what's happenin'?" Slick asked Dell.

"I ain't gonna lie. I just got two of 'em, and they are so goddamn pretty. Damn, the other shit was like that too. I just looked at the top when I busted 'em open, but Wilson and Big T said everybody loves it."

"For real?"

"Um hm. I ain't been fucking with nobody. I gotta get my plays up there."

What a great end to the day. Dell was just sitting there looking at two kilos of pretty cocaine, and apparently everyone just loved it! I knew we were on our way to taking down the whole damn organization but there was still plenty of work to be done. We hadn't even begun to identify all of Shawn's or Marlon's buyers. Identifying all those people would make it a true conspiracy case.

So, the next day I was ready for some action to go down to start adding to the list of names. I'd made no plans for my Saturday other than following deals and catching up on paperwork.

Unfortunately, the day started and basically ended with a quick call that Lewis placed to Dell.

"Where you at?" Lewis asked.

"Man, we gonna have to wait 'til the morning. Shawn just texted and said his son just had a car wreck."

"Who did?"

"Shawn, man." When Lewis didn't respond Dell said, "You know, Creep. His son was in a wreck."

"Your boy's son? Oh, shit damn!"

"Yep, shit is crazy."

"In that Camaro?"

"I don't know what he was in. I don't know if it was in that or the Infiniti. I know he told me he was doing shit, goddammit. I probably need to come to you though so I can put the bread up. You feel me?"

"Yeah, just holla at me later."

Even though no deals were going down, I did verify that Shawn's son had been in a single car accident involving a 2010 Chevrolet Camaro. Not much for the case, but I knew we were getting closer.

Since I didn't have a deal for the day and the phones for Daniel, Lewis, Slick, and Marlon were all being taped, I waited until night had fallen and then went to Brooketrace Drive to visit Marlon's stash house. No one was home, so I spent an hour hooking up a couple cameras to watch the property. I drove by his other residence and Marlon was outside on the phone, still in a boot from his motorcycle wreck. Racing bikes and dealing kilos of coke sounded like a recipe for disaster, but I guess the guy liked to take big risks.

I headed home, calling my dad on the drive, and hoped for more action in the morning.

Chapter 21

I got lucky Sunday morning when I was alerted of the first call of the day between Lewis and Slick.

"You heard from him?" Slick asked.

"Yeah, he going to call me."

"Is it a go today?"

I tried to not get too hopeful as Lewis paused. He ended up saying, "He told me to standby. I'm going to go over and look. Don't bring your chips just yet. I am going to go look and see what all he can dish out and then I'll let you know everything."

"Aight, let me know."

"I'll be able to mix it right quick and get my tab out of the way with you."

"Sounds good." Slick said. "So, what was Dell talking about bringing you one of his people's shit."

Lewis said, "He said he was going to fuck with it this morning. I ain't even touched it. I don't want it to be short. Know what I mean?"

"I was going to call and see how it looked."

"I'm going to let him work this shit. He's the one saying it's dead. Dell is trying to make $50 off ya man, and I'm like he should bring it to me for $1,200 or $1,250, so get your money, Dell. It ain't nothing personal."

"Well, what's your dude charge?" Slick asked.

Lewis answered, "$1,075. I know he can get $1,100 or $1,150 from people. I am waiting on my guy so I can show out. Shit, man, you know how I am."

"Aight, I am fixing to get my shit together, just let me know how it looks." Slick then hung up.

It sounded like Lewis was going to Marlon's to get a kilo, so I headed to the residence off Buena Vista Pike. We weren't sure the deal would go down there, but it was worth watching to see. A couple of my team helped to spread out surveillance, so Hughes stayed at Buena Vista, Titus headed to watch Brooketrace and Sgt. Cox went to Lewis' house. We drove around aimlessly, hoping the next phone call would tell us where they were meeting.

We needed eyes on Lewis. The tracker on his Malibu was working fine, but we needed pictures of him doing a deal. I caught up to Lewis as he met a female at the Publix in West Nashville. For once, I don't think he did a dope deal. Lewis and the female went straight to his house in Franklin and then he dropped her back at her car before heading home again. It wasn't until 3 pm that the real action began, and I let my dad know I might be late for Sunday dinner.

Lewis left his house and headed to Buena Vista Pike. Hughes got some good pictures of Lewis arriving in his Malibu and parking, and Titus and Sgt. Cox headed our way. There was a white Hummer and black Ford Mustang parked at the residence, too.

"Hold up!" Hughes said. "That's the same Hummer that was on Brooketrace the day that Lewis was there last month, right in the middle of his kilo sale."

"Who's in there?" Sgt. Cox asked.

"Shit. There is like no visibility."

As I drove by and looked at the Hummer, I radioed back, "There are two black suitcases sitting by the Hummer. I'm going to circle back and try to get a picture."

I turned around and headed back as Hughes said. "Oh shit, we've hit pay dirt! Two male Hispanics just came out to the Hummer. Bobby you see them?"

"Yeah, couldn't get a picture, though."

"I got one." Hughes said. "No suitcases, but I got a couple of them. Oh, and here comes Marlon on a new little scooter."

Titus laughed. "Man, I love those things. That's hilarious."

"Lewis is there now, too. He's got a bag." Hughes said.

For a second we were all four silent. We were probably all thinking the same thing: Marlon can't run, there's two Hispanic males, two suitcases, and Lewis holding a kilo of cocaine wrapped in black tape in broad daylight . . . this could have been the perfect chance to take some guys down.

Chapter 21

"Let's see where they go." I said as the players got into their cars. The Hispanic males got into the Hummer with Marlon and Lewis in his Malibu.

We definitely didn't want to get burned, but we needed to stay on them. They traveled in tandem on Buena Vista Pike towards Clarksville Highway. They hung a left and headed towards Marlon's other house on Brooketrace Drive. I gave them distance, laid back just a little, and let the tracker on the Malibu lead us. The two cars pulled in to the bricked driveway and they went inside. Lewis came out and left again. We just let him go. I wanted to stick on Marlon and see what he and his Hispanic buddies were going to do.

About an hour later, Marlon left his home still in the Hummer, and he headed back to the house off Buena Vista Pike. It got a little boring at this point, and we didn't see any activity for the next couple hours. It was not all glitz and glamour.

I talked to my dad on the phone to give him an update and he understood why I'd be missing dinner.

"Danielle's on her way over to you, though, so you all be nice."

"When have we ever not been nice to that angel?" He shot back. "You be safe tonight, though, son. If things wrap up early we can keep a plate out for you."

"Thanks, Dad. I'll let you know."

It seemed like nothing else was going to happen, but at dusk we saw some movement. A black Mustang arrived and the two unknown Hispanic males got in. Marlon got in a Saturn SUV and backed out of the driveway. I eventually found out that this residence had been owned by Marlon's grandparents and the Saturn belonged to Marlon's granny. The Saturn led us down Buena Vista and the Mustang followed close behind. They went straight to Brooketrace Drive. Good thing we had a camera on that place. Since they were just moving back and forth between the two properties, we called it a night and I headed to my parents to at least get there in time for some dessert.

22

A couple of days later, Lewis was back at it, and before the afternoon settled, he had already set up deals with two buyers. Both were looking for more cocaine to move and Lewis was the go-to guy. Like with all the other buyers making calls, we traced the numbers to get their identities and added them to the list.

My desk was starting to look like a fort with stacks of papers from all the pulled records and paperwork required every step of the way. Titus offered to help with some organization so, as he put it, I wouldn't die from a "paper avalanche." We got a couple bins and labeled them to help me still know where everything was going, and I had to admit it was nice to see the picture frame of my wife, which had been buried for a couple months.

A call between Lewis and Slick revealed that Slick was getting low on "bricks," and how neither were sure they could trust Dell because of his loud ass mouth. But, they both relied on Dell because he was their ticket to Shawn. If Marlon couldn't come through, they wanted to have a link to Shawn. It took forever to transcribe their long calls, but their filters came off when they were mad, so we gathered really good intel.

Slick talked to Dell in the afternoon after having the bitch-fest with Lewis, and he acted like normal with Dell. It felt very middle school to see how these guys played their games.

"Sup, man?" Dell asked.

Slick said, "It's the same old shit, trying to figure something out. You hear that Stretch is trying to holler at you? He said it was important."

"Who's trying to holler at me? Brian? Knowing him, he probably wants some money."

"There you go, that's how important it is, it's about some money."

"Man, whatever." Dell said. "Let me hit this boy up, he keeps calling. He done got locked up, got out, now having to recharge!"

"We ain't fuckin' with them now, but he alright. He might've got his paperwork now."

Dell said, "I want to know what he got on his mind."

"Just heard Gucci is fixing to get out, too. You know, the boy 'Taz' that got caught with the money. Taz's bitch with the big ole ass who drives a brownish Maxima. Thick as a mother fucker."

"Yeah, that's her."

Honestly, sometimes I couldn't even keep up with their conversations. On the one hand they were talking about moving cocaine and then on the other hand, they were talking about everything under the sun. It was funny, though, because I was involved in the wire case that got Taz arrested a couple years prior. I remembered how much of an asshole he was. He was dealing kilos and fighting dogs. I think he got more time for animal cruelty than he did for the eight kilos.

"What is Creep doing?" Slick said, getting back to business.

"Shit, *diamonds*. When you bust it open, it's all diamonds."

"All the way through glass?"

"Yep. Can't be buying no more cars. Only glassy antiques, you feel me? Go and look at it over at Harry's house."

"I'm still in the house."

"Well, goddammit, you ain't three hours away in Memphis. Get your ass over here."

"Man, didn't I just say that I'm in the house? I'm *good*." Slick said, losing his patience for a second. He then said, "I talked with Lewis and he has two good ones for me already." I knew Slick was bringing Lewis up because of the cost issue. Dell charged over one hundred dollars more than Lewis' supplier.

Dell seemed to shrug it off, though. "Aight. I'm going to have to put you on."

"If your boy grabs nine, how much will he want? Will he go lower?"

"He might." Dell paused, letting that sink in for dramatic effect. "He knows you my boy because I constantly tell him."

"Aight, my man. See what he can do if I get eight or nine."

"I'll call you right back." Dell said before hanging up.

I waited in anticipation for Dell's callback. This would be a solid deal to watch go down.

Dell called Slick back just a few minutes later. "He said that this weekend he can get you however many you want. I can get you one or two right now of what he has put up for me. Shit, I can probably get you as many as four by the weekend. He did put ten of them up for me, but I've already run through six of them."

"Sounds good. I still have a little bit."

"Man, I suggest that you get one and then wait until this weekend. If you have to play now, I will get you this one, but you should wait until this weekend so you can save some money. If you get that many, he will fuck with you. He didn't tell me a price, but he will fuck with me."

"Cool, I will need a little two piece."

I knew Slick wasn't talking about a bikini.

"Man, I ain't trippin'. Anything for you." Dell was getting more sentimental about being buddies with Slick. He added, "Hey, I forgot to tell you that Rock was coming to meet me. He got pulled over with a half-ounce and there was still a quarter in his balls. Had his gun on him, but he has a gun license."

"My boy in Cali was going through the same thing." Slick said. "They were trying to get him an eight. It was a gun, weed, and a DUI. I won't send him money, though, because he should be richer than a mother fucker. You supposed to be a millionaire if you in Cali."

Dell laughed. "People are crazy."

"Aight, go on and get the two of them, I'll call these dudes and see what they want to do and will then call you back."

A deal was set up for early afternoon, and since Dell mentioned he was at Harry's, Director Davis and I headed that way to do surveillance. There was a white 2009 Acura TL with a TN temporary tag parked in the driveway. I also observed Dell's white 2015 Kia Sorento rental SUV, NC tag, parked on the street in front of the location. I got the rental info later and, of course, it was rented in the name of one of Dell's gal friends.

Davis was watching from another angle, and an hour later he reported that Dell was walking out of the front door. Dell drove off in the Sorento and I followed Dell closely as I didn't want to lose sight of him. I can't tell you how many red lights I had to run to keep up with him. He never cared about getting pulled over by the police because he would never stop, and he knew Nashville PD wouldn't chase.

We followed Dell to the bar Chuck had tipped me off to called Donkey's on Trinity Lane. Dell ordered some wings at the bar. After ordering, a guy pulled up and got out of his car and Dell came out to meet him. It wasn't Slick, though, and I realized the car matched the description of what Helton said Shawn Perry drove. I could not believe my eyes. There he was in the flesh, Shawn Perry aka "Creep," aka "The Diamond Guy." The man with the plan, the all-knowing cocaine mastermind, was just standing here outside of Donkey's like it was a regular Tuesday. I guessed, for him, it was just a regular Tuesday.

I radioed to Davis, "You know, I think this is as close as a detective gets to starstruck."

He laughed and said, "We ain't getting his autograph, yet, so reign in your enthusiasm."

After a short meeting, Dell left the bar. We let Shawn go because we had all his information, and we needed to keep on Dell. It hurt to let Shawn drive off, though. Luckily, it began to rain, and Dell drove a little slower towards Slick's stash house. The rain helped keep us concealed, too, so once he was parked I drove by the location and saw Big Mack's truck was also parked at the residence.

"It must be a meeting of the minds." I said.

"Shit, I bet Dell is strutting about gabbing about all the good words Shawn had to say over at Donkey's."

"Probably. You think Slick and Big Mack are starry-eyed?"

Davis laughed. "Not as much as you were fifteen minutes ago."

We both laughed.

We headed back to the office in the rain. After we got inside, I told Davis, "I don't know why but today's felt so long. Actually, this month has felt long."

"It's just halfway over, Bobby."

"I know. I just feel like this is a lot. I mean, we had to follow Dell, but Shawn went off to God knows where tonight. We needed more guys there, but everyone also has their own cases."

Davis took a moment to answer as we stood in the hallway by my office. "We are all tuned into this case, Bobby, but it is a lot for one guy to lead, especially with two big sources involved."

I nodded. Director Davis had a point. I was so focused on Marlon Cummings, and I needed to give his chain a lot of my focus with all the people running around under him. But, Shawn was just as big a dealer, and other than getting some information from Helton, I'd barely been able to spend time on his part of the case.

"It's becoming two case's worth, isn't it?" I asked. Normally, I would ask a question and listen to advice, but I would rarely actually take it. This was how I'd earned a nickname of "ask-hole" at SID. I would ask for opinions, but I would really just do whatever felt right in my opinion. It was something I knew about myself, but I realized I honestly wanted Director Davis' take on the current situation.

He thought for a second and replied, "Maybe so. Just think on it. I know you'll do what's best for the case, Bobby. I trust your judgment completely on this."

"Thanks, Davis." He headed to his office and I went into mine.

Cops are usually Type-A personalities, which means asking for help just doesn't happen. As much as I didn't want to admit it, I could not do this alone. It would be selfish of me to try and work both drug trafficking organizations because one of the cases wouldn't get the attention it deserved. I had no doubt at this point that there were two separate cartels operating in and around Nashville, but I could devote my attention only to one.

As soon as I realized this, I felt a weight lift from my shoulders. Only minutes before I felt like I was being crushed by the enormity of the decision to ask for help, but once I knew I had to do what was best for the case, I didn't have to think much to decide on who to ask for help.

Chapter 22

Most people had left the office for the day, but I knew Mike Hughes and Melissa would still be there. Melissa was the Batcave's Alfred Pennyworth, so she was always there for us when we needed her assistance. Hughes just had the same work ethic I did, which was why I respected him so much. He was one of those first ones in and last ones to leave. Truly a hard worker. Plus, he had been doing this longer than me, and he had more connections and more experience. He had spent six years at the Drug Task Force already, and, per Metro's official policy, an officer was only supposed to be assigned to a task force for four years. Hughes was such a badass, so good at his job, he got two one-year extensions. Right after I had joined the 20th, though, he was worried the department wouldn't give him another extension, so he left the police department in July and was hired on as a full-time agent with the 20th.

I knew he was the right guy to help me carry this case. I got up from my desk and headed to the kitchen to grab a drink. Hughes' office was beside the kitchen, so I stuck my head in and asked him if he had a minute.

"What's up?" Hughes asked.

I stepped inside and sat down. "I need some help."

"Okay, shoot."

"So, we've got Marlon dealing kilos and he has a Hispanic plug, but Shawn is dealing just as much if not more, and I'm positive he's got a separate plug. Dell's the link between both crews. I called my buddy at the DEA and he said that Shawn pulled some weight back in the day but hasn't been caught at it in quite a while. He's got connections across the border, too." I realized I was rambling and slowed down. "Basically, we've got two halves of the same case, but I can't lead both of them. Can you help with leading the Shawn half?"

"Absolutely." Hughes smiled. He gestured to his screen and said, "I was working on the Rocket case, but I can't figure out who his plug is just yet, so I'm happy to help."

"Thanks, man. I got that ping signed on Shawn's phone. I talked to his PO, and I'm supposed to be getting some good info from DEA agents in Texas soon. I'm waiting on tolls on one number still, too."

"Sounds good. I'm in."

"Great. I'll focus on Marlon and once we take him down then I can jump back on Shawn. I'll get you everything I have on Shawn so far."

"Let's do this!"

It took almost a week to finally hear back from our DEA guy, Special Agent Matt Lober, who was assigned to the McAllen, Texas area. Matt explained that in mid-July he took a guy off near the border with ten kilos of cocaine. The person, referred to by him as "Charlie-4" subsequently cooperated and gave statements about the recipient of the cocaine. Charlie-4 admitted to agents in Texas that for the past five years he had been delivering large kilogram quantities of cocaine and tractor-trailer-sized loads of marijuana to two different individuals in Nashville, TN. One of those persons receiving the loads in Nashville was a male Hispanic, only known as "C," and the other was a large black male, only known to him as "Big Country."

He told agents that, at first, it started with small loads of cocaine, just two kilos twice a month. Then, after Big Country showed that he could be trusted, the number was bumped up to six. Over time, the size of the load grew. These deliveries to Big Country started in the beginning of 2013 and stopped, well, when Charlie-4 was arrested in 2014.

Charlie-4 gave agents two phone numbers utilized by Big Country, and that was all we cared about. Coincidentally enough, both numbers matched the same ones we had for Shawn Perry.

Matt said they tried a controlled call with Big Country, but it was obvious he knew something was up and didn't talk about dope at all. Charlie-4 said that Big Country had a "right-hand man" who would move most of the loads. The close associate was described as a tall, black male with a lot of tattoos. Charlie-4 even said that Shawn's right-hand man drove a gray Nissan sedan when picking up the dope. Charlie-4 knew that the car had an electronic trap or hidden compartment in it.

Charlie-4 thought Big Country's source of supply was a male Hispanic that had been in federal prison with him, and he believed the source was out of federal prison and running with the Los Zetas drug cartel in Mexico. It was easy for Charlie-4 to give up the buyers or recipients in

Tennessee, but he didn't give much information about what was occurring on the other side of the border. If the cartel had found out Charlie-4 was cooperating with authorities in Texas, he would likely be decapitated!

I found a Facebook photo of Shawn and a friend (who wasn't tagged in the picture). I sent the photo to Matt and he identified the short large guy in the photo as Big Country and the other guy, a tall guy with tattoos, as his right-hand man, Edwin Fields. I thanked Matt for all the information and passed it all along to Hughes before writing up the report of the conversation.

23

While Hughes continued working on Shawn intel and drafting the wiretap order for his phones, I focused on another part of Dell's dealings. An expensive jeweler was scheduled to arrive from Memphis for a few days called "Iceman" with his rapper brother. The rapper was putting on a concert, and Dell was organizing a party to sling some bling for the afterparty. It worked out perfectly because Slick had some California-based friends coming in with some high-grade weed, and they wanted to chill with the jewels.

After intercepting several calls between Slick and the Cali weed dealer, it was apparent that the dealer needed to fly out the next morning and Slick needed to go get his shit. Davis, Collins, and I went towards the airport where the dealer and rapper were staying in a Marriott. We arrived at 7 pm and went straight to the front desk. After flashing our badges, the clerks were willing to give information on this guy named Tony, and one said they had the cell phone number of the dealer.

"Actually, he just texted me," the clerk said looking at his phone. "He's asking why there are police in the lobby." He looked quickly up at Director Davis' tall, intimidating frame. He sounded panicked as he said, "I swear I have no idea how he found out. He's probably going out the back. He drives a Camry."

Hughes and Titus were just arriving at the hotel, too, and Collins radioed to them to keep an eye out for a Toyota Camry. I left my number with the clerk for more information as Director Davis and Collins disappeared down a hallway towards the back. When I caught up with them, we listened to Hughes report, "There's one driving around from the back. And it's heading around the hotel to the back again. And here it comes again . . . Oh, a black male wearing a gray hoodie came out the back and just jumped into the passenger seat."

"Stay on him," Collins said. "We're going back to our cars."

We ran back to our cars while Hughes and Titus followed the car out of the lot.

I guessed the employees at the hotel felt guilty because the clerk called and was overly cooperative. He said quietly, "Tony's left, but his promoter's still here. He's in the lobby."

I hadn't gotten out of the parking lot, yet, so I made a U-turn, parked, and ran back inside. I was wearing only a t-shirt and jeans, but I had my gun and badge. I went to the front desk and the clerk gave me a key for a third floor room.

"In the black. On the phone." The clerk whispered, gesturing to the elevators. I turned and saw the target waiting for the elevator. I walked to him and stood beside him. I could feel myself sweating as the doors opened, so I started to sway in place, and I rubbed my face to pretend I was drunk.

The doors opened and the promoter said, "I'll take care of it," as he stepped in. I shuffled in behind him and leaned heavily against the wall and closed my eyes. He mumbled "yeah" a few times before the doors opened. I followed him down the hall and went past him when he stopped at a door. He didn't open the door immediately, and I got the sense he was listening for me. I found my door and scanned the card, then opened and shut the door without going in. I stayed against the alcove wall to stay hidden and heard the promoter go into the room.

I walked back down the hallway and heard a lot of shuffling from his room.

I went back to the alcove to wait. I went ahead and called in a K-9. Less than ten minutes later, his door opened and I shut my door loudly and pretended to be on my phone.

"No, honey, listen, listen to me." I slurred my words as I shuffled back down the hallway. The promoter dragged two big bags out of the room and towards the elevator, eyeing me for a second. I continued, "I'm fine. Like, more than fine. Totally. Flipping. Fine. You just worry too much. I'm just gonna have a smoke and hit the hay."

When the elevator arrived, I said, "Okay, I gotta go, I gotta—I love you, too." We got in and I added, "I miss you, too. Sleep good." We reached the bottom and the promoter thankfully went towards the front doors, as I did. Once outside, I raced to my car and grabbed my police vest, and then I hurried through the parking lot in the direction he'd gone.

He was just hauling the second big bag into the trunk of a Lincoln Navigator when I stopped him and held up my badge and gun.

I think he shit himself in fear. He had looked nervous in the hallway before, but now that a trashed guy had just turned into a cop with a gun, he looked on the verge of tears.

He gave me his ID and immediately denied ownership of the luggage that he just put inside his own vehicle. Right on time, the cross-trained drug K-9 arrived in the parking lot and headed towards us. The K-9 alerted us of narcotics in the trunk, so I had the promoter, now identified as Mohammed, open the trunk back up. I pulled the luggage out of the Navigator and began searching.

The two bags revealed twenty-seven vacuum sealed bags of marijuana (weighing 28.9 pounds), a loaded Springfield .40 caliber gun, a digital scale, eight pieces of jewelry, and $7,000 cash.

Meanwhile, Hughes and Titus had stopped the Camry in East Nashville. They didn't find anything on Tony, but I told them to make it a point to let Mr. Tony know that we got all his weed. Tony told Officers that he was staying at the hotel, but he was in town from California because of his "t-shirt line" and not here to sell marijuana. I wondered if Titus laughed in his face. Hughes told him that if he wanted to reclaim the marijuana, along with the cash and jewelry, then he could absolutely come to a future court date and we would be happy to take his statement.

I ended up letting the promoter Mohammed go. We knew it really wasn't his stuff, but I gave him the appropriate paperwork that goes with a civil forfeiture. Dell may have thrown a hell of a party, but we had a party of our own seizing all of Iceman's shit.

The following day, we had a new point of celebration: We flipped the switch on Shawn Perry's phone and were starting the wiretap. This would make the case even more chaotic, but it was essential. Hughes and I agreed to rename his arm of the investigation as an extension of the regular control number: TF-1422 "B." Collins would continue to write the wiretap affidavits for the first half, or the "A" half, and John Phillips would write the wiretap affidavits for the "B" half. Hughes had a leg up with Phillips writing his wiretaps because he'd been writing them since he joined the 20th in the 90s.

Our first real action with Shawn happened a couple days later. I was monitoring some calls when Dell and Shawn planned to meet up at a Waffle House. Shawn had first driven around town, speeding as if looking for a tail and losing our guys in the process. I headed to the Waffle House and left someone else to listen in on further conversations.

We set up surveillance and watched as Dell arrived in a white Acura. Shawn was already posted up in a maroon Jeep Grand Cherokee. They had both backed into the space, which was typical of both dealers and cops. Shawn and Dell looked in Dell's trunk at something, but we couldn't see what. I wished we could bust in and arrest them right then, but I held my breath and waited until they left.

Thomas and I followed Dell while Hughes and Collins followed Shawn.

The wire room let me know of a call coming in from Dell to Slick.

"Come get them now! It is diamonds. My boy is going to sell to you, but he needs you to come on. He called me straight over, and, man, they are pretty. If you want these diamonds, you better come on. Going to go ahead and grab a couple."

"Get some. I'll be a minute, gotta go and grab some money. I'll call you right back."

We'd gotten to Dell's house and waited for the next call. Unfortunately, ten minutes later Dell told Slick, "Gotta grab a new phone real quick."

Damn. That meant another line was being dropped just as it was getting good.

"Where you at with Shawn?" I radioed in.

"We've observed him meeting several people and visiting a storage unit on Whites Creek Pike." Hughes reported back.

"That's a good sign."

"Yeah, doesn't seem like he's keeping furniture there." Collins said. "He went to a car shop next and a guy joined him in the car. Looks like they're going to Walmart now."

I was across town, still watching Dell's house. I knew he'd be meeting up with Slick, but now I had no idea if he was going to drop his phone. Thankfully, Dell used the number we'd tapped to call Slick back to set a meeting place.

The wire room relayed the call, and I learned that because Slick was not a regular of Shawn's, he wasn't going to cut him a good deal, but the quality was still diamonds. Loyalty was the most important thing to dealers. Well, that and money! One kilogram, 2.2 pounds of cocaine, was going for $36,500, so you better believe there had to be loyalty when dealing those "diamonds." They ended the call saying they'd touch base in an hour. They were so careful saying "him" over the phone usually, but we knew who "him" was: Shawn.

My stomach grumbled. It was almost lunch time. At SID, lunch was the most important time of day for the detectives. It was an hour of relaxing, cutting up, pausing the day's activities, enjoying time out at a restaurant. I rarely took the hour though, and now on the 20th I rarely took even five minutes. I reached over the console to the bag on the floor and pulled out an Uncrustables PB&J and a bag of chips. The most down time I experienced between calls was a few minutes, so I scarfed down the food. Regardless of the uninspired lunch, I would have chosen the intense work with the 20th any day over SID's extended lunch hour.

Collins radioed as I worked through my chips and said Shawn was now at an apartment building on the west side. I waited on Dell and Slick while Collins and Hughes followed Shawn to a used car lot.

"Damn, they're all over the place. I'm coming to that side," I told the team. "Slick is just dragging his feet with the money, and Dell's waiting for Shawn to call him back."

Hughes said, "Shawn's been on the phone almost constantly."

"Guess Dell's not his focus." I then remembered Dell talking about another phone and added, "Or, Dell's got him on another line and is making Slick wait around."

Dell must have left his house right after me because only a couple minutes after I reached the car lot, Dell pulled in.

Collins jokingly asked, "He following *you* now?"

I laughed. "I guess Shawn finally called him back?"

Dell talked to Shawn for a bit and they were laughing and acting like they were catching up after forever of not talking. Then we watched as Dell, mid conversation, headed to Shawn's Jeep and grabbed a bag out of the passenger seat. He tossed it into his trunk while they continued talking like everything was normal.

A few minutes later, Dell returned to his Acura and pulled off. Collins and I followed Dell as he headed towards Antioch, and Hughes and Thomas stayed to watch Shawn at the car lot.

The wire room let me know Dell had called Slick to say he was on the way over.

Dell turned into the driveway of Slick's residence and pulled into the garage. On his drive-by, Collins reported that the garage door was closing.

Since it was a neighborhood, we parked nearby, but Dell left only a couple minutes later. We didn't have to be rocket scientists to know what had just gone down.

We followed Dell to the Wal-Mart, and Hughes said Shawn seemed to be heading there, too. Shawn needed his payment fast to get it back to his source. I estimated Dell was carrying over $100,000 for the kilos he just moved. Dealers wanted to do deals as fast and efficiently as possible to get rid of the evidence. No one wants to sit on kilos of cocaine or hundreds of thousands of dollars cash. That was too big of a risk.

Dell parked near the end of the lot, and Shawn parked directly next to Dell on his driver's side. Dell exited his Acura and retrieved a bag out of the back. This looked familiar! Dell entered the front passenger seat of Shawn's Jeep for only a moment.

They left the Walmart and we had our photos of the transaction. Paired with the phone conversations, we had more than enough to prove each step of the deal. Slick got his diamonds thanks to Dell, and Shawn got his money and was heading home for the night with his big payday. Just another day in the life of the top dealers.

Director Davis had assisted us by getting the tracker warrant signed for Shawn's new Jeep while we were trailing him around town all day, so I made a plan to get the tracker placed that night.

24

"Tracker time!" Jack Milliken said as he got in my car at 2 am.

"Shit, you got a lot of energy." I laughed as I pulled away from the Batcave.

"I'm just excited, man. Director Davis is really doing me a big one, so I'm glad to help with whatever, whenever." Jack Milliken had joined our office about a month before as a secondary tech guy. He had been in the DA's office but hadn't gotten along with the financial manager, so he got transferred to work for the 20th. Director Davis had immediately taken a liking to Milliken and his high energy because he always wanted more work and went outside his normal duties to assist the team with whatever we needed. Because of this, Davis offered to sponsor him for a ten week police school program and a future position as an agent with the Task Force. Milliken was thrilled, to say the least.

"Well, I'm glad you're into this." I said. "And it's good to give some of the guys a break at night."

"Understandable." Milliken nodded. "It's great experience for me, too. The classes are great and all, but seeing the work in action is even better."

"Well, in that case, how about you do the tracker placement?"

"Hell yes! I studied a diagram of a Jeep undercarriage before you showed up, just in case you offered."

He grinned, which made me laugh again. He then added, "This guy should be asleep by now, right? Don't dealers work late?"

"He had a busy day making $100k, so I'm banking on him sleeping like a baby tonight."

Milliken nodded.

We set up surveillance close to Shawn's home, and all was dark inside. There was no fence, which meant it was less likely he had land-sharks, and the Jeep was parked in the driveway.

I shivered against the freezing cold night. My heart was beating fast even though I'd done this a hundred times before, but we never knew how things would go.

I handed Milliken the tracker and had him review how to place it.

"Okay. I got this," he said with a deep breath. He got out of the car and headed towards the driveway. It was like déjà vu, but this time I was the one keeping a lookout and I was nervous for Milliken. He walked stiffly to the Jeep, got down on the pavement, and stuck the tracker into the frame. He then hurried back to the car, rubbing his hands together.

"God, what a rush." He laughed.

"There will be plenty more of that in your future." We headed back to the Batcave, and I dropped him off at his car before heading home to get a couple hours of sleep.

Later that morning, I called my dad on the way to work to give him an update on the tracker placement, and I got a ping in the middle of the call. The tracker was already on the move. I wrapped up the call with Dad and watched as Shawn hit his storage unit, which we found out was under his sister's name.

That afternoon, Shawn hit the used car lot again.

I went to Hughes' office and said, "Surely he's just getting his Jeep detailed?"

Hughes grimaced. "Maybe we should go check."

We watched in shock as Shawn the Asshole drove off the car lot in a different vehicle.

"He turned the Jeep in already?" I almost yelled. "You've got to be kidding me."

Hughes pulled out behind Shawn to tail him back to his house. "You don't think he knew about the tracker, do you?"

"I highly doubt it. The house was dead last night. Shit. It's going to be a late night again."

"Yeah, I kind of doubt the car lot owners will cooperate. I'll help with this go round."

"Thanks, man."

That night, we stayed late and came up with a plan to retrieve the expensive tracker from the Jeep. The gate topped with barbed wire would be locked up tight, but there was a tree beside the lot. Hughes said he would scale it and drop down into the lot. It wasn't something I'd do, but it was his idea so I said okay.

At the lot, I watched Hughes scramble up the tree when no cars were around. He dropped into the lot and disappeared for thirty seconds while he found the Jeep and got the tracker. He then had a hell of a time getting back into the tree, and when he got back to the car he was scratched up to hell.

He pulled the tracker out of his pocket with a grin, "Worth it. How about you get some extra sleep tomorrow and I'll get this placed."

"Fine by me. Thanks, man. Actually, I bet Milliken would be happy to help with the placement. He got a kick out of it last night."

"That guy is awesome. He'll be a good agent."

Even though I still only got five hours of sleep, I slept hard and woke up ready to go.

I spent the next day watching a deal go down at Lewis' new house. He had graduated from his mom's house and now had his own duplex in East Nashville. He was on the phone constantly, so people were coming and going from his trap. One guy, in particular, caught our attention and Sgt. Cox followed him all the way to Lebanon. His call with Lewis had told us he went by "Glance" so I called up the Lebanon Police Narcotics division to get more information on him. It turns out we had just met Jacoby Knight, aka "Glance," the largest cocaine distributor from the Lebanon, TN area.

When I got back to the office, I reviewed a long call between Dell and Slick. Slick had supposedly been short on his payment for his recent load, and Shawn was pissed! Even worse, Dell had Shawn on speaker phone to give Slick a piece of his mind.

Shawn said, "One of those five dollar stacks was only four. When you said you counted it, that's not possible cause you would've seen it was a stack off. It's $1,700 off!"

"$1,700?" Slick sounded nervous.

"From now on I gotta be the machine man." Dell said, "I'll go on and count them. I know you gotta machine, but sometimes it can be off."

Slick said, "When I went and bought the Chevelle, I gave up the machine. All by hand now homie, so that's my bad. My mistake. So, it's $1,700?"

"I know you honest." Shawn said.

"Yeah, man." Dell chimed in, "We ain't trippin'. You my boy, Slick. I know you don't play no short games."

"I know you honest, too. If you say it's $1,700 off, then it was. I ain't going to dispute it. I'll take care of it."

"I miscounted before, too." Shawn said, a little cooled off. He was still bitter, though, because he added, "Just sayin', if you counted, you should have noticed."

"I hear ya," Slick said. "If it's off, it's off. My bad. I know you not playing games with it. I'll get it to you."

A second call between Dell and Slick revealed that Slick was headed to the "A." He must have been heading to Atlanta, GA to visit his daughter for her birthday. Even with all the drug deals and stash houses, Slick still played the father role. It was clear that Slick was still a little put off, maybe a little butt-hurt by the amount of cash he had miscounted.

In listening to these calls, it was easy to get caught up and forget the fact that these drug dealers were human beings who were trying to provide a life for their family. Even Slick had talked about "getting out of the game," once he had enough money. However, in the end, it was always about the drugs, the greed, and the next big score.

I also reviewed a call between Lewis and a small-time dealer named Mike Armstrong. In Nashville he would be known as a small-time dealer, but where Mike was from, he was famous. He was a local rapper from Tullahoma, TN, and he ran his area. When he wasn't selling records, which wasn't often, he was slinging crack. I liked some rap, so I watched this dude's YouTube videos. He was terrible! I guess that's why he sold dope. As for Lewis, he was trying like hell to get rid of nine ounces and wanted Mike to come through for him.

When Mike said he wanted the "nina," Lewis played it cool and set up a deal for 3 pm, so Titus and I headed that way to see it go down.

Titus observed a black Chevy Impala pull in the driveway of Lewis' new dig but then pulled back out and left immediately. While waiting for Mike, Lewis had been busy as usual. Several clients had gone in and come out like clockwork, but this was the first car not to actually do a deal. According to intercepted phone calls on Lewis, Mike had attempted to call four times without an answer. Mike and his "dude" could be heard talking about a suspicious vehicle possibly following them. And by suspicious, Titus and I realized he meant us.

"These folks hot as a mother fucker." Mike said.

"Where are you?"

"I'm on Trinity, being followed. I can't get in the driveway. A Maxima kept hitting the block. They went down the block and turned around and a blue Altima followed all the way over on Trinity."

"You just pulling into the driveway?"

"Yeah, but this guy is riding slow. About to hit the block again."

"What happened?"

Mike said, "I turned around in the road real slow and then went to the store and turned around. I wasn't even going to pull up. They be riding like that up here?"

"No, man. I ain't seen 'em."

"Well, they're riding. Was trying to get in the driveway and was also trying to call you to let you know."

"Come back in the morning real quick and be gone early. 9:00?"

"Bet."

Shit, that was too close. I knew Mike had seen us, but it was too late by then. We got burned. We just went ahead and terminated surveillance for that night. Either they deal dope today or deal it tomorrow. It never stops, and we couldn't be on every deal. We needed to start using some other cars if we were going to catch a deal between Lewis and this Mike guy.

Titus and I got back to the office and slumped into our chairs.

"It's funny. When we get burned, we're more on edge than these low lifes."

I sighed and tried to laugh. Then I realized the office was almost silent. "Wait, where's Thomas? Why is it so silent?"

I stood and walked towards the kitchen but saw nobody and Hughes wasn't in his office. Titus followed and we headed to the meeting room where we heard voices.

Everyone was sitting at the table, talking over each other, and Sgt. Cox saw us first and gestured to us to sit.

"What's going on?" I asked as we sat in two of the empty chairs and the room quieted.

Before Director Davis or Sgt. Cox could answer, Thomas blurted out, "Weakling's been promoted."

I didn't quite know how to respond, so I looked at Director Davis. He nodded and looked at the table. "He's now with the Office of Professional Accountability."

My mouth fell open. The guy who hadn't wanted to have any part of the leak investigation was now working for OPA? "When, or, how—" I trailed off.

Hughes filled the silence and said to me, "He moved all his shit out of our office this afternoon. He wouldn't tell me what he was doing."

"And he stopped by my office on his way out to let me know he was promoted." Sgt. Cox said.

Director Davis added, "And I got the official transfer email from OPA fifteen minutes after Sgt. Cox let me know what happened. So, that's that."

This was more than shady and backhanded. Weakling had been sneaking around and acting strange for over a month, and he never stopped being pissed and defensive about the leak issue. But, still, to leave the team so suddenly and disrespectfully like this was shocking even for him. Clearly everyone was still processing the information.

"You know what?" Thomas said with a sigh and then a slow grin, "Good riddance. I know he was a good detective and was dedicated to this team for a long time, but, damn, that guy gave us a hard time. Well, everyone but Hughes; he loved you, man."

Hughes laughed and shook his head. "I don't know why he hated you."

"And me." Sgt. Cox laughed, probably remembering the drunken phone call Weakling never owned up to.

"He could be very difficult." Director Davis added tactfully.

"That's putting it lightly." Collins said, rolling his eyes. "With all due respect, he did good work but only sometimes. He was never invested like we are." He gestured to the table. "I felt like he was always trying to stir the pot or prove himself as better than we are." He shook his head and leaned back in his chair with his arms crossed. "I liked him sometimes, and he could be funny as hell, but he sure pissed me off."

Hughes said, "No kidding. You were downright scary when you got pissed at him, but I'm not saying he didn't deserve it. You'd be in a rage and I'd get worried you were either going strangle him or have yourself a stroke."

Collins laughed and said, "He was bad for my blood pressure."

We sat in the quiet that followed for a moment, and then Thomas said, "Poor little guy."

We all laughed then, even Director Davis who usually tried to keep impartial.

It didn't take long for the office to agree that this was for the best. Director Davis said they already had a new agent in mind and would get started on the process to add him in. Milliken could assist where needed in the meantime while he was still in training. Davis then gave a brief pep talk about the good work we were doing and how solid a team we were. It was a positive end to a really strange day, but I still left the office wondering about Weakling's sudden departure to join OPA. It didn't feel right, but I was glad he was gone.

Chapter 24

NOVEMBER 2014

25

November started off rough. DA Chad Ball had been working over us for two months without issue, but he suddenly made a decision that made our jobs a lot harder. He announced that no Assistant District Attorney from our county could assist in the wire room. We had to have a supervisor in the room at all times if calls were being monitored, which was basically all day every day. Usually someone on our team could step in to supervise during the day, but from 5 pm to midnight, Assistant DAs looking for some side income would step in to supervise. Our team was stretched thin as it was with the huge case that it would really hurt if one of us always had to be in the wire room. It felt like DA Ball was trying to sabotage us, to make our jobs impossible.

The team was on edge all day the first of November as we figured out what to do. I couldn't help but think about how close Sgt. Bagg was to DA Ball. They were tight buddies, and I knew if Bagg had a chance to make the 20th's jobs harder, he would. From what I heard from Adam back at SID, he was still pissed Sgt. Cox had been hired for the position instead of him, and I could only imagine how he felt about me going on to the 20th and leaving him behind. His words still echoed in my head from our last meeting: *If I have to take it down myself, I will, and I'll make sure you go down with it.*

I had no proof he was behind this current situation, so I kept my mouth shut. But I had a feeling he had something to do with it. Knowing him he probably made up some rumor about Assistant DAs sleeping with the monitors or some bullshit.

What neither DA Ball nor Sgt. Bagg could expect, though, was that by the afternoon of the announcement, our team had reached out to all the DA offices in the counties surrounding ours, and several people came through for us right away. It was easy money for an Assistant DA, and they were more than happy to help with the case. It would take another week to get the schedules all worked out, but we got back to being a well-oiled machine soon enough.

It was just a reminder that Sgt. Bagg could wield his power and influence in inconvenient ways, but I felt proud of our team for pulling through regardless. Sgt. Bagg wasn't taking us down.

During all of this, we had finally gotten the order for tapping Shawn's phone, and we were quickly gathering more numbers, names, and evidence for the conspiracy charges.

Lewis had been quiet because he was about to turn himself in for five days of jail time. The dumbass missed his booking date and then a court date. I guess he got caught up in all the dealing. Dell told Lewis to leave him his phone when he was in jail so he could "take care of his clients." What a sweetie.

When we finally had our first out-of-county Assistant DA in to supervise the wire room, the team and I headed towards one of the biggest and most popular shopping malls in Nashville. No, not to go shopping. Shawn wanted to make a big deal, and Dell was ready and waiting. They made a plan to meet, and then Dell had called all of his guys for orders, including Slick and Lewis.

Dell told Slick, "I got half of the money from Harry and now I'm waiting on Rowan. He's about to pull up on my guy now."

"Get five of them, but can I have my money back?"

"Yeah, but I told Lewis where it came from and he said he'll come and get it, if you want."

"Oh, okay. I ain't trippin'. However you and Lewis want to do it."

Dell said, "Shit, I would prefer to give it back to you because I don't have anywhere to put the bread, and I don't want your bread sitting around. I'll call Lewis and I'll grab that for you."

Unfortunately, Dell couldn't reach Lewis for quite a while and the meet time was coming up. Finally Lewis picked up. I was so relieved that we were still up on his phone. We were too deep at this point to chase new numbers down.

"Where the hell have you been?" Dell asked. "Been trying to get with you all day."

"Phone was on silent. About to get out now."

"Are you ready? Because my guy is good to go. I'm about to call some motherfuckers, but should I wait for you?"

Lewis said, "Go on and get it and do what you do and whatever is left over I'll get. Will make some phone calls right quick."

"Aight, I'm pulling up anyway. I'll hit you back soon."

Titus radioed in and let us know Dell had arrived, but we hadn't seen Shawn's vehicle. The wire room was keeping us up on all the conversations as we set up at various points in the huge parking lot.

The wire room let us know Shawn was by the ski place in a yellow U-Haul truck, not the most inconspicuous vehicle. It was November so the mall was packed that afternoon. Tons of cars were driving around looking for parking spaces, so we fell in to the flow of traffic and circled around the U-Haul at a distance. It was storming which made the parking lot more difficult to maneuver and almost impossible to take pictures, so we made our way closer in to the U-Haul. We needed pictures of a 5-kilo deal!

Dealers assumed busy mall parking lots were perfect to do a deal, but they didn't know we knew their faces, voices, cars, and we were watching them like hawks. We knew this deal would require several undercover cars, so we asked the Gang Unit to help us out. Gang Unit Detective Weis observed Dell exiting the passenger side of a yellow U-Haul, carrying a bag. Detective Weis watched as Dell got back in his Acura and drove away. More than $150,000 worth of cocaine was exchanged in a matter of seconds.

We followed behind Dell as he headed to Slick's house.

"Headed your way," Dell said in the phone call.

"You already got them? I don't have all the cheese yet."

"I took care of it. My guy wasn't tripping. Had to go down."

"Alright, well I ain't got all the bread, but come on."

"Cool, you got any weed over there?" Dell asked. "This rain's a bitch."

"A little bit. Come on, man."

Chapter 25

We followed Dell as he took I-40 through town to Hickory Hollow Parkway. GPS tracker surveillance of Slick's Buick showed that the vehicle was already at his stash house. We watched Dell as he headed into Slick's house for an evening of smoking, and then we pulled off. It hurt to have so much money and drugs walk, but there was a method to the madness. As soon as we pinned Marlon and Shawn's sources, we could round up everyone once and for all.

For the next week, we continued recording all the deals we could. My favorite conversation played out between Daniel Harding and a new guy, Damon, who referred to his dope as football players. He asked for a "Peyton Manning," who wore the number 18. Eighteen ounces was half a kilo, so we knew what he was buying. It cracked me up.

What didn't crack me up, though, was that the monitor thought they were legitimately talking sports and didn't let us know in time to cover the deal. We made sure the monitor knew to look for *any* kind of code language because most of the things these guys talked about was dope, even if it didn't seem like it. Hughes said he had seen Damon at one of Shawn's stash spots recently, so Damon would still have it coming to him.

When Lewis got out of jail, he needed to replenish his stash and we knew he'd be calling Marlon. We were up on a number we had for Marlon, but it seemed to be limited to interaction with Lewis only. Marlon had a second number that he used only to talk to girls, but we knew he had to have a third number for his deals. Until we found that number, though, we would have to rely on Lewis and his big mouth.

In a barrage of phone calls, Lewis got in contact with as many people as he could to let them know that he was "good." Lewis even told his good bud Tommy, aka "Pincher," that he just got two kilos and the quality was glass. The monitor on duty didn't alert us of this phone call, though, maybe because it was a Saturday, and I was pissed to miss the deal go down between them.

Lewis' other big phone call was to Jacoby Knight, the big dealer from Lebanon who went by "Glance." Lewis told him that he was good and had some A-1. The monitor knew to look for Jacoby's number and to alert me of any contacts, and I was tired of being antsy at home on a Saturday, so I headed to the office.

While I waited to see if the half-kilo deal would go down between Jacoby and Lewis, I worked on paperwork and monitored Lewis' tracker. He finally moved and headed towards Marlon's house. After the last deal there when we couldn't see shit, we got smart. Work smarter, not harder right? We put a camera up across the street from Marlon's other house one night to catch any action happening there. There hadn't been a good spot for this camera, but we made it work. The camera was far off, but it still caught Lewis arriving and meeting with Marlon, who was already there in his Hummer. They went into a little barn at the back of the property. Of course, it didn't take long, and Lewis was out of there: he had some shit to sell!

While I was filing away what had just occurred, the monitor came to my office and told me Slick was about to meet with Mike Armstrong, the sub-par rapper from Tullahoma. I wanted to take someone down, and Mike would be a good target since he worked mainly outside of Nashville.

I didn't always know how it would work out, but I loved the fact that I could arrest someone knowing 100% that they would be holding dope. I was going to need some help, so Thomas came in for backup. Mike was a heavy hitter in his county, and we knew he would get decent weight, so I contacted my buds at the Task Force in Maury County. I told the Director what I knew, and he was all in immediately and had his team head towards the county line.

"I got five bands. I'm trying to get four of them." Mike said to Slick.
"Headed to get it now."
"Meet at the same spot?"
"Bet." Slick said and hung up. He went to his stash house in Antioch and then headed towards the mall.

Thomas and I set up at the mall near Slick's Buick while he waited for Mike to show, and I knew the Maury County team was probably set up and waiting, and I just had to give them the info on the vehicle.

"Keep your eye on him, Thomas, and try to get his tags."

"Got it."

We saw a guy walk through the lot and get in Slick's Buick. He then walked over to a white Ford Explorer, and neither Thomas or I could get the tag but we pulled out and followed as closely as was safe. When we finally got the tag, we reported it to the other Task Force. I didn't want to get burned on this one, but I also didn't care if he thought I was following him because I wasn't going to be the one stopping him. The guys from Maury County were counting on this.

A whisper stop is a traffic stop that is conducted by a uniformed officer on a vehicle that another officer knows contains something illegal. In this case, we didn't give any of the out-of-county officers the particulars of the case and they were not involved in the wiretap interceptions, but if they could pick up this car, this white Ford Explorer coming back into their county, then there just might be something in there. Wink!

About forty minutes later, when Mike was well out of Davidson County, the blue lights came on. Thomas and I, an hour from Nashville, sat and watched from a distance. It took some time, but finally the uniformed officer placed Mike in handcuffs. They searched the SUV and let me know that Mike's girlfriend had "stuffed" two ounces of cocaine. Mike was on paper and they did not play down there. He was taken in and booked into jail.

What Mike did next was risky and just plain stupid. The Task Force Director called me laughing.

"As soon as this guy was booked, he ran straight to the toilet. This dumbass pulled two more ounces of cocaine from his ass and threw it in the toilet. As if we wouldn't notice!"

"Did they get him?"

"Hell yeah! The jailers were fast on their feet and tackled him to the ground before he could hit the handle to flush the dope."

I shook my head. "He's not the brightest guy, is he?"

"He's also hella single now. After trying to put the coke charge on his girl and telling us he was just trying to help her make money, I doubt she'll be answering his calls any time soon."

"Well, at least he's caught now."

"Thanks for the tip-off, Bobby. You ever need help, you just let us know, you hear?"

"Thanks, Director. We'll have a lot of warrants coming in at some point, so I'll let you know."

It felt good to have a guy behind bars, even if he wasn't one of our targets. Sometimes it just felt good to put some fire under these dealers to remind them that no one gets away with this shit. I knew there would be some talk, and Slick might be shaking in his boots, but I was glad to have assisted in a big arrest halfway into November after such a rough start to the month when we lost our Assistant DAs. This takedown just reminded me of how good it was going to feel when we took our big guys down.

26

The following morning, an unknown male called Slick. "Buddy, you heard what's going on?"

Slick said, "Naw, what's up?"

"Shit, my cousin got pulled over last night. It wasn't the regular people, know what I mean? He was followed from Nashville."

"Shit."

"His girl went down, and she had it stuck in her little too-too, but they let her go. He kept it in his ass and got busted. Is it hot up there?"

"You already know it."

"Okay, well I was thinking your goddamn wires ain't straight, you hear?"

"I gotcha buddy. Thanks."

I never found out who this "cousin" was, but I wanted to kick his ass. Or, I mean, hit him with a conspiracy charge. After this early morning call, Slick dropped his phone—never made another call on it. We had enough on him to take him down anyway, and we still had the tracker, but we couldn't follow more of his deals unless he called Lewis, who, thankfully, was still a "chatty Kathy" on his line.

Lewis had been extra chipper after a recent deal. Those kilos he got from Marlon must have been something spectacular, not the shake or re-rocked shit but real glass. Jacoby from Lebanon was convinced that the product was superb, and he called Lewis to let him know he was on the way to buy a couple.

Lewis, always the salesman, said, "It looks real good. It's soft, easy to touch, but you see glass all through it. I just dropped two of them, and I got back like ten of them over and that's just cooking it down to everything. Trying to get yo' ass in and get on to turning up!" He knew Jacoby was already convinced, but he was insinuating that Jacoby was such a good dealer that he was thinking about "turning up" how much Jacoby could get. In the drug dealing world, he was basically offering Jacoby a promotion.

Lewis then added, "I go to church at noon and I have to do something after church, but I can't remember what it is. You can come before church or after church. If I know what you want to do, I will know what to put in it, if you will need a little extra with it."

"I will call you and let you know what I want to do, and we can go from there." Jacoby said.

What a winning combination: church and dope. These guys didn't look like big time kilo dealers wearing their Sunday best. They set a time for after church, but Lewis and Jacoby were not the only two with a plan.

Since Jacoby was the big dealer in Lebanon outside of Nashville, I had contacted the Wilson County Narcotics Unit who knew him very well. When I told them that he may be coming to Nashville to get a half kilo of cocaine and they could stop him on the way back, they were all over it. They didn't care that it was a Sunday. Drug dealers never stop, well maybe some pause to go to church, but the cops never stop either. I was feeling good. The previous night we took off four ounces of Slick's dope and arrested Mike, and now we were going to try and get Jacoby with a half kilo from Lewis. Jacoby wouldn't be getting the promotion he was promised.

Thomas and I set up off Jones Drive to monitor Lewis' house at noon. An hour later, a white Toyota Camry pulled into the driveway and idled. A female was driving, which was a good sign because Jacoby was known to flee from police. Jacoby got out of the passenger seat and went around to the back of the house. Thomas watched him come back out carrying a plastic grocery bag and then radioed to me, "By the way, there's a kid in the back seat."

"That piece of shit." I responded.

They started heading back towards Lebanon and drove slowly. I alerted the Wilson County Narcotics when they exited so they could take over.

They got a couple marked cars to make the initial stop, and the Camry pulled over quickly and safely. I passed them up, turned around to watch and held my breath!

Thank goodness Jacoby didn't run. The officers had the two adults get out of the car with the child. As they stood next to the Camry, Sgt. Curt deployed his drug sniffing K-9 on the car. Didn't take long. The trained K-9 scratched the shit out of the passenger side door. Of course, it did, there was only a half kilo of cocaine, exactly 509 grams worth, just lying under the seat in a plastic bag. Jacoby was put in handcuffs. After being advised of his rights, Jacoby admitted it was his dope and that he would have run but didn't because his child was in the car. So honorable.

Like clockwork, sweet Lewis sent a check-in text to Jacoby to see if he made it "safe." However, this one was not going to make it. Surveillance was terminated and I laid my head down that night knowing that we had just cleared the street of some of that shit.

It wasn't long before Lewis found out we had Jacoby. Hell, the Lebanon newspaper made this out to be the bust of the century; it was all over the news. Lewis had to know we were on to him, but did he stop dealing dope? Nope. He did freak out, though. He had just lost a good portion of his product. In addition to his "boy" getting thrown in the slammer for the half kilo, Jacoby still owed money for it, which meant Lewis was in the hole. Debts were debts, and it didn't matter if you were in jail or not. That was their chosen life, and it was risky.

Lewis called up his boy Tommy to tell him the news about Jacoby. "I lost a half truck yesterday. Dude's little brother that fucks with Lebanon came down here and made it back, but as soon as he got off . . . man, that shit is potent, the police searched and got it."

Tommy didn't like the sound of that but Lewis said, "Let's give it a day and I'll get a brick and let you mix some shake with it. Try to get off with that." Lewis had to get the money back, and if serving up some cut shit could float him, he'd do it.

Tommy said, "I can get it off, but my people will be whining."

Lewis got off the phone, and the following day, his phone was unnaturally quiet for once.

After taking off two "loads" of dope, we had the whole gang spooked. Slick's phone was down and it was looking like Lewis dropped his, too. We hadn't gotten a call on Daniel's or Dell's phones since taking down Mike, and Marlon was barely doing anything on his own.

It was still early in the day but I went to Hughes' office and poked my head in. "Is Shawn still talking?"

He shook his head. "I think he's dropped his line for now, too. I'm working on getting a new number for him. I'll let you know if I get anything new for Marlon or the other guys."

"Marlon seems to still be good, but if you get Dell I can probably link back to Lewis and Slick easily enough."

"You got it."

I headed back to the office. I knew the dealers would play it safe after we had hauled in two of their associates, but taking down two guys linked to our targets already guaranteed we'd have dirt on the big guns later on.

It took two weeks to get back on with the wiretaps. We took advantage of the slow wire room by getting out in the field and doing some good ole fashioned police work. We followed everyone that we had identified thus far and took pictures and videos of everyone and their cars. We gathered as much intel as possible while we were rifling through phone tolls to find our targets again.

The hard work and late nights paid off. I was able to find new numbers for both Slick and Lewis, and Hughes found a new number for Shawn. The wiretap affidavits were knocked out just in time for the Thanksgiving holiday.

I spent Thanksgiving day with my family, cooking and eating a feast. Ashley was still weak from the pregnancy, which was different from her previous three, so she had to take it easy. The rest of us took on entertaining her three girls to keep them out of the kitchen where Danielle, my mom, and Angela were wrangling every dish imaginable. Angela was doing more talking than helping, but she was there. After stuffing ourselves, my dad, Ashley's husband Randy, and I did the dishes. Then I took a food-coma nap on the couch and was woken up by Ashley's girls poking me thirty minutes later, wanting everyone to get up and have a second round of pie.

That evening, Danielle and I went to her parents' house for a light dinner, drinks and more pie. I kept checking in with my trackers and the cameras we'd set up on Lewis' house and Marlon's properties, but even the dealers seemed to be focused on family time for a couple days. The wire room was quiet, too, so I was forced to try and relax, not something that came naturally to me.

We got back to business after the long weekend, and Weakling's replacement started with the team. Anthony Diesel was a workout freak who quickly got the nickname "Swole." Right from the start I liked him because he was a team player who was easy to work with. He was laid back and not argumentative or dramatic, basically the opposite of Weakling. He hated trash talk and gossip, and he had a history of beating up people like Weakling who acted like assholes. It was definitely best for Weakling to not have been on the same team with Diesel, and we were all happy to have "Swole" on our team. He joined Hughes in his office and quickly became his right-hand man.

Thomas, Titus, and I were killing it on the Marlon side, TF-1422 "A," and Diesel and Hughes were plugging away on the "B" side. I might have been a little biased, but I thought this had to be the best crew at the 20th Judicial District Drug Task Force in its 28-year history. We were the dream team, and I said as much in a meeting one morning.

Sgt. Cox added, "The Dream Bat-team . . ."

I glanced at Melissa in the corner who was shaking her head at us, but she was smiling.

Now that the Dream Bat-team was back up on phones, we easily got back into the work. It was only a matter of time now before we could take the dealers down on the "A" side of the case. Part of the waiting was Sgt. Cox making sure we could conduct all the search warrants at the same time, which took a lot of scheduling with other teams both in our county and the surrounding areas. The other part was waiting on a big haul where we could identify Marlon's source.

Chapter 26

Meanwhile, Shawn had a sleek looking Chevy Impala, his fourth car in only two months, and it still had a temp tag of course. We acted fast, got a tracking order signed, and got it placed that night.

Shawn made a plan to do a deal with Damon, the dealer who always asked for a "Peyton Manning." Our monitors knew to look for sports references now, so we organized to follow the tracker wherever Shawn went. He headed east to Hermitage, which was new for the case. Neither Hughes nor I had seen Shawn head to this area on the outskirts of Nashville before. Hermitage was in Wilson County, the same that Jacoby had just been arrested in.

I headed that direction, though, to get an eye on his location. He stayed a long time at a house off Central Pike, so it gave me time figure out the best surveillance spots on the heavily travelled two-lane road. The house sat far back from the road where it came to a sharp right curve. Future surveillance would be a real bitch. However, I noted there was a telephone pole directly across from the driveway. There were a lot of trees but having a camera up would be better than nothing.

Hughes and I trailed Shawn back to his house and then headed back to the office. Hughes did a work-up on the address that Shawn just visited, and he came by my office.

Hughes was grinning as he said, "It's owned by a male Hispanic named Jose Lopez. He has another house in Smyrna and bought this Hermitage house last summer for $170k."

"Dude." I said. "Could this be his plug?"

Hughes shrugged. "I highly doubt Jose Lopez is actually involved, but hopefully we'll find out. I think it is very likely this house is important, though."

I nodded and Hughes headed back to his office. For a moment, I processed the information. Hughes was right. No dealer had more than one house in his actual name. And, after running a report on the guy his name came up clean. It was likely he "rented" his second house to some friends, the actual plugs, and probably got a kickback from the deals. Either way, this place was looking like it could be Shawn's cartel's basecamp. That was huge!

Man, there was so much shit going on I couldn't see straight. That's not always a good problem to have. It meant no sleep and no time with family. We were literally living other people's lives, so how could we have time to keep up with our own?

Only a couple days later, the Goodlettsville Police Department got the seizure of the year. Ray Suggs, Shawn's little nephew, got stopped for running a stop sign. Officer Sony immediately detected a strong odor of marijuana coming from inside the vehicle when he approached the window. He asked Ray to step out. Ray complied and was placed in handcuffs. Officer Sony, who had been on the force for a decade, called for additional backup. He knew that he was going to be conducting a search of the Honda Accord.

What shocked him, though, was that there wouldn't be much of a search. When he opened the passenger door of the Accord, he got the surprise of his life: five bricks of cocaine just sitting on the passenger floorboard. That was $160,000 worth of cocaine! Officer Sony couldn't believe his eyes. He transported Ray back to the police department where he called agents from the Drug Enforcement Administration.

During an interview with DEA agents, Ray stated that he had been in Murfreesboro all day, staying with a girl at a hotel. Ray said that his plug was some guy who went by "B" and drove a black truck. Agents continued to interview with Ray for some time, but it became clear this dude was lying through his teeth. When our team heard about it, we wondered if the DEA knew who this kid's uncle was. As we expected, Shawn got so spooked by this he dropped all his phones. Hughes had to start from square one all over again.

It wasn't that we didn't want to work with the DEA or other agencies, it was just a fact that if a bunch of units were involved in one case then people would start trying to call the shots. By keeping everything in house, we were able to work our cases on our terms and play by our rules only. In many instances, federal agencies could not allow a load of dope to "walk" because their priority was to not let it hit the streets. But if a dealer was hit too early or only the runners or mules got taken in, then nothing would be done about the drug trafficking organization at large.

The day after Ray got popped, we knew we had to reach out to the DEA to let them know where we were at in handling the case as a whole. We called a couple guys we'd worked with in the past who'd never caused a problem before. But this time, it was different.

DEA Agent North and DEA TFO Tolbert arrived at the Drug Task Force office to talk over the situation. I knew Tolbert because he was really tight with Sgt. Bagg, and I got a bad feeling as soon as he walked in the door. He and Agent North waltzed in with puffed-up chests, thinking they were going to take over the Shawn investigation. They explained that they had received a tip from the Texas DEA back in the summer about Shawn receiving loads of dope from a Hispanic organization over the border, so they wanted responsibility for the case.

Well, we countered by showing them the sheer mountain of investigative work we'd already done on the case and how many phone lines we'd wiretapped on him already. Director Davis was nice about it and said that they could assist with later searches, but they were not going to call the shots. I knew Tolbert was going to report to Sgt. Bagg everything we said, but what mattered the most was that we showed we had the hot hand and they needed to back down. We weren't about to let them walk away with our case.

After the meeting, the two DEA guys left our office with their heads down and literally grumbling.

I turned to Director Davis as we watched them leave and said, "I kind of doubt they're going to help us take down these guys now."

He laughed. "Poor Sgt. Cox is trying to organize everyone and their moms for these search warrants, too. He'll be bummed the DEA may not be on board to help."

I didn't reply but thought to myself, *He won't be so bummed when he learns one of the agents was a Sgt. Bagg puppet.*

DECEMBER 2014
27

Titus and I arrived to the Batcave at the same time on the first of December. I said, "This is our month, I can feel it!"

"Our month to get capes?"

I nudged him. "Just wait for Christmas, son. You'll get your cape."

We headed to our office and I said, "I can't wait to take these guys down. I'm sick of their voices."

"Same. They just talk constantly. You'd think they'd have slowed down after the November busts in Wilson and Maury counties."

"Oh, come on, they never learn. Besides, as soon as they slow down, they're out. They lose clients and status and money."

Titus nodded, "And we got Christmas around the corner, so they'll need that money."

"Exactly. Expensive time to slow down business. They'll slow over the holiday, but up until then they'll be hustling to make their green. I'm not the only one who's gotta buy a Batman cape for his kiddos."

Titus smacked the side of my chair as a warning, but we laughed.

There was a chance there wouldn't be a huge load to come into town since the dealers did slow down as Christmas got closer, but I had hope. I was so drained and ready to take down these guys. The last five months of my life had been spent working fourteen hour days on this case. I didn't want to force something to happen, but I was feeling the effects of running such a huge case, and I needed something to come of all the hard work.

Since Shawn had gone dark once again, Hughes and I decided to focus on the stash house in Hermitage owned by Jose Lopez while we tried to find his new numbers.

We spent the day waiting near the house, and I saw a silver Altima pull out so I followed it. Unfortunately, I lost it in heavy traffic. Hughes found it at the Maple Leaf Apartments complex nearby, so I headed that direction. Hughes was always in the right place at the right time.

He radioed to me, "A male Hispanic is leaving the breezeway and heading to the Altima. He's holding a black trash bag and a big duffel bag over his shoulder." I pulled into the lot and stayed back by the dumpsters. "He put both bags in the passenger seat. Looks like he's heading your way."

"I see him." I slumped in my seat out of his sight, and I watched in my rearview mirror as the guy threw the trash bag into the dumpster. "Homerun!" I said to Hughes. "It's our lucky day. You ready for a dumpster dive?"

A trash bag could be like a gold mine for a detective. Dealers were bound to get sloppy at some point, and when they did, we were there. After throwing away the trash, the Altima pulled off and I made sure he was out of the area before I hurried to the dumpster. We could hardly wait to recover the bag and find out what the hell these dealers were up to. Let's just say it was an early Christmas present for me and Hughes.

I pulled the bag out and threw it in my trunk before we headed back to the office. We went through the bag and found a ripped-up receipt and a brochure for a bus trip from Dallas, TX to Nashville, TN on 11/21/14. The bus company was so well known to the Drug Task Force that we joked it should change its company name to "Mules." After I taped the receipt back together, the name on the receipt was Mateo Vargas. We also found a baggage receipt from the bus company with the name "Luis, Nashville" handwritten on it. This was a good sign, but we had a long way to go if we were going to take down Shawn, his source of supply, and the entire organization.

This was the gritty, smelly detective work that I loved. My favorite part of the job was bringing dealers to justice and getting drugs off the street, but I really enjoyed putting the puzzle pieces together, even if it meant going through another man's garbage.

The next day, though, I was glad to be back on the phones. Even though Marlon had stayed quiet, I had combed through phone tolls for days before figuring out Slick's new number. Collins got the warrant done really fast, too, so we were already back up on Slick's phone and it was damn good timing.

I identified Dell on one call, who told Slick, "Buddy is waiting on me and I'm waiting on you." We didn't have to guess who "Buddy" was anymore. We were certain that the only source of supply for Dell was Shawn. He wasn't even reaching out to Lewis anymore because Shawn always came through for him.

"Go ahead and grab nine of them." Slick said. "I'm fixing to pick up money from Barry and them, and I have two of them already situated."

"Man, don't worry about that. I will grab it all for you."

"How long will it take you?"

"Fixing to call him now."

I stared at the wall in front of me as I processed the call. Slick just asked for nine? Sometimes this meant nine ounces, but I knew Slick wasn't working in ounce amounts. We were going to have to make a big decision. Letting one or two kilos of cocaine walk was one thing, but letting nine kilos walk away and hit the streets of Nashville was a whole separate ball game. We didn't want to do a takedown during the transaction, but in the back of our minds we knew that it was certainly a possibility.

While Slick was lining up his buyers on another line, I got Titus and Thomas to come with me to set up surveillance at Slick's house. If we didn't stop the deal, we would at least have it documented on record. I just had to decide if it was worth waiting to see if Marlon was going to get a big shipment soon. Lewis was always gabbing on his phone and slinging deals left and right, but we still didn't have a solid lead on when a motherload was coming in, yet. This wasn't an easy position to be in.

The wire room relayed summaries to me of calls coming in, and it sounded like Dell was running late, once again. There was something off about Dell and the other dealers seemed to see it too. Even as a dealer, he just seemed a bit sketch. It'd been three hours of Dell pushing it off and pushing it off, giving Slick the runaround, and we had just sat there patiently waiting. On Slick's end, he was making calls left and right pushing his guys back, too, which was just frustrating for everyone.

We knew Shawn wasn't home because his Impala was out and about according to the tracker. Director Davis reported to us that Shawn was at his favorite car lot off Charlotte Pike.

"He better not be switching cars again." I radioed back.

Hughes added, "Yeah, we're a bit over waking up at 3 am to slap trackers on cars this guy keeps for two weeks."

"He's been inside for a while, so . . ."

The radio garbled with everyone groaning and complaining at once. When it cleared, Director Davis said, "Okay, y'all done? Good. He just left looking mad, so no new car today. Edwin was with him and followed him out." Edwin Fields was Shawn's right-hand man, and we followed them to Shawn's barbershop off Clarksville Highway.

About that time, the wire room let us know Dell called Slick and said, "Come look at them! He's got three for you and they are all proper."

"But I want to get nine." Slick responded.

"He can do that, but he will want the bread."

"I'm only a few stacks short, but I'm picking it up now."

"Aight. I'll let him know."

Nine kilos equaled twenty pounds of cocaine, worth more than $320,000. When Slick picked up his last stacks, he'd be rolling around with more money than what my house cost.

An hour later, Slick let Dell know he was on his way, unknowingly with us on his tail. "I had a damn funeral I got caught up in. I had to divert." It was no joke attempting to follow Slick amidst a funeral as he wound around side streets trying to head it off. We pulled off and turned back in the direction of Shawn's barbershop. We knew Dell would have to get the bricks from Shawn, so Shawn would be involved at some point.

Slick told Dell, "I'm coming buddy. I got the check to give you."

"I'll give him a call and see if he's ready. I don't know where he'll want to meet."

"I hope these motherfuckers are pretty."

"They pretty as hell."

Almost the whole team was posted up near the barbershop, and we watched as Shawn finally made a move. He went to the Infiniti, the car that Edwin was driving, and left solo. We didn't have a tracker on the Infiniti, and it was hard not to feel that Shawn was somehow one step ahead of us. But, there were six of us out there, so if we lost him then it was on us.

Shawn went straight to his storage unit, but we watched him go to a new unit. Hughes had guessed that Shawn had switched units to one in the back, and it seemed like he was right. We could barely get eyes on him at the back of the facility. I had a fancy camera and my binoculars, so I tried to get some clear pictures. Sgt. Cox went around to a side street and could see through a house's yard, straight to Shawn's unit.

"He got a black backpack from the unit. Man, you can see a lot more from this angle."

"Maybe we need to get a camera there." I said.

"Yeah, I'll come back to this spot tonight and find a good spot. He's heading out again."

Shawn drove fast but not crazy. He probably didn't want to end up like his nephew Ray and get popped with so many kilos because of a stupid traffic offense. We followed him all the way to the mall, which had turned into his main dealing spot. We fanned out as Shawn parked near the movie theater and walked towards Buster's Bar. I wanted someone to follow him in on foot, and Hughes was already on top of it.

He said, "We need someone to get a close look at the car, though."

"I got it. I'm close." Sgt. Cox said as he parked and headed towards the Infiniti. After looking in the windows, he went back to the car and reported, "The backpack's in the back seat, partially covered by a black jacket."

Hughes then radioed from the loud bar, "He just headed back out. He went to the bathroom and came out whispering on the phone."

The wire room notified us Dell had just told Slick he was headed to the mall. Dell was in Antioch, though, so it took him forty minutes to get to the mall. What didn't make sense was that he must have met with Slick before without us knowing because he must have already had the money on him. He parked his Acura right beside the Infiniti, and Shawn got out of his car and into the passenger side empty handed. Dell drove off, clearly checking for a tail while Shawn counted his money. We followed them to the other end of the mall and back to the Infiniti.

Shawn got out with a camouflage bag, threw it in the back, and grabbed the backpack, which he tossed into Dell's open window. They both pulled away, and Hughes and Milliken stayed on Shawn while the rest of us followed Dell back to Slick's house. Dell pulled into the garage and the door shut behind him.

We decided to terminate surveillance on Dell because the deal was clearly done.

Hughes and Milliken had followed Shawn to the possible stash house on Central Pike, so the rest of us headed towards Hermitage. Shawn hadn't stopped at the bank or storage unit, he went straight to the house with that big bag of cash, which seemed to confirm that we'd found Shawn's plug and the cartel's basecamp.

Hughes was able to time it just right so he saw Shawn walk from his car to the back of the house, carrying that camo bag. All that money made it safely to its intended destination. Also parked at the house was a backed-in silver Nissan Altima, a Dodge truck, and a GMC Denali. The Altima was facing the street, but we got the tags for the truck and Denali and planned to run them at least.

Fifteen minutes later, Shawn left and Hughes and Milliken followed.

Milliken reported, "Wait, I just saw three people get into the Denali, and it's leaving, too. Are you guys close?"

All of us who had followed Dell and were making our way to Hermitage were still too far to help with the Denali. Milliken turned around in traffic in order to pick up surveillance on it.

When a couple of us caught up to Milliken, we followed it all the way to Murfreesboro where the Denali pulled into the Department of Corrections, probation and parole.

"Sweet!" Milliken said. "This must mean that one of them is on paper already."

Sgt. Cox added, "Looks like it. I have a good spot. A male Hispanic got out and is heading inside. Milliken, you get it's tag?"

"Yeah. I just got the registration. It's owned by someone named Arturo Gonzalez. And, he's got a lengthy rap sheet." Milliken then laughed, "Man, he sold a kilo of cocaine to an undercover cop at a truck stop. That's desperate."

The Denali left the probation and parole office and jumped back on the interstate, heading back to Nashville. They went directly back to the mall, where we had started the afternoon.

Milliken offered to follow them into the mall on foot and radioed ten minutes later, "They stopped at TGI Fridays. I think they're just hungry."

I responded, "After a long day of distributing kilos and counting money, who wouldn't work up an appetite?"

"Well, shit, I'm gonna get something, too. I'm starving. Maybe I'll even have a beer. Who's with me?"

We laughed and said the rest of us would stay outside while he went undercover. I split off to head back towards the office.

Sgt. Cox said over the radio, "This will be good experience for you, Milliken. Don't look suspicious. If they seem to catch on, just act drunk or something."

"You got it."

A couple minutes later, Milliken called Hughes on the phone and he put him on speaker phone over the radio. Milliken gabbed about nonsense to the group, and we cracked up because almost nothing he said was making sense. We kept asking questions that he would barely answer, and then he texted the group photos of the three guys eating, so we knew he was trying to focus on being sneaky with the photos. It was still fun to give him a hard time.

Back at the office, I scarfed down another Uncrustables and started researching the three guys, starting with Arturo's file and trying to make connections from there.

After some magic with the databases available to us, I was able to identify one of the other male Hispanics. The owner of the Dodge truck was named Francisco Hernandez. The third one, the tall and skinny

Chapter 27

male Hispanic with the gelled hair, was the same one we saw throwing the trash away, so we could assume that was Mateo Vargas based on the receipt we'd found. We also could assume he owned the silver Altima that was backed into the driveway, but we couldn't be sure, yet.

After an hour in TGI Fridays, it appeared that the three guys were in it for the long haul, drinking and celebrating their daily accomplishments, so the team decided to terminate surveillance and pick it up another day.

Milliken was clearly feeling warm and fuzzy from the one or two beers because he texted the group thread a series of emojis after the photos. It was a good last laugh before wrapping up for the night.

Before I left the office, I stopped by the wire room to pick up the records I'd missed while we'd been out all afternoon. Lewis had been a little busy bee calling all of his customers telling them that he would be "good" this week. Apparently, the last batch of kilos were "bad" or had a bad taste, so now Lewis was making it a point to tell his people that the new shit would be better, A-1 quality. One of his calls revealed he'd be getting the new batch on Thursday morning. It was Tuesday, so we had exactly one day to get everything together and find out if this was going to be the motherload or not.

To say I barely slept that night would be an understatement.

28

The next morning, I called a meeting and everyone in the office needed to attend. This wasn't a decision I wanted to make on my own. Once everyone was seated in the kitchen, I told them that we had been intercepting numerous phone calls on Lewis. He has been calling several of his customers, letting them know that "it" was going down the following day. Marlon had to be getting a load, and it was time to take this sucker down!

Everyone was on board, and the whole team helped me put tactical folders together, which consisted of operation orders, threat assessments, intel info, and pictures. It took me all day to update all fifty-one search warrants. The warrants were spread across six counties, and we planned to execute them all as quickly as possible so nobody would get tipped off. I had been updating the documents every Sunday for the last several months, so I didn't have to start fresh, but Sgt. Cox was freaking out a little since there were so many. It was his responsibility to organize personnel to hit every single house and trust me, it wasn't easy, but he'd somehow done it. He got on the horn and notified everyone that we would be doing numerous search warrants on the morning of Friday December 5th at 6 am.

We were ready as we would ever be as we set up to monitor Marlon the following morning. The entire plan hinged on Marlon's shipment, which Lewis had said would be coming in that morning. We knew Marlon had a Hispanic plug, but we were not up on the right phones and we were just taking a shot in the dark. The only person we could rely on was Lewis. We hoped that his big mouth would lead us to the kilos.

Sgt. Cox arranged a meeting at out office for all of the warrant supervisors at 10 am. The meeting would consist of our team briefing everyone on the operation and handing out specific location packets to each unit.

It felt weird to be in the same room as Sgt. Bagg again after five glorious months of not seeing his ugly mug. I couldn't tell if the tension in the room had to do with just him or the anticipation of all the supervisors to time their parts of the case just right.

When Sgt. Bagg got his assignment, he complained loudly, "This threat assessment is scored too low. It needs adjusting before I can do anything." Out of the other fifty-one search warrants, no one else had any issues or scoring problems, but I kept my mouth shut, like he'd taught me. We did the last-minute adjusting to accommodate his request. I was glad to see him leave the Batcave. I hoped it would be a *very* long time before I had to see him again.

After the meeting, I asked the team to help me follow Marlon for the day. We had the cell site locations on his phone, but that was basically it. I never got a chance to put a tracker on any of his vehicles; we had tried once but nearly got caught. Just as the dealers were spooked when one of their own were caught, almost getting caught under a criminal's car could really spook an undercover detective.

It was still early for Marlon, and he had not left his compound on Brooketrace Drive yet. Several Gang Unit Detectives helped us on surveillance for the day, too. I knew that if we could follow Marlon to meet with his plug, then we could just swoop in and take them down immediately, and then we'd follow up with the mass warrants the following morning. This was the ideal plan, but there was no telling how things would actually go.

Eventually, Marlon left his house, but it was in a white box truck. This was a good sign he might be going to get a big load. Hopefully fifty kilos of coke!

Marlon pulled out on Clarksville Highway and proceeded towards Rosa Parks Boulevard, where he got on the interstate. As soon as he got on the interstate, he kept switching lanes.

I radioed to everyone, telling them to stay in their lanes and not to move when he moved because I knew he was watching. Marlon took I-65 to Dickerson Road where he exited and pulled into a Lowes parking lot. He didn't get out, he just sat there for a few minutes. We spread out and waited.

Suddenly, he floored it and swung through the parking lot right to where one of the Gang Unit Detectives was parked. Marlon whipped his cell phone out and started yelling at the detective about his attorney and why he was following him. Man, this dude had some balls. The detective got out of his car and he pointed to his phone. He told us later he said, "Dude, I'm going shopping for materials for a crib, and I was texting my wife. Paranoid, much?"

He then walked calmly into the building and Marlon yelled after him. Marlon then looked around the parking lot, wanting to find someone else to yell at.

We were burnt. Crispy and fried to the core.

At this point, we had no choice but to pull off. I was pissed, but I thanked the Gang Unit for helping. It wasn't their fault that Marlon was on high alert and zeroed in on one of them.

For the rest of the day we thought through our options. It was late in the evening, and we didn't have any indication that Marlon had picked up the load. Since our original plan was foiled by one of our surveillance vehicles getting burned, I made the decision at 10 pm to call off the warrants for the morning. The team texted and called all fifty-one supervisors to put a hold on the warrants. I hoped they would still happen soon, but it was just too risky to do it the next morning not knowing if Marlon had alerted his organization.

I was so angry. All the hard work had come to this. It should have worked, but we got burned. Because the morning had been such a wreck, I didn't go to the judge to get the warrants signed, which was good because once the paperwork had the signature, we'd only have five days to execute them before they expired. We could sit on them a little longer. One silver lining was that Marlon didn't know about the camera we had on his residence at Brooketrace Drive. If anything was going to happen, we'd be watching.

Everything was quiet on Friday, and it wasn't until the following morning that action started back up. At 7:30 am on Saturday, Marlon arrived at the Brooketrace Drive house and moved the white box truck from the side of the home (where it was backed in front of the garage) to the front driveway. As Marlon walked from the box truck towards the side of the residence, a silver Ford Fusion was observed backing into the side driveway and to the garage. An unknown male exited the driver's seat and entered through the garage as it opened.

I rolled out of bed watching this go down from my cell phone. Once I noticed all this early movement, I threw on some clothes and ran out the door. I literally drove 90 mph to get to the office before anything else could happen.

Fifteen minutes later, I watched Marlon leave the residence in his white box truck. I waited and checked the live streaming video of his other spot off Buena Vista Pike. Thankfully, he pulled up a few minutes later and headed inside. If this guy went anywhere else, we were screwed, but I was hopeful something would happen at his house.

The moment the monitors flipped the switch on for the day, I asked them to check the cell site locations on Marlon's phone. I told them that he had been on the move that morning and it was unusual. They radioed back and told me the pings showed that he had started moving before 6 am and had hit a spot near Nolensville Road before going to his other house and staying there. I wondered what the hell was so important to travel to Nolensville Road so early in the morning.

I got on the horn and rallied the troops. They already kind of hated me because this case had most of us working every weekend, but dope dealers don't stop, so we couldn't stop either. I was all alone as I headed to set up on Buena Vista Pike. Of course Marlon wasn't there for five minutes before he decided to leave. I was shaking in my boots. Diesel and Thomas were on the way, but I wasn't sure they would make it. Lucky for me, Marlon went straight back to Brooketrace Drive, so the team headed that direction.

And then we sat and sat and sat. As usual, the team gave me a lot of grief for it, but our number one priority for our "A" case was catching Marlon in the act, and hopefully with a big load.

After lunch, the wire room let us know Harry had called Lewis to confirm, "Is it for sure?"

"Hell yeah." Lewis said. "He called me at like 6 this morning and told me his people have landed. I was damn asleep though."

Harry said, "I'm going to tell Dell to stand down then because he was gonna grab me two from Shawn. Get me two, man."

"Bet." Lewis said. "I'll let you know soon."

It didn't take long for Lewis to let Harry know he was leaving for the deal. Sure enough, we watched as Lewis' GPS indicator moved away from his house and came straight to Marlon's. We watched as Lewis arrived and went in the front door. Fifteen minutes later, he left and headed to Harry's house to make the delivery.

Others were coming and going from Marlon's, and Collins joined our crew on surveillance. I made a drive-by to grab a Florida temp tag off the Ford Fusion that had been parked in the driveway the whole morning. It was definitely a rental. Only a moment later, Thomas radioed that the garage door opened and three subjects got into the car. With the way Marlon parked the car, there was such a small window to see what was going on. When they pulled out, we picked them up. This had to be the best chance at surveillance we would get. If we got burned on this, then we might as well shut the whole thing down. We played it smart, though, and followed Marlon straight to the Radisson Hotel near the Nashville Airport. I didn't want anyone to follow him in there and risk getting burned, but we had to see what was going on.

Thomas went into the hotel lobby and saw two male Hispanics waiting by the elevator. He created a ruse and told the young female desk clerk that he was part of a warrant task force. He said he had reason to believe that a violent fugitive had recently checked in to the hotel. The clerk bought it, hook, line, and sinker. Within thirty minutes we had identified the two people that had just gotten out of Marlon's rental car: Roberto and Oscar Perez. We did a quick Facebook search and found they had public profiles, one even had his cell phone linked to his account. They were brothers and from San Benito, Texas, located right on the border of Mexico and the US. The hotel clerk was so cooperative, she even gave Thomas their portfolios. This showed all the dates and times that the brothers had checked into a Radisson Hotel in the past. At first glance these guys were coming to Nashville at least once a month, and sometimes twice a month. This looked like serious evidence that we had just found Marlon's Hispanic plug.

While Thomas was inside gathering material, a wire room monitor came over the radio and told me Marlon was calling from a new number according to a recent call picked up from Lewis' line. Marlon told Lewis to start calling him on the new number, and then he started talking about his "go bag" and how he left his "sack" in his buddy's car.

This day was almost too good to be true. After our big hiccup on Thursday, this felt like a gift, and I could barely believe things were falling into place finally.

Now, I had to make a decision. Do we kick in the motel door, storm in, and arrest the brothers? I would need them to talk, to cooperate, and help me out. I was certain they brought some kilos of cocaine into Nashville, but I had no idea how many, how they got here, or where the product was currently located. I had to play this cool.

Collins spotted Roberto coming back out of the hotel to smoke, and he reported that he recognized him from surveillance at Marlon's house on October 13th. I checked the Radisson portfolio and sure enough, they were here in Nashville at that time.

Oscar joined his brother a few minutes later, and they got on the airport shuttle van without any luggage. We followed the van to the airport and tried to make a plan as the brothers entered the airport. This was going to be complicated.

Thomas leapt out of his car and ran inside, but he couldn't see the brothers anywhere. I tried not to panic and reminded the team that they didn't have bags, so they probably weren't going anywhere.

Director Davis arrived to assist and just in the nick of time. He contacted Airport Police who were able to replay the surveillance videos. They confirmed that Roberto and Oscar entered the airport, went downstairs and got into a cab. Collins contacted the cab company and the driver stated that he took the Perez brothers to the mall nearby. Thomas and Diesel went to the mall to look for a needle in a haystack, and the rest of us returned to the Radisson Hotel to wait.

That evening, the Perez brothers arrived back at the Radisson Hotel with bags from the mall. As it was getting late, we called in some back up. We asked some of our friends on the SWAT team and the Gang Unit to come in and do surveillance for us while we went home and got a few hours of sleep.

29

I got a call a few hours later from Gang Unit Detective Bowles, who let me know a black Mustang arrived at 2:30 am and Oscar came out to meet it.

"Oh, shit." I said, still waking up. "Did he leave in it?"

"No, he got in the passenger side and got out a few minutes later with a bag and an obvious bulge under his shit. He went inside and the car left."

"Did you get the tag?"

"Yeah, I waited until the Mustang made a turn and then pulled out to catch up. Here's the tag . . ."

I thanked Detective Bowles and hung up. I ran the tag and almost laughed. Of course Marlon had another vehicle that he'd do late night runs in.

I managed to fall back asleep until 6 am when I got ready and headed to Marlon's house, talking to my dad and updating him on the case finally coming to a head. The Fusion wasn't at the house, though, so I headed to the hotel to relieve the SWAT team guys and Gang Unit. A couple guys from North CSU joined me and Titus on surveillance. My dad wished me luck as I parked in a surveillance position near the hotel.

Only an hour later, Roberto and Oscar came outside the Radisson rolling their luggage. Shit, shit, shit!

Titus came on the radio, "What do we do?"

I tried to keep my voice calm as I said, "We need to follow them. I don't think we can let these guys leave town at this point."

There were only four of us out there, and I drove on ahead of the van to get to the airport before them. I called Sgt. Cox and Director Davis but neither answered.

I parked illegally and ran inside right before the van pulled up. I watched as the brothers exited the shuttle and came towards the building. I saw Titus pull past them and stop where my car was. I stared at my phone, my brain racing with making a decision, and I watched in my peripheral vision as the brothers headed to the Southwest ticket counter with their luggage in tow.

Titus and Detective Harris from North CSU came inside as Roberto stepped up to the counter.

"Okay," I said to them, "you two head over and start talking to Roberto. Just, make some shit up to get him talking. I'll go to Oscar. We can't let them get on that plane."

We three headed in the same direction but separately, and I went right up to Oscar who was digging sleep out of his eyes. Getting up at 2 am to make deals really messes with the sleep cycle.

I flashed my badge, realizing I hadn't planned what to say, and what came out of my mouth was, "I'm a detective with a task force in Nashville, and we have information that you are involved in a robbery crew in Texas." For a second I just stood there, facing a kilo dealer and maybe even a cartel member. Was this going to work?

I went on and rambled more about random dates and details of made-up robbery cases and how his appearance matched the robbery ring leader. The more I talked, the more dazed Oscar looked. He was visibly sweating and shaking, and he was dressed in a winter coat when the Nashville December weather had given us sunny 60 degree days. He even had a pair of black cotton gloves on. Regardless what Oscar was wearing, I could tell he was sweating from the pressure, not the temperature.

I had talked long enough, though, that our team had attracted the attention of the Airport Police. Thankfully, they were willing to assist. I asked Oscar if we could search his person and his luggage and he said no problem, that he didn't have anything to hide. Roberto was asked the same thing and he also cooperated. We were directed to a more private room around the corner. There, I sat both of them down in the room. Neither were cuffed or restrained in any way, yet, but it felt good to know it was only a matter of time.

I opened Oscar's bag first. Within seconds I came to a pair of socks that obviously contained something more. When I unfolded the socks, a wad of $100 bills fell out. I could almost hear their hearts sink in the beat of silence that ensued. I set the wad aside and kept digging, all the way to the luggage liner. When I unzipped the liner, I found additional cash hidden along the pockets. After finding about $18,000 in Oscar's bag, I moved on to Roberto's bag. I took a minute to count the money, and the Perez brothers had $34,577 between them. I then explained money laundering to the two.

To put the nail in the coffin, I called in K-9. The cross-trained K-9 was a narcotic cop's best friend. Officer Jay arrived with his partner "Liberty" who was a pretty black and tan German shepherd. I placed the two large black suitcases with other suitcases in a controlled environment. Liberty tore straight for the brothers' bags.

I was happier than a kid in a candy store, but the Perez brothers had realized they were sunk.

Thomas and I stepped outside to talk.

When we were out of their sight, we both started to laugh and high fived. Thomas even did a little jig and I said, "Did these idiots think they were going to come to my city and leave on a plane with loads of cash? Hell no!"

"Hell no!" Thomas repeated. We got our excited energy out, and then we made a plan for our questioning. Even though this bust felt amazing, we knew there had to be someone larger pulling the strings. It just didn't seem like we had closed everything. There were still a lot of questions that needed to be answered.

After reentering the room and securing the cash in a tamper-proof bag, we put the brothers in different rooms and did some paperwork. I knew there was a DEA satellite office in the building, and I noticed the DEA badges on the wall, but a state charge of conspiracy to distribute over 300 grams of cocaine or more in a drug-free school zone in the state of Tennessee would land them more time than a federal charge.

Hughes arrived on the scene, and we interviewed Roberto after advising him of his Miranda rights.

I started with, "Can you tell me how you came to be in Nashville?"

"Oscar and I came here on the Lightning Bus from Texas on Saturday. We are from San Benito."

"What do you do in Texas?"

"My family owned a transmission shop, but we had to close it down because my father and I couldn't pay the rent anymore."

I nodded and said, "Well, we received a tip from the DEA that you and your brother have been moving drugs from Texas to Nashville. Who picked you up at the bus station?"

Roberto paused but said, "A guy named Joe."

"What does Joe look like?"

"He's a white guy, bald."

Roberto was really sweating and I knew he was lying through his teeth. We knew Marlon had been dealing with these guys for years, so I showed Roberto a photo of Marlon.

"Is this the guy that picked you up?"

"No."

"Are you sure?"

He paused for a long time. I was not going to put up with lies much longer, and he must have sensed it. "Yeah, that's the guy."

Hughes then asked, "Okay, so how many times have you been to Nashville in the last ten months?"

"Four or five times."

"Where did you go after Marlon picked you and your brother up at the bus station?"

"He took us to the Radisson Hotel."

I looked at Hughes and nodded. We were ready to switch gears a little. When searching the luggage, I'd found a Holiday Inn notepad that was obviously a drug ledger. The handwritten notations included gram amounts and corresponding prices. And the gram amounts were large, as in around 1,000 grams, which was a kilo.

Hughes asked, "Have you ever been to a Holiday Inn in Nashville?"

"Yeah."

"Is that where this notepad came from? Is this your handwriting on it?"

"Yeah."

Hughes nodded and pointed to the paper. "So, here on the paper where it says, 'red tape' and 'black tape,' what does that mean?"

"It means that some bricks were marked with black tape and some with red."

Hughes asked, "And, what does 'LTF' mean?"

"That was what was stamped on the brick." He didn't explain further.

"Look," I said, "we know you and your brother have been coming to Nashville with cocaine in your luggage. We know about every trip you have made up here. We have the records."

Roberto looked at the table.

"Is he right?" Hughes asked. "Have y'all been bringing cocaine with you?"

"Yeah."

"So, where are the kilos now? Does Marlon have them?"

"Yes, he has them."

Hughes then asked, "Do you talk to Marlon?"

"No, I don't deal with him." I wondered if this meant that Oscar did all the dealing interactions, like he'd done at 3 am.

Hughes continued, "Does Marlon deal with people in Texas or Mexico?"

Roberto looked up at him and asked, "If I tell you all this, what is in it for me?"

"Well," Hughes said, pacing the room, "cooperating with us always plays well with the DA, and they will decide what can be offered. So, do you know if Marlon deals with people in Texas or Mexico?"

"He deals with the other side."

We knew he meant Mexico even if he was being very tight-lipped about this information. If we had to dig this hard for info on Marlon, I couldn't imagine how hard it was going to be to get info on the next level. The guy on "the other side" was likely directly tied to the cartel and Roberto could get his entire family killed if he cooperated with us.

I considered if we needed to get info another way. We had recovered three cell phones from the luggage, and they would be very helpful. Collins was working on cell phone search warrants as the interview continued.

"I want to talk to my brother." Roberto said. "We need to be on the same page."

I almost laughed out loud. Everything was recorded and "getting your story straight" was not something a suspect usually admitted. He really didn't get how this worked. We already had plenty of evidence to put him away for a very long time.

"We'll talk to your brother later. What happened after Marlon took you and your brother to the hotel?"

"I stayed at the hotel. Marlon and Oscar took the kilos."

"So, you don't know where they went?"

"No, I don't deal with Marlon. I just carry the stuff to Nashville. It is fronted to Marlon and he deals directly with our boss."

"So, what happens if you don't make it back to Texas on time? Will your boss notify Marlon?"

"Probably."

Hughes and I exchanged a look. He then started asking more questions.

"Have you ever brought more than ten kilos?"

"No. Ten every time."

"Why does the handwritten ledger say seventeen kilos here?"

"Well . . ." Roberto shifted in his chair before saying, "most of the time it was just ten but once or twice we brought more."

"So, did you bring seventeen kilos this time?"

"Yeah."

"Do you bring anything up for anyone else other than Marlon?"

"No."

I cut in then and said, "Let's break."

Hughes and I stepped out of the room and I told him it was unlikely Roberto had the answers we needed. "We need to know where the hell those seventeen kilos are located now."

Hughes nodded, and we got Thomas to sit in with Roberto while we went to Oscar's room. We had to see if their stories matched at all and what information Oscar was holding. I began by advising Oscar that he was under arrest and reading him his Miranda rights.

We then asked him about the third cell phone, the one Roberto said belonged to his brother, and Oscar said it was his. Hughes asked for the code and Oscar voluntarily gave it. Already he was being more cooperative than his brother.

We asked for his story of coming from Texas, and he also said they came on the Lightning Bus and "Joe" picked them up. He added, " He took us to a brick house with a wall."

I showed him the picture of Marlon. "Is this the guy that picked you up?"

"Yeah."

Hughes asked, "Do you have any ID? A driver's license? Social security number?"

"I don't have those things."

I then said, "Well we got a tip from the DEA that you and your brother have been bringing drugs up here from Texas. We've seen y'all here in the past, and I know you didn't just come up here to meet a buddy at the mall. We have talked to a lot of people about you and what you've been doing up here. You need to be honest with us before you create more problems for yourself. We know about you being at the Radisson and the Holiday Inn."

Hughes then showed him the Holiday Inn notepad and asked if it was Oscar's writing. He said yes. Roberto had already tried to take ownership of the notepad, so we were already finding inconsistencies in their stories.

Hughes continued, "Did you know there are special laws in Tennessee that you two have violated that are going to carry a lot more weight? We know where you dropped the drugs off and it was very close to a school. Tennessee has special laws about moving drugs in a school zone, and it can land you in jail for a lot longer than other charges. So, are you going to talk to us about Marlon?"

Chapter 29

"I don't deal with him; he talks to someone in Mexico."

"Does he get his drugs from more than one source?"

"No."

"Do you bring drugs for anyone else other than Marlon?"

Oscar shook his head but said, "I didn't bring the drugs. I was just sent to oversee them being dropped off."

"You just came up here to oversee them? So, you spent fourteen hours on a bus just to weigh the kilos?"

He nodded. "That's right."

"If you didn't bring the cocaine, did your brother?"

"No, we didn't bring it, it came on a truck."

We knew there wasn't a truck full of cocaine. They brought it in their luggage! Shit, his brother already told us that part and the K-9 had confirmed it.

Hughes said, "Well, we have had a K-9 dog inspect your luggage, and he indicated that he smelled drugs. We know you brought the drugs up here in the bags."

Oscar didn't respond.

I cut in and said, "Did you meet Marlon when he came by in the black Mustang last night?"

"Yeah."

"Were you getting the money?"

"Yeah."

"Okay." I said. "Well, we are seizing all the cash you had. Will your bosses be upset about that?"

"That was just money to buy cars. Marlon has the money for our boss. If we don't call him by noon to let him know we are back, he will probably contact Marlon."

"How will the other money get back to Texas?"

"It will go back on the truck."

We continued to interview Oscar, but it was getting to be a waste of time. He was barely confirming information we already knew. He told us about Marlon's cars, gave extremely vague descriptions of Marlon's houses, and talked about how some of the drugs were bad on the last load.

Nothing helpful. He only wanted to know what was in it for him if he cooperated. That's all these guys cared about. We wondered if we could get them to talk if they were in the same room, so we tried that. Oscar, Roberto, Hughes, and I were all staring at each other in a cramped room.

When we asked questions this time around, Oscar led with answers and Roberto agreed with him.

The interview didn't last much longer, but they both were certain on one thing: Marlon would receive notification from his source in Mexico that the two did not make it back to Dallas.

Well, no shit! But we were not going to just let them go on home. These two were responsible for bringing hundreds of kilos of cocaine into Nashville over the past year and a half.

"Hey guys, I got one more question before I go. Is the person in your phone named 'Tortus' actually Marlon?"

Oscar looked up at me and said, "Yep, that's the good line."

I informed Oscar and Roberto that they would not receive any type of deal or consideration if they tipped off Marlon by making phone calls from the jail. To make this look as legit as possible, and to distance it from the 20th, I asked North CSU Detective Hall to obtain one warrant for Oscar and one warrant for Roberto. Both were charged with felony money laundering.

At 8 pm that night, Marlon was getting worried. His source from the other side in Mexico had messaged him that his mules had not made it back. Marlon called the one person that might be able to figure out if they had gotten caught, his attorney Jack Moorehead.

"What are you doing?" Marlon asked casually.

"Just getting a little exercise, taking a walk around the neighborhood."

"I wish I could take a walk around my neighborhood at 8:30 at night."

Jack snorted, "You could, but you're a felon so you can't carry a gun."

Marlon huffed. "I don't even feel safe with that motherfucker. Hey, what time are you going to be in the office in the morning?"

"I got court at 9:00, then I'll be back to the office after that."

"I can meet you down there, you know across the street."

Chapter 29

"What kind of problem is it?" Jack knew something was up.

"I just need you to see somebody. I'm going to come down to court to meet you."

Even though we had tapped Jack's phone calls, he would be getting off easy because he wasn't directly involved yet. A few more conversations and he might have gotten caught in a conspiracy case. He got lucky though, because he and Marlon wouldn't be meeting the next morning. Little did Marlon know, I was going to make sure that Marlon got to visit his two pals in the slammer before sunrise, but it wouldn't be for a visit.

30

After Roberto and Oscar headed off to jail, I spent the previous evening rallying the troops for an early morning bust. The Metro Nashville Police SWAT team made entry into Marlon's residence at 6 am.

Within minutes they reported to me, "The target is in custody."

That was music to my ears! After nearly a year of work, judgement day had finally come for so many of my targets. Months of surveillance, long nights in the streets, no sleep, tuck and rolls to place GPS trackers, almost being attacked by vicious dogs, multiple dropped lines on every suspect, a dead guy who drank his cocaine, and a freaking leak causing constant stress on the team hadn't stopped us. We'd done it.

After the residence was deemed safe, officers from the 20th and the North Precinct's flex units were allowed inside. I had promised those flex officers they would have their day, and I made good on the promise.

Now, it was my turn to come face-to-face with this big bad drug dealer. He had been slinging dope in my streets for a long time, and I'd been working towards bringing him in for almost a year. This guy had multiple stash houses around Nashville and connections with the cartel in Mexico. He was the biggest guy I could take down, and it wasn't even over yet. The best part was that his case had led me to the other biggest fish, Shawn. It was only a matter of time before we put a huge wrench in the Nashville drug machine, and this was just the first big blow.

When I asked if this coward had anything to say, he kept his mouth shut. Well, he did ask if he could put more clothes on because he was cold.

I laughed and took out my cuff key so he could put on more clothes. I think a small part of me was hoping that he would try to take a swing at me because I was ready to flatten that ass. After he put on a velour sweat suit, I put the handcuffs back on and in the front. See, I am nice.

We started to search the house, and I wasn't leaving until every inch of that house was inspected. I knew he had something, and my team and I just had to find it. A CSU officer located two bundles of money in vacuum sealed bags and a red velvet bag that had even more cash in it. Thomas located a loaded Desert Eagle .45 near the nightstand, ready to go with one in the chamber.

The 2014 Ford Fusion rental vehicle that Marlon had been driving was parked behind a fence at the house next door. I suspected he knew something was coming and tried to pull a fast one on us. Marlon was transported to booking and charged with one count of conspiracy to distribute over 300 grams of cocaine. A Black Ford Mustang and a white Hummer H2 were seized from Marlon, and they were transported to the tow-in lot where a hold was placed on them pending forfeiture proceedings.

By 7:30 am, I felt like I could finally take a breath. Marlon was being booked, and I could now make some rounds. Fifty other locations were also being searched at that very moment, and I had to pick wisely because I could not hit them all. Luckily, for every search warrant inside Davidson County, I could sign as the affiant and executioner and didn't technically have to set foot inside the home. I got to pick and choose which locations I went to. I knew I wanted to interview Slick, Lewis, and Dell, and I heard they were already talking.

Just before I left, I received a picture message of eleven kilos of cocaine from the guys at Marlon's property off Buena Vista Pike. I raced over to take a look at them. They were found in a small motorcycle trailer, and as soon as I walked in I was hit with the acetone-like smell of cocaine. I took a quick photo with the bricks to show my dad, and my nose burned slightly from the sour chemical odor. It was the sharp smell of success! The coke looked good, just like the guys had described on the phone, and they were even stamped with some cartel insignia. I got chills. This shit was so cool; who got the opportunity to do a job like this?

I then headed to Slick's house because one keen Gang Detective found a "trap" or a hidden compartment inside the stairs of Slick's house. The compartment had ten more kilos of cocaine and over $100,000 cash.

Who knew all that could fit under your stairs? The teams now knew how closely we needed to search. These guys were pretty savvy! House after house I kept getting calls that traps were being discovered and more kilos and cash were being seized, along with other drugs and guns.

That afternoon, I worked with the team to label and organize the seized items from each house. We took funny photos with the cars and drugs, and it was like we were all on a high. The case had turned out so much better than any of us could have expected, and it was only half done. When I finally wrapped things up and headed for the stairs, Sgt. Cox met me at the bottom of the stairs, grinning.

"You did it, Bobby."

"*We* did it, James!"

He then whooped up to the roof of the warehouse and it echoed like crazy. Then I followed with my own whoop and before we knew what was happening, we were jumping up and down, laughing and shouting to the ceiling, "SUCK IT, BAGG!"

Taking all those drugs and dealers off the street felt good. Really good. But, shouting with James about our success and how we'd done it despite Sgt. Bagg's meddling was the highlight of the whole case. Sgt. Bagg had completed his part in the warrants, so I knew he'd see just how big my case had turned out to be, and I was glad of it. I was succeeding without him. I wasn't under his thumb anymore, and I had done a damn good job despite him. I felt on top of the whole fucking world.

We had a lot of paperwork and court dates ahead of us, and Shawn still had to be dealt with, but that afternoon I felt like a huge weight had been lifted off my shoulders as Sgt. Cox and I laughed and jumped around the warehouse like excited kids. I knew that the night would be full of celebration, but I also knew I'd finally get some much-needed sleep.

I felt so rested and rejuvenated the next morning when I checked my phone and Hughes had sent me the media release on the case:

> *A major Nashville drug distribution organization believed responsible for dealing in more than 200 pounds of cocaine this year alone*

Chapter 30

has been dismantled after an 8-month investigation led to the identification of 19 mid to upper-level dealers, all of whom are now jailed.

The investigation, led by Metro police officers assigned to the 20th Judicial District Drug Task Force, culminated Sunday, Monday and Tuesday in arrests and the execution of 51 search warrants throughout the area. Seized were 59 pounds of cocaine, 71 pounds of marijuana, more than $449,000 cash, 70 guns, 19 cars, 15 motorcycles and 5 All-Terrain Vehicles.

"We know this drug network was responsible for funneling large amounts of cocaine to street dealers throughout the greater Nashville area," said Chief Luther Smalls, who serves as a Drug Task Force board member along with District Attorney General Chad Ball.

"Violence often associated with street cocaine sales endangers innocent families and drags down neighborhood quality of life," Chief Smalls said. "Disrupting this type of cocaine traffic is very important for the overall health of our city."

"Regardless of a drug network's complexity, we will devote the resources necessary to fully investigate and prosecute those involved in sending and distributing cocaine, marijuana, heroin and any other controlled substances on Nashville's streets," General Ball said. "We will never know for sure the number of crimes that have been prevented by the interdiction that has taken place over the past few days."

The case began in April after undercover detectives confirmed that Edward Peterson, 33, of Clarksville Pike, was selling multi-ounce quantities of cocaine. Intense surveillance and investigative work revealed that one of Edward's cocaine suppliers was Daniel Harding, 27, of Nashville, who was dealing in multiple kilogram quantities. Harding's supplier was determined to be Lewis McDonald, 31,

> of Franklin. The man supplying Lewis was identified as Marlon Cummings, 35, of Brooketrace Drive, who is alleged to have been receiving cocaine from Mexico via Texas.
>
> Two Texas brothers who just days ago are alleged to have delivered cocaine to the organization, Oscar Perez, 32, and Roberto Perez, 26, were arrested at Nashville International Airport Sunday as they were about to board a plane to Dallas. Seized from them was $34,000 in cash. Both were then charged with money laundering and, like the other defendants, will be facing charges of engaging in a large-scale cocaine conspiracy.[1]

I texted Hughes back, "They didn't mention the houses and land we seized."

Hughes immediately wrote back, "Haha, dude seriously."

"Just saying."

"Just get to work. We still got one to go." He was right. This was only the first big haul; we still had Shawn's organization to bring down.

We were still up on Shawn's phone, and now we could focus on him with Marlon, Slick, Dell, Lewis and other co-conspirators out of the picture. I was ready to take on the next part of the investigation. We didn't think it would be long before Shawn and his buds went dark for a bit. Dell wasn't really with the "in" crew, but he was directly connected to Shawn, so if Shawn decided to lay low, that meant that everyone was going to lay low.

It didn't take long for Shawn and his buddies to get wind of what happened the day before. I'm sure Shawn was shaking in his boots, as he should, because Dell had been picked off. Hell, Shawn had distributed more than ten kilos of cocaine to Dell in the last month alone. Even though Dell was not known as a snitch, we would set him up to make it look that way and soon we could call checkmate.

For the rest of December, though, we needed to work on the paperwork, court cases, and picking up a new number for Shawn yet again. We could relax as much as the 20th knew how to, which meant we didn't work every single waking moment and took a few evenings off a week. It was nice to spend several nights at home with my wife leading up to Christmas, and I spent a couple days practically living at my parents' house during the holiday. Family was going in and out of their house like it was Grand Central Station.

I also was looking forward to making a trip to Miami with James right before New Year's. During our search of Marlon's house, we had found evidence of a new car he had purchased in Miami, which was at a celebrity body shop to get tricked out (most likely with special compartments for drugs). We contacted the shop and let them know who we were and that we were going to show up on December 29th to pick up the vehicle and drive it back to Nashville. Technically, it would be a work trip, but it would also feel like a minivacation.

The night before we left, though, I held a going-away celebration for Adam Bristol who was being deployed on the last day of the month. He'd been deployed before, but this time around I was feeling more nostalgic because, unlike his previous deployments, we hadn't been working in the same office right up until he left. I'd been at the 20th for six months and hadn't gotten to see him every day and now he was shipping out. He'd probably come home fine, but it was never a guarantee with deployment. I wanted to make sure he knew he was still one of my best friends, even if my head had been so filled with the case for so long. The going-away party was the perfect opportunity to just relax and have fun with him before he shipped out.

I rented a room at one of his favorite bars and invited everyone I could think of (except for Sgt. Bagg), and I told Adam to come meet me for a drink before he left. When he walked towards the back of the bar, I had the twenty or so guys jump out to surprise him before we then spent the next several hours drinking, hanging out, and playing darts. It was a huge success and I could have sworn Adam almost had tears in his eyes when he thanked the group.

I stayed until Adam was ready to go home and then I caught a few hours of sleep before heading to the airport to meet up with James for our mini-vacay to Miami. James' family lived near Miami, so our plan was to get the seized car, stop by his family's house, and then spend the evening at South Beach before driving the sixteen hours back to Nashville the following day.

The Miami police picked us up from the airport and took us to lunch and then to get Cuban coffee, which was like a power punch but in the best way. The Miami police had been a huge help in going to the body shop and picking up the vehicle, and when we arrived at the tow lot, we understood why the Miami police had made so many jokes about it. It was a diesel Chevy Kodiak 4500 truck, which seemed only slightly smaller than a tractor trailer. Welded to its truck bed was a fifty gallon auxiliary gas tank.

"This baby could probably get to California and back without having to hit a gas station," the officer said, laughing.

I looked at James and said, "Gee, Sarge, I can't imagine why a drug dealer would want that special feature."

He laughed and asked the officer, "Is there gas in the auxiliary tank now?"

"Dunno." The officer shrugged. "It says it's got half a tank, but I'd fill up before heading to Nashville. I don't know if the gauge works for the auxiliary tank or not."

We then took the keys and climbed our way up into the truck, laughing at the ridiculousness of its size. We were big guys, but this truck made us feel small. We settled into the front seat and looked around. It hadn't gotten all the tricks done yet because Marlon hadn't paid, so the interior was bare, all the door panels were removed, and the back seat was missing completely.

James called down to the officer, "Well, you're right. It looks like a piece of junk from the inside."

We thanked the officer and headed to James' family's home and had a nice visit with them. When we headed back towards Miami central, we were on the Florida turnpike when the engine started to sputter and we lost speed. James pulled over into the grass median.

"It still says it's got half a tank!" He said as he poked the gauge.

Chapter 30

We were too far out for the Miami police to come to our rescue, but they said, "We'll send a ranger to help you."

A half hour later, a ranger car parked behind us and an ancient guy with leathery skin walked along the highway towards James' window.

The old man yelled up to us, "Need some diesel in this babe?"

James nodded and told him about the broken gas gauge. The old guy had already hobbled to the back of the truck and was opening one of the gas flaps.

We got out of the truck and stood by the tailgate. James asked, "How do you know that's not the auxiliary tank feed?"

Ranger Rick, as we came to call him, wheeled back on us and yelled, "I know what I'm doing, damnit! I been doing this longer than you boys have been alive!" He stood half in the road, pointing his finger at us, as cars flew past him going 80 mph or more.

We attempted to apologize, but Ranger Rick waved us off as he shuffled to his trunk. I swore I heard him grumbling, "Couple of sissyboymen . . ."

We stayed quiet as Ranger Rick continued grumbling as he put five gallons into the tank. James went to start it up and it sputtered out.

Ranger Rick had us pop the hood, and then we watched as this tiny, ancient man hoisted himself up onto the bumper and half into the engine. He then went back and forth between his trunk and our truck's engine for a long time, walking half in the road and seemingly unphased by the cars zipping by within a foot of him.

After a particularly long stint with his head in the truck's engine, I whispered to James, "You don't think he died in there, do you?"

James looked momentarily worried. The last thing we needed was to have this old ranger die on us in the middle of nowhere, right as it was getting dark.

He went to the front of the truck and called up, "You okay in there?"

Ranger Rick responded with a slew of curse words and then he tossed a wrench down without looking, narrowly missing James who jumped out of the way.

We sat on the side of the road and waited. Finally, Ranger Rick hobbled over to us, sweating and looking angry as a cat, and said, "I put the damn gas into that there aux tank. Backup's on the way."

Before we could respond, he went back to his car and sat down in it, leaning back in his seat.

It had gotten fully dark at this point, so James and I climbed back into the truck to wait and laugh at the ridiculousness of the situation. It got less funny as more time went by, though, and our stomachs were grumbling loudly at us.

Almost an hour later, a car pulled up behind Ranger Rick's car.

"Let's just wait in here." James said, and I agreed.

A figure approached my side of the truck and I opened the door. It was a less leathery, fourteen-year-old Ranger Rick. "Which tank ya need this in." He said as he held up a can.

I got out and showed him the right tank, and the kid put the gas in and then silently headed back to his car and drove off. I looked at Sgt. Cox and he shrugged and tried to start the truck. It didn't start.

"So, should we check on Ranger Rick?" We assumed he had fallen asleep in his car, but neither of us were too keen on going to find out. I headed to his car and knocked on the window. I saw him start up from a deep sleep, but he rolled down the window and said, "That boy shoulda been here by now."

"He came and left actually. He put gas in the other tank. It still won't start."

Ranger Rick spit out his window and then pulled himself out of his car. I followed him back to the truck and watched him climb back into our engine, holding only a rag this time. Thirty minutes later he got back down and closed the hood. He stood outside James' window till it was fully lowered and handed the rag, covered in oil and gas, up for James to take, which he did with two fingers.

Ranger Rick said, "Try her."

James turned the key and the truck magically started.

Chapter 30

When he looked back down, Ranger Rick was already almost to his car. James leaned a little out the window, still holding the dirty rag, and yelled a confused, "Thank you?"

We watched as Ranger Rick pulled out onto the turnpike and slammed his gas.

James and I couldn't help but laugh until we almost cried. After all that, Ranger Rick had taken a rag to the engine and made it work. James threw the rag into the nonexistent back seat, and we finally headed back to our hotel, almost three hours later than planned.

Since the truck didn't fit in the hotel's garage, we drove for several blocks looking for a parking space that could possibly fit us. Then we took an Uber to South Beach to get a very late dinner. Every bar and restaurant was full to the brim and people were dressed to the nines. We were in cargo shorts and didn't get in anywhere, and after walking almost two miles, we stopped in a small, grungy bar, had terrible jumbo margaritas and some chips, and then got an Uber back to the hotel. We were too exhausted to do anything else.

Before we split off to our rooms, James said, "Man, I hope this damn truck gets us back to Nashville tomorrow."

"We'll see if it gets us out of the city." I forced a laugh.

He forced a laugh, too, and said, "Well, us 20th guys really know how to take a vacation, huh?"

"Man, I can't wait to get back to work."

Then we both laughed and slept a few hours before waking up at 5 am to drive the sixteen hours back home.

JANUARY 2015

31

Getting back to casework was a huge relief after spending most of December working on paperwork and court cases. Plus, work felt like a dream compared to the exhausting "vacation" in Miami with Ranger Rick and the truck from Hell.

I tried not to be bitter in thinking about how some of the guys I'd worked so hard to bring in might already be on the streets again on bond. When I testified in court as to the probable cause of the wiretap case, I faced nineteen defendants, all wearing orange jumpsuits, and my goal was to get the case bound over for the Grand Jury. I was successful after six hours of testimony, but it took a lot out of me. Nineteen defendants meant just as many attorneys berating me with questions.

Even though the case was bound over, I was disappointed when DA Chad Ball refused to prosecute the Drug-Free School Zone law. In this case, there were several homes directly across from elementary schools where kilos and weapons were recovered. Not prosecuting on this portion of the law dramatically reduced the possible sentences for these individuals, and some received almost no jail time.

There was nothing I could do about this, though, so I tried to focus back in on the "B" section of the case and finish the paperwork on the over 100 seizures from our warrants in the "A" section.

We had tapped six different phone numbers on TF-1422 "B," but we were not getting any closer to the head of the snake. We had one of Dell's numbers, one of Damon's, and we were on Shawn's fourth number. Clearly the most important lesson he learned in federal prison was to never keep a phone number longer than a month. It was a real headache.

After our huge bust, the whole city seemed on edge. We dismissed Dell's conspiracy charge in mid-December, thinking he would lead us right back to Shawn, and Dell sure did try. But Shawn wasn't taking the bait. Dell looked like a snitch since his case was the only one to get dismissed by request of the state, and Shawn wasn't interested in chancing it. He never talked to Dell again, so Dell had to find a new big-dealer friend, which was unlikely given we'd just taken Marlon down, or change careers. Either way, he was of no use to us anymore unfortunately.

We already had plenty on Shawn to arrest him and execute search warrants, but we wanted to get his source and the whole crew. No use in working a wiretap conspiracy case if we couldn't take out the whole organization. We still had three male Hispanic guys on the drawing board: Francisco Hernandez, Arturo Gonzalez, and Mateo Vargas. Milliken referred to them fondly as his TGI Fridays boys now. We also knew Shawn's possible plug house was owned by Jose Lopez, so it was only a matter of time before we had enough evidence to take everyone down.

Since we had taken down some of the cameras from the "A" side of the case, we decided to use some on this half. A picture may be worth a thousand words, but a video is worth a million.

We put one camera over off Due West in Madison where Shawn had an apartment that we thought he was using to re-rock his kilos. Then I took a second camera and went to Jose Lopez's property on Central Pike where Milliken's TGI Fridays boys were living. There were so many damn trees around the house, though, that it was tough to get a perfect line of sight. A tech met up with me and we found a solid spot for the camera on the telephone pole looking at the side of the property.

Luckily, later that afternoon after we had placed the camera, Arturo's white GMC Denali pulled into the driveway and parked. The camera was up and running, but between the trees and the red metal carport, we were screwed when we realized Arturo was heading to the back of the residence. At least it was winter and the leaves were gone so we could at least see that he went to the back, but we couldn't see anything happening back there.

Arturo headed back to his SUV with two large white bags that looked heavy. My initial thought was that we would have more trash to go through, which would be awesome. Unfortunately, he got into his car with the heavy bags and drove off. Collins followed, but Arturo made four right turns within a mile, so we knew Collins was being watched. He pulled off. It was way too early in the second half of the case to get burned. We didn't want them having any suspicions they were being tracked.

An hour later, another van pulled into the driveway, and two females went in through the front door with a couple of dogs. Francisco came out from the rear of the building and began throwing a tennis ball for the dogs in the fenced back yard.

The females reemerged with white bags that looked nearly the same as the ones Arturo left with an hour earlier. They placed the bags back in the van, put the dogs in the back seat, and pulled out of the driveway so fast it was lucky another car wasn't driving by because those dogs might not have survived the day. Collins stuck on them and Hughes and I stayed put, watching the house.

"These girls are driving like maniacs," Collins radioed in. "They're bobbing and weaving like crazy. If I was working patrol, I'd pull them over just to find out if the driver was suffering a seizure."

Collins soon lost the girls, and it was getting so dark that we couldn't see anything, so Hughes and I pulled off for the night.

For the next few days, I stayed back at the office while Hughes was out doing his thing and getting all the intel to keep the case rolling. Hughes was one of the best, if not the best, at gathering intel and putting together pieces of the puzzle. We already had a dozen properties and parcels of land all over the surrounding counties that we knew related back to this Hispanic drug trafficking organization, so Hughes did surveillance on all the locations while I got buried in paperwork from the "A" case. For every moment I spent out on surveillance, I was getting more and more behind at the office. The more I worked on the paperwork, the more the pile seemed to grow.

It was during one of these long paper-filled days that Thomas paused in his work and said, "Bobby, I've been thinking about the leak thing."

I groaned as I turned my chair around to face him, relieved to have a break from the papers but also not thrilled to talk about the leak. OPA was still periodically doing interviews and it seemed like this investigation was going to last forever. Thomas had been interviewed twice more, with only a slight variation in the questions, and I knew the leak issue weighed a lot more on him than me.

"What're you thinking?" I asked.

He turned his chair to me and said, "Okay, just hear me out. I'm not making any accusations, and I definitely haven't brought this up to OPA. I just, I need a soundboard for the idea."

I nodded. "Shoot."

"Okay, so, remember at the end of July when we still thought Hector was something big?"

I nodded, remembering the embarrassment of how certain I was he'd gone to Texas for business, not a funeral, only for nothing significant to come out of it.

"That was right before the leak happened."

"Yeah, about a week before or so."

"Well, remember how Director Davis finally found a translator through Sgt. Lazaro? His wife and niece came in and translated what turned out to be Hector's personal phone calls."

I nodded, the pieces starting to form in my head.

Thomas continued, "I just remembered recently that Davis had said Lazaro recommended his niece because it would be good for her since she was starting to head down the wrong path. He was trying to set her right, and he thought police work would help show her the dangers of the drug game."

"Oh, shit, man."

Thomas put his hands up, "Like I said, I'm not making accusations, and I don't think Sgt. Lazaro is responsible for anything, but his niece . . ."

"She could have totally been the leak."

Thomas nodded. "That's what I'm thinking. She knew we were looking for ties between Hector and all those other guys. She would know their names, and the timing lines up perfectly. They came in a couple days before Officer Vong. I remember that because I had talked to Vong about how he was the second translator we'd had in, but the first Vietnamese one."

My mind felt like it was spinning, but not in the same way that paperwork made my head spin. "That makes perfect sense. Why didn't we think of that? Shit, we need to find evidence though."

"Finding evidence on Sgt. Lazaro's niece would be pretty risky. It's not case work."

"Dude, it's worth the extra effort. Vong's still on the green mile, and I don't know how he's survived this long in that situation, but if we can pin it on the right person, he'd be freed!"

"Exactly!" Thomas looked relieved. "I'm so glad you're on the same page. With all these OPA interviews, I just haven't really stopped thinking about the leak and if it's my fault and all. I thought maybe I was going to lose my mind." He laughed and said, "But then the other day when Hughes mentioned in the meeting about finding another Spanish-speaking translator for these calls from Milliken's TGI Fridays boys, I realized the possible connection."

"Well, shit, let's do some investigation! Do you remember her name?"

Thomas showed me the records from the day back in July, and then we searched her on the internet and Facebook. Within a few minutes, we'd found out her boyfriend was mutual friends with Ken on Facebook.

Thomas said, "Coincidence?"

"Hell no! Let's look through pictures." It didn't take long to find photos of her and her boyfriend at the exact same bar that Ken frequented. Then we found pictures of her boyfriend with Ken himself at the bar.

"Yeah, I don't think this is a coincidence." Thomas laughed. "Man, I think we've found our leak."

I grinned but then deflated. "We do have one major problem."

After a beat of silence, Thomas said, "Sgt. Lazaro."

I nodded. Sgt. Lazaro was the department's golden boy. He had only been an officer for a couple years before being promoted to sergeant, and we knew he was close friends with a lot of the higher-ups.

I said, "I say we bring this to Sgt. Cox and see what he says."

Thomas nodded and we took screen shots and printed what we'd found. When we approached James with the evidence, he was both supportive and wary. He complimented us on doing the investigation more effectively than OPA, but he repeated what Thomas and I already knew: Sgt. Lazaro was a favorite and it would be difficult to question or investigate his niece without it coming across as threatening to the sergeant himself.

"This information has to be dealt with cautiously," James said. We nodded. With how Sgt. Korbin was treating our team in his interviews at OPA, and the fact that Weakling was now a sergeant over there spreading rumors, we didn't know if we could trust OPA with the information or not. Our other option was to get the report directly to the Chief, but that would undermine the chain of command.

The only thing that could be done was give the information to Sgt. Korbin and hope for the best. Thomas and I brainstormed with Sgt. Cox about how to phrase the information and how to make it clear no blame was being placed on the golden boy, Sgt. Lazaro. Since it was OPA's investigation, we had to rely on their resources now to investigate Lazaro's niece.

We chose to write up a report, supporting our claims with evidence from Facebook, and have Sgt. Cox sign off on it. Then we brought it to Director Davis so he could be in the know and get the report to Sgt. Korbin. We waited in the hopes that the information would clear the whole leak mess up.

Unfortunately, nothing in the police department works that cleanly.

We waited in anticipation for a week after Davis handed the information off to Korbin, and then we got good news from the grapevine: The Chief had formally apologized to Officer Vong and had taken him off the green mile. The embarrassment of the last few months on the green mile would forever trail Officer Vong, but at least he could return to work.

As happy as we were, we still hadn't heard anything more from the Chief or OPA about Lazaro's niece. An announcement was never made that the leak had been determined, either. We waited all month and never heard anything else about it. Maybe the whole thing would just be pushed under the rug? We'd just have to wait and see.

32

Because Shawn was a high-rolling kilo dealer, he celebrated the new year with another brand spankin' new car: a black Dodge Charger.

"Man, he must have a loyalty card to that Charlotte Pike dealership," Collins radioed after Hughes gave the news.

Because we had already gotten at least two dozen trackers for the case, drawing up a new one was simple and we got it signed that same day. I offered to place the tracker to have a break from my stack of papers, and the road rash and gravel in my pants was well worth the change of scenery. The hard part was done for now and we could just sit back and let the tracker do the work. At least until Shawn decided to buy a new car.

After the tracker was up and running, the first place Shawn went to was his storage unit. With the number of times he visited the unit, one would think he was keeping something alive in there, but since Sgt. Cox had set up a camera with a direct view of the unit, we knew the only thing living in there was Shawn's lucrative business.

Shawn and his right-hand man Edwin were the only two that ever visited the storage unit. These two must have been tight and that was fine; they would have plenty of time together once they were taken down. Both men had lengthy rap sheets, and Shawn was on federal probation. I mean, really, how many times do you have to be caught? How much of your life do you have to live in jail before it really sinks in that you should just quit dealing drugs?

While I dealt with Shawn's tracker placement, Hughes was putting one on Arturo's vehicle. We'd learned that Arturo didn't live at Jose Lopez's house like Francisco and Mateo did. Arturo owned a trailer in Smyrna and had three kids that were always running around the property, according to Hughes.

"He spends nothing on his home, but, shit, you guys should see these cars he picks up. It must be where all his cash goes."

Titus said, "Flashy cars are a terrible investment. He should really look into diversifying his portfolio."

We all laughed and Collins chirped, "Nerd."

"When I retire before you, old man, we'll see who's a nerd."

Collins laughed it off.

I asked, "So, Hughes, how did the placement go?"

"No problems."

I was like a magnet for landsharks, but Hughes never once had an issue placing a tracker. He and his best friend, Special Agent (SA) Trey Jones with Homeland Security (HSI), had gone out early that morning to place the tracker on Arturo's GMC Denali. They were both flawless in their work, and of course they got the job done easily. Hughes literally saved SA Jones' life several years prior during a shootout, so they were as tight as blood brothers.

That afternoon, Collins came running into my office.

"Where's Hughes?"

"I don't know, why?"

"You keeping up with the tracker on Arturo's Denali?"

I gestured to my mountain of papers, "Not for a minute."

"It just pulled into a dealership off Murfreesboro Pike."

That got me up. "Shit! Let's go!"

When we got to the dealership, we saw Arturo's Denali parked by the shop.

Collins said, "Maybe just an oil change?"

"We should find out for sure. If someone saw Hughes this morning, they might be looking for the tracker. You got nicer clothes on, so maybe you take the lead on this. If we can avoid letting them know who we are, all the better."

"Yeah, don't want them to get spooked and say something to Arturo."

We walked inside and the manager was the only one available thankfully. Collins chatted him up for a couple minutes before asking if the nice Denali SUV outside was for sale or getting fixed up.

"It was just dropped off for a wiring issue." If it was an electrical issue, they wouldn't be dealing with the frame, so we were in the clear.

"Nice vehicle," Collins said, rubbing his chin. "Thinking one day I might like me a Denali."

"It's always something we can get special ordered for you here."

"I'd have to talk it over with the wife." Collins then asked about specs and the size of the interior cabin.

The manager blurted out that since three Hispanic guys dropped it off, it fit them comfortably enough.

Collins nodded and then changed the subject. After a couple more minutes of bullshitting, I nudged Collins and he said we were just on a lunch break but would come back by when he knew what he wanted. The manager gave him his card and we were out of there.

"Easy as pie!" Collins said as we buckled up.

"You loved that a little too much."

"If I could get paid to bullshit around in car dealerships all day, that'd be a dream job."

I laughed and we headed back to the office. When we arrived, we found Hughes and let him know the situation. He then updated us on the new number he had for Shawn, which ended up being his son.

Hughes said, "Man, that kid texts a lot. We finally got Shawn's number when this boy texted his 'daddy.'"

I asked, "Isn't the kid like eighteen?"

"Nineteen." Hughes shrugged. "Daddy's boy I guess. He's a low hustler, too, though."

"The apple doesn't fall far from the tree."

"Yeah. So, we dropped him but now we have Shawn's new number for sure, so Phillips is working on the wiretap order."

We were up on Shawn's new number before the end of January. The slight break over Christmas and New Year's had made it harder to get back into the long days of surveillance and tracking, but it felt good to be back on our game finally.

It was the last day of the month and Francisco was on the move early in the morning. Titus and I made a guess as to the Dodge truck's

Chapter 32

direction, and we headed to the Lightning Bus Company building. We realized we didn't make it in time because we got an alert that the truck was heading back to Hermitage again.

We found them at a McDonalds, and we saw Francisco inside with two other male Hispanics. We got great pictures of them as they came out with their food bags, and we followed them to a gas station.

Francisco gassed up while the other two sat in the truck. Diesel joined me and Titus as we headed on to the Central Pike house, anticipating their next stop.

Instead, they headed to Maple Leaf Apartments where we had dumpster dived and first found Mateo's name on a receipt. Like other occurrences at this location, the Dodge pulled into the complex and parked in front the same breezeway as last time. Francisco and the front passenger exited the truck and looked around the parking lot as if their life depended on it. After "securing" the area, both Francisco and the unknown male walked up to the third level.

A few minutes later, Francisco came out and left the guy in the apartment. We followed Francisco back to his house. While I circled the block, Diesel reported that Francisco was on the move again and had two white trash bags with him.

"Shit, he's probably making a dump off." This was when dealers took their garbage to other trash cans around town to try and cover up a trail.

We followed Francisco out of town to Smyrna and then to the city dump. Titus was in his pickup truck, so he got in line right behind Francisco. It would have looked sketchy to pull up to the dump in my sedan, so Titus was our man.

He pulled past Francisco when he stopped at a dumpster, and he watched in his rearview as Francisco tossed the bags on top. He turned and headed back to the bin when Francisco was out of sight. The bin was full, so Titus just had to grab the bags off the top and throw them in his truck.

He got back on the radio and said, "Got 'em. Man, you guys should see this old employee's face right now. He's looking at me with so much judgment and disgust."

We all laughed as we headed to a nearby grocery store and pulled behind the building to their dumpsters. We were on an adrenaline rush. Snatching someone's nasty ass trash was the most exciting part of the day.

Titus let the tailgate down and we all gloved up. Diesel arranged the greasy items we pulled out of the bag on the pavement to take pictures. We found torn boxes of Foodsaver heat seal rolls, torn Foodsaver vacuum sealed bags, torn boxes of Glad press and seal wrap, used Rubber gloves with a torn glove box, numerous used rubber bands, cut vacuum sealed bags, and used carbon paper.

This was a homerun! We had already suspected that the Central Pike house was a stash, but this evidence sealed the deal. Heat seal rolls meant they were vacuum sealing dope or money. Rubber gloves mean that they were careful; they took precautions to not touch any of the cocaine or grease, and they didn't want to leave fingerprints. The rubber bands were used to separate the money in "stacks."

The grease and carbon paper were the best part, though. Drug traffickers believed that if they smeared the kilo bricks with grease then a trained K-9 would not be able to find the drug scent. Of course, that shit did nothing but create a mess. K-9 dogs have noses 1,000 times stronger than a human's. Trust me, they smell right through bullshit. In addition, traffickers thought that if they wrapped their product, whether dope or money, in carbon paper, then it won't be detected by an ion scanner at the border. Also not true.

Diesel got the evidence organized and brought it back to the office. It was a busy morning and while we were running around, gathering up another man's trash, we had also noted Shawn making multiple trips to his storage unit. He was a busy bee, and we could see everything he did at that unit thanks to the camera!

The following day, I went to do surveillance on the Central Pike house and pulled up right in time. A black Buick Lacrosse pulled into the driveway, and, from previous dealings, I knew this was one of many vehicles operated by Shawn. It was always odd to me that Shawn would do most of his work on Saturdays. It seemed like he thought we didn't work on Saturdays, but the joke was on him.

The wire room let me know of some texts between Shawn and an unknown male who owed him money. Shawn was a pretty laid-back guy, but when it came to business, he ran a tight ship. If he had to wait, I wouldn't have put it past him to charge interest for his time. This time, though, he waited for over an hour for this guy to show. It was so unlike Shawn who just sat, waiting, and only lightly complaining when the unknown male pushed the meetup time to noon. I drove around a bit to blow off some of my own impatient steam.

The wire room then relayed to me a new conversation between the two.

Shawn said, "I need you to go check one for me."

"I just got one to the screen door. He don't have one to the wood." This could mean that the unknown male had a key but not for the main door. Or, it could be "keys" of cocaine. I had a guess.

Shawn replied, "Can't hear you."

"Okay. What is it or do you want me to call you when I get over there?"

"X-man. Take KKC from last night on that 4-4-2."

"KKC last night on the 4-4-2 X-man."

"Yeah."

"Alright."

Half the time I didn't know if they we're talking about drugs, cars, movies, or shows. I felt like all the lingo just ran together sometimes. From my experience, they were trying to set up another deal, and X-Man was a nickname of a small-time dealer. This cryptic speech was unlike the Shawn I knew who was a man of few words and liked to get shit done fast. Before I could figure out what was going on, though, the deal was pushed off until "everyone gets their shit together," according to Shawn.

I headed back to the office, my eye twitch getting worse. Getting a little bit of sleep over the holidays was nice, but the eye twitch had remained. Plus, I had officially gained fifteen pounds from the never-ending Uncrustables I relied on.

When I got to my computer there was a rough cartoon drawing taped up on the screen. An arrow pointed to one figure with a Braves baseball cap and crazy eyes with my name and the added note, "super power: eye twitch." Another arrow pointed to the other figure holding a giant trophy and looking chill. The label said, "Hughes, winning award for Bobby's work."

I laughed and took a picture of it to text to the team. I wrote, "Y'all are idiots."

They bantered back about how I looked wrecked first thing in the morning and Hughes looked refreshed even at midnight.

It was all in good fun, and it felt good to be able to laugh about it. Hughes did manage to always look in control, and I knew I wore my emotions on my sleeve.

As I drove home that night, I wondered how long the case would go and how I would look by the end of it. January had gone by in a flash, and it was almost a year since I started the work on this case. We were almost there, but I could tell my body was running on empty.

FEBRUARY 2015

33

New month, new opportunities. Shawn, Arturo, Francisco, and the male Hispanic we hadn't identified yet were spending most of their time going between the Central Pike house and the Due West Apartments complex. I doubted they were making each other turkey sandwiches, sitting down, and playing cards. Hell no, they were in there breaking down kilos of cocaine! Really "skilled" dealers could take a whole kilogram of cocaine and turn it into two. It would be cut to hell and probably all lumpy, but if it was wrapped up real tight it would look okay. That shit could sell for double the price then. What's better than $36,000? $72,000 for the same investment.

Ray, Shawn's nephew was even coming around regularly to the apartments. After the traffic stop that sent him to jail in November for five kilos of cocaine in his passenger seat, one would think he might have learned his lesson. Nope, here he was, back hustling like nothing had happened. My guess was that Shawn bailed him out and now Ray was indebted to his uncle for life. Or, at least until he worked off whatever bail Shawn had to pay. If Ray was in debt to Shawn, it meant he was in debt to a cartel, too.

We watched a lot of other people coming and going from the complex, too, including Shawn's best buddy Edwin who seemed to be attached to Shawn's hip. Smaller dealers and users stopped by daily for quick deals with Shawn, and we always picked up their tags and added them to the conspiracy list. We had lots of photos at this point of Shawn standing outside of the Due West apartment by his car, talking to one guy after another. Even if a deal didn't go down, we were always looking for connections.

One afternoon, Shawn's GPS tracker spent the day at his favorite bar Donkey's. Maybe he just needed a few drinks, we all did at this point, but when we intercepted a call between Damon and Shawn, we knew a deal was in the making.

Damon, being the predictable dealer, asked for a "Peyton Manning" again, and Shawn left the bar about an hour later. He stopped at the suspected home of Damon, and we watched as Damon came outside and retrieved something from his black truck before inviting Shawn inside.

When they came outside later, cutting up and laughing about who knows what, an unknown male was with them and he got into Shawn's passenger seat. I considered following Shawn to try and identify this new guy, but I knew the tracker would show me where they went, and Damon was acting really weird. He walked back to his house, but he kept looking over his shoulder. When Shawn had pulled out, Damon booked it to his truck and peeled off in the opposite direction. This was too weird not to look into.

I followed at a distance and watched as this guy drove like a bat out of hell, like he was a cat who got spooked by his own tail. He conducted some heat runs to move the product, but I ended up losing him as he swerved all over the interstate and made a quick exit before I could follow.

I should have followed Shawn instead of trying to chase that dumbass, but he was acting so suspicious it threw me off course. Chalking it up as an opportunity lost, I headed home. It was after 6 pm but, considering the other nights in this investigation, this was an early one for me. Just when I thought everyone was done for the evening, Shawn had business on his mind like usual. I fell asleep after two hours of watching his GPS tracker travel to several locations. He was a money-making, hustling machine.

It felt like no sooner had I laid my head down for the night that another ping came in. When I checked my phone, though, I saw it was already 7:30 am. I must have slept like a dead man. I was so tired, but I couldn't afford that attitude. Shawn was up and moving early, so I got up too. I didn't want to miss a beat!

As I headed towards Shawn's area, Collins touched base that Shawn's tracker was giving delayed pings. A moment later, I got a new ping and saw he was in a different part of town.

"Shit." I said. "We can't lose his tracker now."

Collins said, "I caught up with him and it looks like he's heading to his storage unit. The wire room got a call that he's doing a deal in twenty."

"Okay, I'm on my way."

We watched as Shawn made a brief stop at the unit and then headed to a buyer's residence way up in Madison. Miles didn't matter though when it came to Shawn's business. Money was money.

Thomas joined up with us as we reached a house in a small neighborhood. Shawn parked but didn't go inside. The buyer, Ayden McClain, was finishing up with a couple other small-time dealers, and the yard looked like a small party. It was clear Shawn didn't want any part of it, so he stayed put until Ayden was done.

Collins followed one of the small dealers to get identification on him, and Thomas and I watched as Ayden approached Shawn's vehicle. Ten seconds later, Ayden was heading back to his house with a bag, and Shawn pulled away.

We then followed Shawn to his gym where he spent the next two hours working out.

Thomas radioed, "Maybe we should be hitting the gym, too."

"For real," I said. "I keep trying to get to the office early three mornings a week to do a quick workout, but I can never do more than five minutes on the treadmill before getting distracted. There's just too much to work on. Or, I get a ping and I can't just ignore that."

"You are the ping king." Thomas laughed. "Maybe when this case is done we can get back in shape. I don't know how Titus and Diesel do it."

"They don't have a wife and kid like you do, man. They probably just spend all their extra time working on out 'swole'-ing each other."

We laughed and continued to wait on Shawn, as usual.

Just as I was trying to enjoy my Uncrustables, Shawn reappeared and got into his car. I stuffed the sandwich in my mouth and we were off.

Chapter 33

We arrived at his damn storage unit again fifteen minutes later. Thomas and I waited at our vantage point and got out the binoculars. Shawn always went into the unit carefully, making sure that no one was around, leaving the unit door mostly closed while he was in there, closing the unit door behind him promptly as he left.

"Man, I can't wait to search that shit," I told Thomas. We knew he had shelves storing tons of bags and supplies, but it would feel really good to go through everything on our own. We then headed to the Central Pike house in Hermitage.

Already parked there was the silver Nissan Altima, as always, which we were almost positive belonged to Mateo. Shawn got out of his car and went around to the back of the house. Sure enough, when he returned, Arturo was right behind him with a bag in his hand. It was clear that this was purely a business visit. Just as Shawn left, Arturo unlocked his SUV and placed something in the driver side. Afterward, he went back inside, and we were back on Shawn. He was clearly distracted, and at first, I couldn't tell why. Then I noticed that the fool was texting and driving.

Thomas said, "For a guy who is extra careful all the time, this is a pretty stupid move. He could get a ticket for that shit."

We followed Shawn to his house and spent the afternoon waiting again.

The wire room let us know that Shawn sent a text message to a whole list of his boys. It was just one word: "Other."

Thomas said, "This guy is famous for cryptic, one-word texts."

Before long, regulars were coming and going every few minutes.

A female arrived at one point, too, which was different. When we ran the car's tag we realized Shawn's sister had just gotten herself tied into the conspiracy. It would be hard for her to say she didn't know what was going on now.

After a couple weeks of almost constant surveillance, our team felt pretty confident we had identified all the players in Shawn's case. I had finally finished my paperwork from the "A" side of the case, and I was ready to help the team focus in on Arturo and his co-conspirators.

One morning in mid-February, we started off at the house off Central Pike. We knew that Arturo had gotten up early to head over there, *thank you GPS surveillance.* I sat behind a nearby church and watched the camera on my phone as Arturo pulled into the driveway. Luckily, he didn't pull his big ass Denali all the way under the carport for once, so we actually had some visibility.

He still went inside through the back door, of course, but he returned with the male Hispanic we still hadn't identified and couldn't be sure if he was Mateo or not. The unknown guy was skinny with super gelled hair, and they were both carrying suitcases. After loading them into the back seat of Arturo's SUV, they went back inside for ten minutes. They reappeared with white trash bags and tossed them into the trunk and they pulled out.

We followed them to Maple Leaf Apartments. We had become very familiar with this complex's dumpster so we readied ourselves for yet another dive. Instead of stopping, though, they circled the complex and we had to pull off. We waited at the front and they reappeared a minute later, and Arturo drove them over to one of his girlfriend's houses.

Diesel was able to pull in the driveway of a vacant duplex across the street and watch. We got pictures of Arturo coming out of the duplex carrying a nice Burberry bag. Arturo threw it in the back seat and then took off. I called one of my friends that worked in the patrol division and asked him to make a stop on the GMC Denali SUV. I told the officer to let him go if he ran because we could track him down and arrest him if so. We had a plan in the works!

Only five minutes from the house, a uniformed officer with the Metro Nashville Police Department got behind Arturo and activated his emergency equipment. There were about five seconds where I held my breath, thinking that if Arturo had a bunch of money in the SUV then he would take off. Slowly, very slowly, Arturo pulled over, just before he got on I-40.

The officer casually approached the vehicle and explained to Arturo the reason for the stop was that he failed to signal a mile back when he changed lanes. The officer obtained Arturo's identification as well as the passenger's Mexico passport. The whole mission was to identify the passenger and now we knew for sure it was Mateo Vargas whose name had been on that first receipt we got out of the dumpster. He was young and from an area just south of Mexico City.

When the officer completed the stop, surveillance officers followed the Denali as far as Dickson, Tennessee where surveillance was terminated. I was ready and wanted to keep going. I had snacks in my car, a jug of water, and a couple empty bottles, just in case. It wouldn't be the first time we followed someone out of state, but we had the tracker and could let it do the work.

Driving home that night, all I could do was wonder where the two were headed. Probably Texas, which was good, but I was still anxious. Last time I watched a guy go to Texas it ended up just being for a funeral. There was no way that I would be able to go to sleep until these two stopped somewhere. I managed to catch a couple hours in between pings, but they drove all night and ended up in Dallas, TX the following morning.

Something major was clearly in the works with Arturo in Texas and Shawn going quiet. We worried he had changed lines, but it turned out he just wasn't dealing for the moment. He wasn't even visiting his storage unit.

For once we had a really quiet day at the office where we caught up on notes and organized our list of co-conspirators. Shawn would move and talk soon and we doubted Arturo would be in Dallas for long.

34

At 3:30 am the next morning, Arturo's GPS tracker sent an alert that it was just outside of Dallas. They were on the move again. It was typical for dealers to travel at all hours of the day and night if they needed to transport drugs.

The route taken by the Denali was not the shortest or the quickest route from Dallas to Nashville. A normal trip, taken by someone who wasn't transporting drugs, would take about nine hours and they would travel 674 miles, mostly by interstate. It took Arturo and Mateo over fourteen hours, and they travelled nearly 800 miles to bring that dope back. That was routine, though. Most dealers transporting drugs travelled the same way, stopping only to fuel up and avoiding the interstate in areas known for higher police activity. It was well known that interdiction units routinely worked I-40 looking for drug couriers.

Since it was Sunday, I had family dinner at my parent's house that night. Danielle and I drove separately because I knew I'd be seeing Arturo soon.

We got to their house a little bit after 5 pm, and I spent a few minutes checking in with my dad and nieces playing in the den before I found Danielle in the kitchen with my sisters. My phone vibrated and I checked to see if it was Arturo's tracker. It wasn't, but it was a text from Hughes letting me know he was going to set up surveillance off the interstate to try and follow the Denali when it arrived to town. I let him know I'd come as soon as I could.

I tuned in to my sisters' conversation just enough to hear Ashley say, "Yeah, but at least I wasn't holding the baby."

"That could have been really scary," Danielle said.

"Wait, what happened?" I asked, giving the conversation my full attention.

Angela said, "Ashley lost the feeling in her legs and fell a few days ago, but she's okay now."

"Yeah, I called my doctor and he thought it might be a blood pressure thing, but it was still weird. Like, disorienting."

"I'm glad you're okay," I said.

Ashley smiled. My mom said, "You should go in for another checkup, though. Get your blood checked and all."

"I will. I'm guessing it was just a weird post-pregnancy thing because I still feel weak and tired so much of the time, but it's just strange it's all still happening six months later." Ashley said this with a shrug. "I'll make an appointment for next week, though, if I can. It can't hurt. And what's one more doctor bill at this point, right?" She laughed.

My phone vibrated again, and I saw Arturo was about forty minutes away. I'd need to eat and run. I tried to focus on the conversation during dinner, but with my phone pinging so often, it was all I could do to get a few bites down before I headed for the door. Arturo was almost at the outer-Nashville limits. My heart was beating fast because I knew that some big shit was about to pop off. They were probably returning with a whole load of kilos, and I couldn't focus on anything knowing that shit was about to enter my city.

A little after 6 pm, Hughes and I entered the interstate and spotted them. The Denali was following a white Ford F-350 work truck. The truck had built-in boxes on the side of the bed and a heavy-duty hydraulic liftgate.

I radioed to Hughes, "This has got to be the 'load' truck."

"Yeah, that's some really precious cargo. You see how they're riding bumper to bumper?"

"Man, you'd think they'd be a little less obvious about it."

We didn't want to lose sight of the Ford truck and followed it all the way back to Central Pike where Diesel joined us in surveillance. When the two vehicles pulled into the driveway off Central, we zoomed the camera in. It was dark and hard to see, but we could make out what was transpiring. The passenger, Mateo, jumped out and then moved the silver Nissan Altima that was blocking the garage. We got a picture of the tag and confirmed it belonged to him. The garage door went up, the Ford truck pulled in, and the garage door closed. Mateo moved the Altima back in front of the garage.

I told Hughes and Diesel, "It is so freaking hard to not run up on them and take this shit down right now!"

Hughes said, "I know. I can only imagine how many kilos of cocaine are packed into that F-350."

The hardest part of our jobs was letting any bit of dope walk. This wasn't our moment, though. We didn't have our team and paperwork together, but we knew we'd take them all down soon enough.

A few minutes later, Arturo and Mateo reappeared and removed what looked to be a heavy box from the Denali. Together, they carried the box inside the garage. I was itching to get in there and find out what they were doing.

Francisco's Dodge Ram truck was parked out front, too, and we were surprised to see Arturo and Mateo come out and drive off in the truck. We followed them to Maple Leaf Apartments, of course, and Hughes hurried ahead to beat them through the gate. He got set up on the apartment on the back side to have an advantaged view.

When the Dodge Ram pulled around the back, it parked near the breezeway. Arturo and Mateo were seen carrying a comforter and a white paper shopping bag into the hallway and up to apartment 311.

"Gee," Diesel said over the radio, "You think anything was bundled up in that comforter or what?"

We laughed and made some jokes about what could possibly be wrapped up in the blanket. Diesel came up with the best guess: vintage Spanish nudie mags.

Twenty minutes later, Arturo came out carrying a white Walmart shopping bag. Mateo was close behind, carrying a large, black garbage bag. They put both bags in the truck, drove to the complex dumpster, and tossed the bags in. They thought they were being sneaky under the cover of night, but we were cheering over the radio about getting to dumpster dive again.

After the Dodge Ram truck left and went back to Central Pike, Diesel took his flashlight and was the first over the edge of the dumpster to retrieve the bags. Hughes grabbed on to his feet right as Diesel almost fell in head first.

We took the bags back to the office so we wouldn't look sketchy hanging around a dumpster with flashlights.

As we started pulling things out of the bags, we realized this was even better than the last trash collection. It was better than getting discarded kilo wrappers with grease all over them, and it was even better than remnants of the kilos themselves. It was the packaging for two cell phones! Inside the Wal-Mart bag, we found a receipt dated 02/15/2015 for two AT&T Go Phones and two SIM cards to activate the Go Phones. The total price for the phones and cards was $144.47 and the receipt showed $200 cash was given for payment. They always dealt in cash.

I knew from my years of experience in wiretap investigations that drug dealers buy "burner phones" regularly. They are cheap and require no contract or subscriber information, so they only use them for a short period of time and then throw them away. It was fucking frustrating, especially when we knew we were about to get to something good, and then the phone dropped. It did throw us off, but we always found a way back in, even if that meant digging through trash.

The following day, we did more research on the trash haul. The bar code on the Go Phone packages showed the serial numbers and the IMEI numbers. The IMEI number is the International Mobile Equipment Identity number that identifies the wireless device. Thank God for those receipts! They should have known better than to leave behind evidence like that. AT&T could locate this device by the IMEI number and identify the telephone number assigned to the device on activation by the customer. We had a good idea of whose phone it was, but we just identified the phone as belonging to "A Member of the Conspiracy" in the wiretap order. Hell, I pulled Arturo's GPS tracker history and noticed where he was at that Wal-Mart where the phone was purchased. We would be up on those two phones in no time!

After putting it all together, at least the information we did have, it was clear to me that the trip to Texas was 100% drug related, and we needed to watch that F-350 *very* closely.

We had only been up on the two burner phones for about fourteen hours, but we were quickly able to identify the user of them both: Arturo.

We watched the tracker as Arturo's Denali left his trailer in Smyrna the next morning and took all back roads to the house on Central Pike. Once Arturo arrived at Central Pike, Francisco also pulled up and parked near the garage in his Dodge Ram. Acting as normal as possible, Francisco immediately started doing light yardwork, but not before looking down the road and checking for any unmarked cars. We hid well, and he couldn't see us, but we could see him.

Arturo and Francisco met towards the back of the residence and I noticed that Francisco had a shovel in his hand. I had seen it all, but now I was even more curious as to what they were up to, but they went out of sight again. I decided to wait before terminating surveillance. I had a feeling that the guys were about to do something, and I wanted to know what. I didn't have to wait long, not even twenty minutes, when Francisco pulled off in his Dodge truck and wound up at a church. Seriously. Was this guy praying on a Monday morning that we wouldn't catch his ass? Or was he repenting for missing church the previous day while his buddies drove to town with a load of drugs?

Shawn had been quiet for over a week, so while Francisco repented of his sins and Arturo did God-knows-what with the shovel and the F-350, I radioed the wire room for anything new on Shawn. It turned out Shawn was trying to make a deal with Ayden McClain again. I headed to Shawn's house to set up surveillance. Mateo's silver Nissan Altima that had been parked at Central Pike in front of the garage was now in front of Shawn's house, as were Shawn's Infiniti and Dodge Charger. Ayden came and went, and I touched base again with the wire room.

They let me know that Shawn and Arturo had made a plan to meet, but Shawn was distracted with his smaller dealers and didn't confirm a time. Arturo had left the Central Pike house and was back in Antioch, and the wire room said he was hitting Shawn's phone constantly. Shawn didn't answer his calls until late in the afternoon.

"Man, where the fuck have you been?" Arturo almost yelled.

"My bad."

Arturo sighed. "I'll be there in thirty."

Shawn hung up. Something was weird between them, and I didn't know if it was just Arturo being pissed at Shawn for not answering his phone or something more. As crazy as Shawn was about his money, Arturo was on a whole different level. He didn't have the patience Shawn did.

Arturo was on Highland Avenue in Antioch, and soon after the conversation ended, Shawn got his ass into gear and booked it over. They had planned to meet at the Central Pike house, and I was glad because Antioch was always a nightmare to navigate. Arturo was on time as always and Shawn arrived shortly after. He got out of his car and retrieved a large red bag from the back seat. I snapped photos because I was sure it was full of money, and by the way he carried the bag, I could tell that shit was heavy. Shawn wasn't in the house long. Arturo was probably still pissed from earlier, and Shawn looked almost depressed as he got back in his car and headed to his sister's house before going to her daughter's birthday party.

Shawn had to keep up the normal act as best he could around the family, but the wire room notified me that right before 8 pm, Arturo texted Shawn, "It's short $3,150. I ran it three times."

Major buzzkill. If Arturo was pissed before, he was probably in a rage now. Not only was Shawn late, but he didn't even have the right amount of money.

Shawn responded, "Okay. I gotta slow down."

"Ya, that rush shit ain't cuttin' it. You need to get your shit together."

"I know."

Shawn left the birthday party a couple minutes later and went to his favorite bar, Donkey's. We waited around a bit to see if Shawn would meet back with Arturo and settle the debt owed, but at midnight I was exhausted and headed home. Shawn must have just been getting hammered in the bar because the last ping from that location was at 3 am. Maybe he thought the cartel was going to cut him out of the business. Or, cut off his head.

35

We had gotten comfortable with our casework schedule since the OPA interviews had paused after the holidays. Officer Thammavong had been reinstated to his position for over a month, but we still hadn't heard anything about closing the leak case. We assumed it was only a matter of time, though, because what more could they do? OPA had thoroughly interviewed everyone on our team over the fall, and in some cases multiple times like Thomas. But, as we realized at the end of February, they still had to interview our bosses, Sgt. Cox and Director Davis, to complete the investigation. Chief Smalls may have apologized to Vong, but it turned out he still needed someone to pin the blame on.

James was called in for his first interview with Sgt. Korbin on February 20th, and he knew anything he said might be skewed to hold him accountable for the leak.

When he returned to the office after lunch, he looked worn down as he walked slowly to his office. I followed him and he told me the questions had focused solely on his job's responsibilities and how he should be running the unit. I understood this to mean that Korbin had accused James of lacking leadership skills and tried to make him take responsibility for the leak. James was an honest guy and one of the few sergeants who actually paid attention to his team and put in supportive effort on cases. He was the best sergeant I knew, so I was immediately pissed to hear how he'd been treated.

"That's not all," James said, leaning back in his chair and staring at his hands. "The interview was recorded and Chief Smalls was watching the whole time. He called me to his office right afterwards. He said it was an emergency meeting." He then sighed and shook his head. "I should have kept my head more level."

"What do you mean?"

"When Korbin kept challenging my authority, I finally unloaded on him. I told him he had forgotten where he came from and that he had no right telling me how to do my job. I told him he didn't know shit and needed to get *his* act together."

I almost laughed, "Well, that's true. Korbin's doing a shit job considering this whole mess has been going on since August. Other than interviewing us, I don't really understand what Korbin's doing to actually close this case, especially since he wouldn't even listen to the evidence on Lazaro's niece."

James nodded and started to organize the things on his desk. "Yeah, but I shouldn't have turned it on him like that. I shouldn't have exploded. It didn't look good."

"So, Chief Smalls wasn't happy about that?"

"That's an understatement." He proceeded to tell me what happened in the Chief's office. Several deputy chiefs sat in on the "emergency meeting" in order to witness Chief Smalls reprimanding James. "It felt like I was on trial," he said as he stood and put a few things from his desk into a bag. "He said he was disappointed with my attitude and our team. He said he didn't like task force units because he couldn't control them. He said that the 20th is out of control and it's because of leaders like me."

"That's bullshit," I said, shocked. James nodded, looking tired, and motioned for me to follow him out of his office. He turned off his light, and I walked with him outside, waiting to hear why he was leaving. It was only mid-afternoon but I assumed he was just ready to head home for the day after such an exhausting experience.

Once at his car, Sgt. Cox said, "The Chief told me to go home because he didn't know what he wanted to do with me."

"What to *do* with you?"

He nodded and wiped his face. He then took a piece of paper out of his pocket and looked at it. He said, "Before he told me to get out of his office, he slid this paper across the table to me and told me not to open it until I was gone. He said, 'That's what I think about you, Sergeant.'"

I took the paper and turned it over. The only word on the paper was one quickly scrawled word: "Arrogant."

I almost laughed in disbelief. "You've got to be fucking kidding me." James was anything but arrogant, and I couldn't believe the Chief had pulled such a dramatic and ridiculous stunt of passing him a note. "This is ridiculous. It's . . . it's wrong and it's inappropriate. It's bullshit!"

"I know," James said. He took the piece of paper back and put it in his pocket. "I don't know what is going to happen now, but I wanted you to know what I just experienced. I've always told you there is so much good in the department and to just avoid the bad eggs like Dick Bagg, but . . ." He didn't finish as he looked at his feet.

"This is crazy, James," I said, shaking my head. I now saw how the department would stoop to a whole new level to lay blame on someone, even if it didn't make any sense. Nothing James had ever done could warrant Korbin and Chief Smalls talking down to him like that. "This is so ridiculous. I mean, we are in the middle of a huge case that's going to bring in millions of dollars and take truckloads of drugs off the street. Why are they doing this to us?"

James shrugged and looked back up at me. "I don't know, but you did just remind me of the good in the department. The work this team does is amazing and directly benefits our city and its citizens." He set his hand on my shoulder. "Thanks for reminding me."

He then got into his car and said, "I'll be in touch. Be good, Bobby."

I waved as he drove off. I stood out in the frigid February air to let the rest of my anger cool off. I then went and told Director Davis that Sgt. Cox had headed home for the afternoon. I was still so angry and shocked at what James had gone through, but I wanted him to be the one to tell the guys what happened. I didn't want to be a gossip, especially not about James' affairs, so I spent the rest of the afternoon unable to concentrate.

Late that afternoon, Deputy Chief Timothy Cream called all the officers on the 20th to the SID building for a special meeting. Director Davis shrugged when we asked him and said he hadn't been invited. The rest of us stopped work and went over right away. I followed the guys to the conference room past Sgt. Bagg's office, but I made a point not to look in. The last thing I wanted was to see his face.

"Thank you for coming, officers," Cream said as we filed into the SID conference room and sat around the table. "I'm going to keep this short, but I wanted to deliver this news in person. Shut the door, please. Thank you."

We sat in silence for a moment as Cream looked at each of us. "Sgt. Cox has been suspended and will no longer be with your team as of today. A new supervisor will be appointed to oversee your cases, and until then, you are not to even speak to Sgt. Cox. He is under disciplinary review, and the details are of none of your concern. If I find out that any of you reach out to him," he paused as he stared at me for an extra beat, "there will be swift and serious consequences. These are orders directly from Chief Smalls, so if you fail to comply with these orders, you will report directly to the Chief for disciplinary measures up to and including instant decommissioning."

The room was silent when he stopped speaking. He stood and paced, just like Sgt. Bagg did when he was winding up for an ass chewing. Cream talked as he paced, "It has come to the attention of the department that certain activities enacted by the 20th Judicial District Drug Task Force during case TF-1422 have threatened the integrity of the Metro Police Department." He then looked back at us directly and said, "It should be common sense that if you are told to do something illegal, you shouldn't do it. Wrongfully blaming an innocent officer for mistakes *your* team made, and then looking to cover it up, compromises the entire department and puts the Chief and DA Chad Ball in a terrible position. This behavior, currently under investigation with the Office of Professional Accountability, *will* be brought to justice."

Cream kept talking, but I was starting to see red. He was implying our team was a bunch of hooligans who were breaking laws and not following orders. He also was saying we were trying to cover up a mistake by putting the tracker on Officer Vong's vehicle, which was an order that had come directly *from* Chief Smalls. Plus, I was in the room when Sgt. Cox had deliberately told Captain Zander, "Do not decommission him, we don't have near enough evidence . . ."

In addition to all this, Deputy Chief Cream was threatening us with repercussions for just *talking* to Sgt. Cox, who had literally done nothing wrong or even questionable. They were silencing him and putting a wedge between him and our team.

When Cream dismissed us, the team was silent as we left the room. I saw Lieutenant Noah Spine enter Captain Zander's office with Deputy Chief Cream, so I told Thomas I'd be staying behind at SID for a bit. I sat down at a table near Captain Zander's office door and waited a long time, trying to let my anger subside. Lt. Spine was who I'd always go to for cash for my deals at SID when I didn't want to deal with Bagg, and we'd always gotten along well enough. I wanted to touch base with him, but I was also wondering why he and Captain Zander had specifically avoided the meeting. Shouldn't they have been the ones communicating with our team since they were directly above Sgt. Cox? I also didn't understand why Spine was now having a private meeting with Captain Zander and Deputy Chief Cream. As I waited, I wondered if Captain Zander experienced any repercussions for decommissioning Officer Vong despite Sgt. Cox's warning not to. I guessed not.

When the door finally opened, Lt. Spine came out, and following him was Sgt. Bagg. Both were smiling.

My whole body felt like it was sinking into the ground. What the *fuck*?

Before either of them saw me, I stood and weaved my way through the back hallways back to the kitchen door. This was a terrible sign. Cream, Zander, Spine, and Bagg had just met for almost an hour right after the 20th was told Sgt. Cox was suspended and taken off the team. And Dick Bagg had just walked out of that meeting smiling. I knew the answer to my question about if Captain Zander experienced repercussions: definitely not. I knew the blame was being placed on Sgt. Cox for sure now, and if I didn't get out of that building, I might lose it and kick down some doors in my rage.

I drove back to the Batcave and called James, who didn't answer his phone.

Chapter 35

It was almost 7 pm by the time I walked in the building, and it was eerily quiet. Melissa gave me a small smile and said, "I'm so sad to hear about Sgt. Cox."

I nodded and headed to my office. Thomas and Titus had gone home, so I sat down at my desk and just stared at the wall. I was at a loss what to do. Sgt. Cox wasn't our supervisor anymore and there was nothing I could do about it. I then pictured Sgt. Bagg coming out of Captain Zander's office smiling, and I knew there was some kind of plot going on and it was only a matter of time before I found out what it was. It had been months since that meeting with Bagg, but his words floated through my head again regarding the 20th: *If I have to take it down myself, I will, and I'll make sure you go down with it.*

The last time I'd thought about his words was when I suspected he was behind DA Chad Ball's decision to take away all our Assistant DAs, and we had to scramble to form a new team of nightshift supervisors for the wire room. How many more times would Bagg meddle with the 20th and our work?

My phone buzzed but it wasn't a number I had in my phone. I read the text, "It's James. On wife's phone. Will text you. Official suspension meeting in the morning."

I typed back, "Good luck. I always have your back."

"Thanks."

I then stood to head back to my car. I went to my favorites tab in my phone and clicked on my dad.

"Hey, son."

"Hey."

"You okay?"

I took a deep breath as I got in my car. "Dad, it's the same old shit. I thought it was different on the 20th, and it is. But, it's—it's not—"

"It's not immune to the department hypocritical bullshit."

I nodded even though he couldn't see me.

He asked, "What happened now?"

I told Dad everything James had told me and everything Cream had told us in the meeting. I described Bagg coming out of the Captain's office smiling. I even told him about that last big meeting I'd had with Bagg when he'd threatened the 20th and how even then, almost nine months ago, it felt more like a warning rather than an empty threat. I also told him about my suspicion that Bagg was behind Ball's decision to remove the Assistant DAs from the wire room.

I then remembered how James and I had yelled in the warehouse, "SUCK IT, BAGG!" after the December takedown. I told Dad how it felt like we had just been duped this whole time. Sgt. Dick Bagg was still around, and I knew he was planning something and had something to do with James getting suspended.

Dad listened and sympathized. He didn't try to make light of any of it, and he didn't tell me to let go of my anger about it. He understood it all. When I was done, he said, "All of that really does suck."

"Yeah." I said, sitting in my driveway in the cooling car. "It really sucks."

"But you know what doesn't suck? The work you're getting to do with the 20th. You have your dream job, and you just make every second of it count. Focus on your work, son. I know the bullshit feels like a lot, but you haven't lost James as a friend, and you've still got your family and we're healthy and you're healthy."

I smiled. "I got this fucking eye twitch, though."

"And I stand by the fact that you drink too much caffeine and don't sleep enough, but you ain't doing shit about that, are you?"

I laughed.

"Now, go kiss your wife and get some rest. Go to bed early. Everything else will work itself out, and it was never under your control anyway."

I nodded. "Thanks, Dad."

"Love you, son."

"Love you, too."

36

Throwing myself back into work did help. Dad always knew what I needed, and I was glad I'd called him the previous night. Things felt really weird the next day with James gone, but we had a new number coming in on Arturo's burner phone, which was a good sign because every major dealer that we could identify buying kilos from Arturo was a win in our book. The unknown person arranging to meet with Arturo was later identified as Giani Bell, who was a big dealer in the area who had gone under the radar for quite a while. It was clear from the text messages that Giani wanted to make a deal, but Arturo was not having it. For some reason Arturo wasn't going out of his way for this guy.

Giani said, "What it do?"

"Out with the family."

Giani brushed off the cold shoulder and said, "I'm going to grannies real quick, call me when you get done."

"Hell no, man, you take care of it! I'm not going to be able to today."

"Okay, what do I need to do?"

Arturo took a long time to respond. He was clearly annoyed with Giani and thought he was a real pain in the ass. But, Giani was clearly trying, so whatever ice was in their past melted slightly as Arturo gave in, "Alright I'll call and see if they're over there."

"Cool. Can the dude meet me in about an hour?"

"I'll give him a call, and then I'll call you."

A bit later, Arturo made good on his promise and called Giani.

He said, "They are over there."

Giani hesitated and said, "Gonna head that way but will be about an hour."

Arturo's voice raised as he said, "Well, try and get there as soon as you can cause they got some things later on tonight."

"Okay, okay. That's why I tried to call you earlier 'cause I was trying to move around earlier."

"Yeah, yeah, I was out and about. You gonna ride in your car?"

"Yeah. You have another for me to try later?"

Arturo responded, "You want to try the whole one?"

"Yeah, that would be good."

"I got it."

"Okay alright, sounds good. I appreciate it, man. We straight?"

Arturo hesitated but said, "Yeah."

The team headed to Central Pike to set up, and Giani wasn't too far behind. I guess his ass wanted to be on time, if not early, after the way Arturo was acting. We watched a black Buick Lacrosse pull into the driveway. Giani, a large black male, got out of the car and went around back. Giani was prompt, he got the stuff and got going. As he was pulling off, I caught wind of the tag. After a quick check, I realized that the car was a rental. Shit, of course.

Since we couldn't immediately track the car, we had to stick on this guy. No tracker, no pings, no helicopter, just good ole fashioned police work. Giani got onto the I-40 ramp towards Nashville and abruptly pulled over onto the shoulder. I was right behind him and almost slammed into him.

I yelled to the guys over the radio, "Stop!"

Hughes and Diesel reported back that they peeled off into a gas station.

I watched in my rearview as Giani jumped out and went to the trunk. If he thought someone was following him, this was a damn good tactic because three of us almost went right past him and got stuck on the interstate like I did. I couldn't exactly pull a U-turn on I-40, so I was going until the next exit.

"He's getting back in his car!" I reported to the guys, and they hurried to get on the highway. They followed him to 28th Avenue where he weaved his way to a triplex in a not-so-great area of town. I really could not believe some of these kilo dealers and their living conditions.

The wire room reported that Arturo texted to check on Giani and make sure he wasn't pulled over.

"U good?"

"My bad. I'm good thanks."

Arturo texted back, "K let me know when u ready to cruise again."

"Bet! Nice detail, man."

Really, this was weak-ass coded language. Giani was just sucking up to Arturo, telling him that the kilo looked good so that Arturo would work with him again in the future.

Since we now had Giani and his address on our radar, I wanted to see what he was going to do with the kilo of coke he'd just bought. He laid low the rest of that day, but at 9 am the next morning, Hughes and I set up across from Giani's home and watched his rental car and a Ford Explorer. There was very little movement all morning, but this guy was a pretty big dealer and if he wanted to start his day after lunch there was no one to stop him. I headed back to the office, thinking I knew a spot for our last camera.

Hughes came back to the office, too, because it was the 20th's annual Soup Day. Phillips held the event every year and had us invite all of our friends and family. He also invited judges, all the District Attorneys from the surrounding areas, and any officers who wanted to come try a bowl of his spicy chili. It was the one day of the year that the Batcave was open to anyone who showed, provided we knew them and trusted them.

I passed my wife in the hallway and gave her a quick kiss. Danielle had made her award-winning chicken velvet soup and was helping Phillips with organizing the event. Working full time and being in law school, I was just reminded as to how much of a Wonder Woman Danielle was.

The kitchen and hallways were packed with people laughing and slurping soup. The guys had told me it was like Christmas at the Batcave and they were right! It was hard for me, Hughes, and Director Davis to take our bowls of soup into the conference room to discuss the case rather than join the party. It was also difficult to have fun with James suspended. I couldn't let myself think too much about that because I couldn't let myself get angry all over again. I hadn't heard from him after

Chapter 36

his hearing, so I put him on the back burner in my mind. We knew that the lunch wouldn't go uninterrupted, so we needed to use our time wisely, even if that meant missing out on the fun. That was just part of the job, and it was worth the sacrifice.

While we were eating, Hughes and Director Davis suggested that we break off the Giani thread of the investigation into a part "C." Giani historically had his own big crew of people and could have been dealing as much as Lewis, if not more. We had already taken down TF-1422 "A" and Shawn's line was TF-1422 "B" but they thought there should be a TF-1422 "C" just for Giani's ring. So few cases ever had multiple parts, so this was already confusing to have it split once. We decided to at least start monitoring Giani as if he could be "C" and see how it went.

Lunch got cut short, no surprise there. Something big was going down!

At 11:45 am, the wire room alerted us that Arturo received a call from an unknown male Hispanic utilizing an 832 number. That was a Houston number.

Arturo answered cheerfully, "Hola!"

The caller responded, "Estoy a una hora de distancia. Prepare las herramientas."

"No hay problema."

"Te llamo cuando llegue a Super 8."

Arturo said, "Okay, entonces nos vemos en los apartamentos. Voy a abrir el garage."

After doing a quick Google translate, we understood the unknown male told Arturo that he was an hour away and to get the tools ready. The unknown male was going to call Arturo when he got to the Super 8, and Arturo was going to go to the Maple Leaf Apartments and open the garage. This was key information because we hadn't realized these guys had a garage at the complex. There must have been one of those detached garages for rent. It sounded like a load vehicle was coming, but it was always a tossup on how it would come in.

By the time the wire room had gotten us the call, it was already 12:30 pm, so Diesel headed to the Hermitage Super 8 since it was closest to the apartments. He drove around back and saw a silver Toyota pickup truck in the back parking lot with a Texas tag. If it was a load truck, though, where were the kilos stored? Since the truck was backed-in, Diesel crept to the back of the truck and got the tag to run. A check of the vehicle showed that it was registered to Manuel Jimenez of Crosby, Texas, right outside of Houston. This was the right truck, so now we just had to wait.

Diesel settled in his parking spot while we headed his way and set up in surveillance spots. Only a few minutes later Francisco's Dodge Ram arrived. It stopped right in front of Diesel, and he stared Francisco down but he kept rolling along without noticing. Manuel jumped out of the passenger side of the Dodge and got into the driver's seat of his Toyota truck. Both left the back of the motel and headed towards the front.

Francisco stopped at the exit like he was watching something. We were watching him, but I hoped he wasn't watching us. We were spread out: one in the motel parking lot, one across the street at the gas station, and a third at the Mexican restaurant. Even Manuel got tired of waiting on Francisco. He went around the Dodge and pulled out onto Old Hickory Boulevard.

We had to make a split-second decision on who to follow. Hughes came across the radio and said that he would follow Manuel in the Toyota if one more person wanted to go with him, and the rest could follow Francisco. Diesel went with Hughes and they followed Manuel as he got on the interstate. They followed him for an hour and finally let him go on I-24 past Murfreesboro. My best guess was that he was headed to Atlanta.

It was back towards Central Pike and the Maple Leaf Apartments for Francisco. Titus was already there and watching Mateo messing around in the apartment's rented garage. Mateo was using his silver Nissan Altima to block the front of the garage just like he did at the Central Pike house, so it was difficult to see what he was doing.

Titus said, "He's smarter than he looks if he's setting up like that. He's probably done this a long time."

When Francisco pulled up at the complex, Mateo took a break. They both ran up to the apartment and then left the complex. We tailed the Altima and Ram back to the Central Pike house.

Chapter 36

As they went inside the house, we saw our chance to take a closer look. We had a short window to walk up to the garage and try to gather any evidence we could. If there were duffle bags in there, we could go on in and take them down almost immediately. I already had it planned out: if we saw something good, then we could whip up a search warrant, execute it in the middle of the night and quietly remove all the items without them ever knowing. Then, I would just strategically leave the search warrant in the garage for them to find later. They wouldn't know what hit them!

Director Davis volunteered to walk by and take a look. He was the tallest of the current group since Titus headed home for the night, so Davis would have the best vantage point to see inside. He walked to the garage, slowly, and glanced in. I saw him pull out his phone and take a picture. Oh shit, must be something good in there. As he walked back to his Tahoe, he sent us a text; it was the picture.

The whole garage was empty!

"Damnit, I was so ready to level this place!" I replied.

"Well, there's not nothing. But, yeah, it's not full of bags of cash." Davis replied.

I looked closely at the photo and could see some items of interest: a small tool box, a hydraulic car jack, a press and seal box and some sort of plastic packaging and a black bag. These were items consistently used to extract drugs from vehicles or, in the words of Manuel, "tools." We could chalk this up as a small win because we were one step closer. Shortly after that, we terminated surveillance, knowing that Mateo could return at any moment.

The next morning, I switched out the SD card in the camera looking at Shawn's storage unit because we'd gotten word that his main man Edwin had just made a deal for Shawn. We'd gotten a lot of pictures of Shawn's cars in front of the unit. As I flipped through the images, I found a great photo of Edwin wearing a sweat suit and walking from the unit to his car. In his left hand, he held a kilogram of cocaine wrapped in black tape. He wasn't even trying to hide it!

Shawn had still been quiet for a few weeks after his rough interaction with Arturo, but he finally had something that put the fire back in him: Arturo had shorted him.

Shawn started the call on a light note, "This shit ain't right."

"Huh?"

"It's not weighing right."

Arturo tried to joke, "It's off like your money count."

Shawn had no sense of humor, though. "I'm for real, man."

"Did you get that from my cousin?"

"Yep. It's the ones with the black cast."

"The new set is coming soon." Arturo seemed to be deflecting, but Shawn wasn't having it.

"What are you gonna do about this one?"

Arturo sighed and then raised his voice, "Bring it back if it ain't good! Just quit bitchin, man!"

"Aight, man, shit."

Shawn hung up. He'd gotten some kahunas and mouthed off to Arturo, but Arturo was still running the show and could still shoot Shawn down with a raise of his voice.

Arturo's confidence sounded like he still had plenty of dope to get rid of, and he didn't have time for Shawn's bitching. He was dealing left and right, and it didn't seem to slow. He must have been sitting on dozens of kilos.

I was still dealing with the eye twitch on the last Saturday of February when Arturo seemed to be setting up a deal with another unknown male, but I had made plans that night to go out with some friends and relax. I was relieved when the deal was pushed off to another day. I needed to let off some steam, and having a couple beers with my buddies was the perfect way to do that. I was entitled to at least one drink after all this shit!

And, what do you know, by the end of the night my eye twitch was gone, and I slept like a baby. Sometimes, self-care was the way to go, as my dad had kept saying, and it also reenergized me to approach March with new purpose.

Chapter 36

The case felt like it was coming to a head, and I knew within a couple weeks, we'd be coming face to face with Shawn Perry, big-time dealer with the second Nashville cartel. Along with Shawn, we'd be taking down Milliken's TGI Fridays boys and a whole list of other dealers, causing a city-wide shut down of the active cocaine dealing business. Even if it wasn't permanent, someone would always step into place with these cartels, it would still be a huge win for the city.

Even though I hadn't heard from James since his suspension meeting several days prior, I knew he would want me to keep going with the work and putting my all into it. As he had said, the good work the 20th did was what made dealing with the bullshit actually worth it. I needed to focus on this case and make it the best the 20th and the police department had ever seen. This was our month. It *had* to be.

MARCH 2015

37

On the first day of March, a Sunday, I headed into the office as usual to find out what my dealers were up to. The wire room had intercepted calls between Arturo and a small-time dealer named Daryl, and they had set up a plan to touch base that evening for a deal. I spent the day listening in on calls and monitoring Arturo with the GPS pings. I periodically checked the cameras for all our locations, too, but it seemed like people were taking a lazy Sunday off for the most part. I even picked up a full-size lunch for myself instead of my usual Uncrustables, which really hit the spot after the evening of hanging out with my friends and having a few beers. I was ready for action, though, and paced the office impatiently. I needed to do work. I needed to stay busy.

I finally headed home and told the wire room to let me know when they received the call. A little before 11 pm, I got the call that a red GMC SUV pulled into the house on Central Pike and the deal was going down. I ran to my car and pulled up the camera footage on my phone and watched as a black male exited the SUV and walked to the rear of the house. I hauled ass to the area so I could catch this guy leaving, but the deal was too quick. I checked the video as I got close and saw the SUV pull away from the camera view.

"Shit." I was close, but not on Central Pike yet. Central Pike fed into the major artery of Old Hickory Boulevard, though, so I took a guess and headed for the intersection. Thankfully, my intuition was on Hughes' level this time, because the SUV appeared a moment later. I sped through the intersection and ran two more red lights to catch up to him. I ran his tag and got all his details for later.

Just because the vehicle was registered to Daryl Williams, though, didn't mean he was driving it. The only way to be sure was to get visual confirmation, so I needed to get up beside the SUV. I had a shot when we both stopped at a red light. I held my phone up to the steering wheel and pretended to talk at it. I turned it slightly and snapped a few photos of the driver. He was completely unaware of my presence, so it was easy to get the confirmation.

I pulled back, switched lanes, and followed Daryl as he meandered all the way home off Neely's Bend. It was a dark, quiet Sunday night, so the drive was peaceful. I wanted to call James because he was always out with me on weekend nights like this, but my last few texts to his wife's phone had gone unanswered, and he wasn't supposed to know about the case stuff anyway. He probably didn't want to at this point. I drove home wondering how Sgt. Cox was dealing with all this shit. He had always been a role model for me in keeping his cool and handling bullshit, but he'd also never dealt with something as crazy as this timeout situation.

Just after Daryl reached his house, he called Arturo to tell him he had gotten the drugs and was safe. They looked out for each other, just like James and I had looked out for each other. I tried to stop thinking about that, though, and focused on how Daryl and Arturo both said they were getting new phone lines. Damn. We were about to lose them, and our game would start all over once again.

On Monday, as we worked these backwards numbers, trying to get up on the ever-changing lines, I got a text from James' wife asking if he could call. I answered yes and headed to my car.

"Hey, man." James sounded tired.

I closed my car door behind me and settled in. "Dude, how are you doing? What happened in the suspension hearing? What's going on?"

He sighed and said, "Well, I just finished a week's suspension, my wife gave me her cell for the day to make a personal call I don't want tapped, and I'm in the bubble for the foreseeable future. So, yeah, things are super normal."

"Shit." Second only to going to the green mile, the "bubble" was an embarrassing demotion for a high ranking and high performing officer like Sgt. Cox. It was the small desk at the front of a precinct where you act as the secretary doing paperwork, answering the phone, and interacting with any random joe that walks in off the street. "That fucking sucks, James."

"Better than sitting at home in timeout."

"You have to wear a uniform every day?"

He laughed. "I don't mind that as much as you do."

"But, wait, I don't understand. Why is this happening?"

"Well, other than being punished for allegedly not managing the team at the 20th properly, there's been another . . . accusation."

"What do you mean?"

"You know our friend Karen Braden?"

"Of course. She was so awkward the few days we worked together at SID, she wouldn't even look me in the eye when I tried to talk to her. Bagg thought I was being bitter and avoiding her, but she was the one giving me the cold shoulder. Plus, she was schmoozing him hard, which was disgusting, so I stayed away from her."

"Well, that was smart. She went to OPA after my meeting with the Chief and claimed that when we were all together on the Hermitage Crime Suppression Unit four years ago, I sexually assaulted her by looking down her shirt."

I yelled, "What the fuck?"

"I know. It's not true. I have never once looked at Karen that way, and I know they can't prove anything because there is nothing there to prove, but she said it and they're making it part of my punishment."

"Shit."

"Yeah. I wanted you to know because it might come up for you, and I thought you should know."

"Jesus Christ, is she accusing me of looking at her? I wouldn't look at or touch her for all the money in the world."

James laughed. "No, but she said you were kicking in doors illegally back then. Again, no proof and I know that's not true, but it was mentioned as an aside during my hearing."

I shook my head and closed my eyes. This was so ridiculous. Then I remembered something that made me sit up straight. "Wait. If Karen's doing something shady like that, Bagg's gotta be behind this shit."

Chapter 37

"That's petty and sick, even for him." This shocked me because James had only ever been vague about Bagg's negative qualities. We had always been open with each other, but it had always been a mentor and mentee sort of friendship. I'd rant about stuff Bagg said or did and James would give advice but withhold his own opinion. I guessed James had nothing to lose being in the bubble now. Plus, he wasn't my supervisor anymore.

"No, seriously." I continued, my anger rising with each word. "After Timothy Cream told our team you were gone, I stuck around SID to talk to Lt. Spine. He went into the Captain's office with Cream, so I waited outside. Well, when Spine came back out, Bagg was with him and they were both grinning like they were planning some bad shit. I've seen that face on Bagg before. It's conniving and bad news, and I think it had everything to do with your punishment and Karen's accusations."

"Wow." Sgt. Cox said. We were both silent for a second.

"James, did I ever tell you what Bagg said in our last meeting before I came to the 20th?"

"You said he ranted at you for a long time, but you didn't give me details."

"Yeah because it was such crazy shit that I tried to just let it go. But, something he said has sort of haunted me ever since. I know that sounds stupid, but it was a threat I can't really shake. When he was talking about the 20th, he said, *If I have to take it down myself, I will, and I'll make sure you go down with it.*"

Sgt. Cox sighed. "You know, two weeks ago I would have said that man was full of hot gas and couldn't actually do anything about the 20th."

"But now?"

He didn't answer right away. "To be honest, I don't know anymore. I'd like to think he doesn't have that kind of power, but I'm on my first lunch break as a glorified secretary and will be lucky to return to my sergeant status any time soon. I don't know if he had anything to do with it, and I may never know, but . . . I don't know what to think anymore."

He sounded so demoralized I didn't know how to respond. This was worse than I thought. James was giving up.

"I should head back in probably," he said. When I didn't answer, he probably guessed at my thoughts and changed the subject. "Another thing I thought of is that I never took down the trail camera I put up for the 'A' side of the case. If you need me to go grab that at some point, let me know. I know I'm not supposed to do anything with the case, but I'm also not supposed to be talking to you." He laughed. "Everything feels so nuts."

"That it does. And, yeah, if you go grab that, that'd be great. I'll tell the team I'll handle it and they won't ask questions."

"Okay. Well, I'll talk to you soon, Bobby. Be good."

"You too, James. Talk soon."

I stayed in my car another minute thinking about the call. I went back inside the office, grabbing an Uncrustables from the fridge and headed to my office.

When I sat down at my desk, Titus turned to me and said, "OPA just called up Phillips and Director Davis."

I rubbed my face. "Of course. I hope this shit just ends soon."

Thomas offered, "It will at some point."

I looked at him. "But only when they've really taken someone down, right? Who's it going to be, huh? Sgt. Cox is gone, but who's next? Will they ever stop or will we all be on the chopping block sooner or later?"

Thomas didn't answer and didn't look away from his computer. I looked at Titus and he gave a half shrug before looking back at his computer.

I knew getting mad at them, especially Thomas, wasn't helping anyone, but I could feel myself starting to boil over. I was so on edge from the phone call with James. I got up and went to find Hughes. I needed some time alone and doing surveillance on our targets was the best way to do that.

My dad had said just to focus on my work when I faced something I couldn't control, and I certainly couldn't do shit about OPA's bullshit investigation. I didn't even know why they were interviewing Phillips. He was our main wiretap writer and had worked for the 20th longer than any of us. He stuck to office work more than field work because he wasn't under the police. He only knew about stuff after it happened or by overhearing bits of our conversations because he was always so busy in the wire room. Whenever we talked, I could always tell he was going out of his way to liven up stories and add his own twists and opinions. This was fine for day-to-day chatting, but I was worried about how OPA would approach his interview, especially since he was the person who'd had to write the tracking warrant for Officer Vong's car. Hughes had said Phillips had voiced "concerns" over tracking another officer, and I worried OPA would really latch on to that and spin it into something more incriminating.

I knew Davis' interview would be less to worry about because he was always unbiased and even-keel. He worked to be fair in all his decisions as Director of the 20th. He was not always a part of the day-to-day operations that went on out in the field, but he knew our team always worked hard to protect and progress our cases each day. He was 100% by the book and knew how important it was for proper documentation, so I hoped he would make sure his summary was as clear and accurate as possible.

Granted, he also had no control over how Korbin would summarize the interview, and it would be a while before we ever found out what conclusions OPA was coming to with these interrogations of our team.

No matter what OPA typed in a report, though, I knew exactly who had my back and that was all that mattered. Phillips and Director Davis were damn good people and investigators, so I had to trust that things would end up working out, even if things hadn't worked out for Sgt. Cox.

38

While Phillips and Davis were called in for interviews, the rest of the team was tracking Manuel Jimenez, who had just gotten back to town. He had given Arturo another call when he was returning, so we posted up at the Super 8 motel for surveillance. SA Trey Jones with Homeland Security was assisting us thanks to his friendship with Hughes, and he located Manuel's silver Toyota Tacoma at a Walgreens down the street. It was nice to have SA Jones helping us with the case. He was great at his job and he wasn't one of those Feds that would try and jack your shit and call the shots. I wished I'd had that luxury on the first half of the case, but I was glad we at least had his help now.

The truck was facing Walgreens on the Central Pike side of the building. I pulled up shortly after Collins entered the store to locate Manuel. Collins found him by the toothpaste section, so I headed inside to get a separate angle. I wanted to make sure if this was a new meeting place for dealers. As soon as I got in there, Manuel had just come out of the bathroom, but he didn't leave. He just wandered around the store like he was lost. If I worked there, I probably would have called the police on him just because he was acting that damn weird.

I got a text on my phone from our group thread. Titus had sent the group a message stating that Francisco's Dodge Ram was at the Lightning Bus station.

I didn't have time to stick around to watch Manuel with Collins, so I headed for the door and made my way to the bus station as fast as I could.

It was hard keeping up with all these dealers because they were everywhere and always on the move. It seemed like every key player had an agenda that day, too. Francisco's black Dodge Ram was on Nolensville headed towards Harding, and Manuel headed towards the Maple Leaf Apartments with Collins on his tail.

Unfortunately, what I thought would be the start to a good night of intel, turned into a night of partying for Arturo, Francisco, Mateo, and Manuel. Clearly, they were just celebrating Manuel's return to town. They headed to the fancy bars in the Gulch to have some drinks then went to a Mexican restaurant off Nolensville Road. I headed home, but several others stayed on them until they got home around 2 am. I wanted to get some sleep because I wanted to be ready for whatever business these guys had planned for the next day.

I had a feeling the garage at Maple Leaf Apartments would be the source of something huge, but the last time we looked, that shit was empty. Diesel and Hughes met up with me at the Maple Leaf Apartments around 10 am the next morning. I'd been watching Manuel's Toyota truck parked right in front of the garage door for a couple hours already. We had GPS pings set up on Manuel's phone, but the radius was spotty and unclear. He was either at the Super 8 or Maple Leaf Apartments. Hughes didn't want to lose this opportunity, so he drove 100 mph downtown to meet the judge and get a GPS tracking order signed for Manuel's truck. We needed clearer coordinates than this.

Within the hour it was granted, and I was prepared already with an extra tracker in my car, ready to go. Diesel acted as a lookout while I slid under the truck. I had to be very cautious on where to place it, though, because if this was the truck that had a trap in it, then I didn't want the tracking device to be anywhere near the trap. It would be game over at that point!

Since the guys had been out late the night before getting drunk, we guessed that they would get moving late. Thankfully, we were right, and I got the tracker placed and we got back into our surveillance positions.

Francisco's Dodge Ram didn't move until almost 2 pm that afternoon. I watched on my phone as he left the Central Pike house, and a few minutes later it pulled into the apartment complex. Diesel reported that Arturo was driving and Mateo was in the front passenger seat with Francisco in the middle.

The Dodge hung a right and immediately pulled as close as possible to the trash bins. Arturo got out, retrieved three white plastic trash bags from the truck, threw them into the bin, and then pulled off. We were itching to get to those bags.

It was shaping up to be a good day already with a tracker placed and now three bags of trash to go through. Titus and Diesel pulled up quickly to retrieve the bags that had just been thrown away, and they stood behind the dumpsters as they searched them. There were many ripped boxes of Foodsaver sealing packaging, but it wasn't the motherload. It was still solid evidence, though.

I caught up with the Dodge Ram as it left the apartments and entered I-40 heading towards Nashville. Thomas and I followed the truck, and I could see it had three people inside: Arturo, Mateo, and Francisco. We wound up at a taco stand off Antioch Pike. My team was very familiar with the stand because it was owned by a well-known cocaine dealer. Maybe this stand coined the phrase, "street tacos."

Thomas radioed to me, "Yeah, hi, can I get a fresh taco with a side of powdered cocaine?"

"Absolutely, señor!" I replied. "One ounce, or two?"

We then waited as they ate lunch and I stuffed down an Uncrustables. Diesel then reported from the Super 8 that someone just came out of Manuel's room, and it wasn't Manuel. The unknown male Hispanic, later identified as someone named Andres Gomez, walked to a Mexican restaurant nearby wearing jeans, a dark brown jacket, and, as Diesel put it, "some sweet shades."

"What can I say, this guy's got style," he added.

When Andres was inside the restaurant, Diesel headed back to the Super 8 to await his return. When Andres got back to the room, he shut all the blinds.

"Maybe he's taking a nap," Diesel said, which made us laugh. We knew this guy was just hiding shit. Manuel was never in town for long, so work was getting done and we needed to find out what that was and how this Andres guy was involved.

On the other side of town, Thomas and I followed Arturo and his boys as they went on errands. They returned to the house on Central Pike and Arturo drove off towards Antioch. Mateo headed the opposite way, and Francisco drove his truck in a whole different direction. We didn't have time to follow them all around town so we pulled off. The trackers would at least show us where they were stopping.

Diesel had been watching Andres periodically come outside to smoke, so Thomas and I headed to Maple Leaf Apartments to see if anything happened there. Thankfully, Mateo showed up an hour later and raced up the stairs to apartment 311. He returned with a blue and black duffel bag strapped over his shoulder, and he went to the Super 8 where Andres got into the car. We followed Mateo all the way back to the damn Lightning Bus station, the source of most of the incoming drugs to Nashville.

Mateo pulled in on the side and parked near the rear of the building. I got lucky and found a great vantage point. I observed Andres exiting his silver Altima and walking inside to get a bus ticket. Andres got his ticket and then came back out and grabbed the bag that Mateo had picked up from the apartment. Mateo retrieved a black Swiss luggage bag with an extended handle from behind his seat and set it behind his Altima on the ground.

This was not your average sendoff of a buddy. This Andres guy was in town for like a day and was heading home with two suitcases? There was no way in hell those bags contained clothes. Even though we were tapping people's phones, it was hard to predict exactly what these guys were going to do and when. If only we had gotten a call hours prior that had said, "Andres is going to take $500,000 back to Mexico," then we would have come up with a plan to take that money off! Hit them where it hurts: the money.

Mateo was explaining something to Andres outside of the Altima. I could tell by Andres' body language that the dude was freaking nervous. The conversation looked intense. Finally, he gathered his bags and headed over to the bus. He handed the black luggage bag to the bus attendant and kept the blue duffel bag with him, which meant the blue bag must be the money bag.

At 6:30 pm Mateo watched as the bus pulled away from the station. I'm sure he didn't give two shits about Andres. He just wanted to make sure that money got back to the cartel safely. If it didn't, it would be his ass on the line.

Once the bus pulled out onto Nolensville Pike, Mateo booked it out of there. I did my best to keep up, but I figured he was headed back to Central Pike.

The day was nuts and we were spread thin trying to keep up with these guys, but we did it. Hughes was still watching Arturo run errands and he followed him back to his trailer in Smyrna. Diesel was now over at Maple Leaf Apartments with Davis, and I followed Mateo back to Central Pike.

Director Davis radioed in at almost 7 pm and said, "Hey guys, I'm going to walk past the garage again and check it out."

Hughes said, "We've been watching it since 9 am but go for it."

"I want to make sure something didn't get put in there late last night."

I said, "Just don't get burned."

"You're funny." Davis replied.

I knew he'd keep it cool; he always did. Last time he peeked in the garage there wasn't shit, just some remnants of materials that indicated a car was being fixed up. Just as Director Davis reached the garage this time around, the motherfucker started to open! Casually, Director Davis just kept walking as if he wasn't an undercover narcotics officer. We saw a white Dodge Caravan with a Texas temp tag approaching the garage, but we didn't know if Director Davis saw it.

I could lie and tell you I was playing it cool, but I was about pissing myself with excitement and nerves. I hadn't been this pumped since the first round of the search warrants. The white van turned into the garage and then the door closed behind it. I don't think they suspected anything; this was a populated complex and it was common for people to be out walking, usually with a dog. Little did they know what was going on right under their noses. Director Davis calmly headed back to his car and radioed in "You jinxed me, Bobby."

I laughed. "Luckily, we now know we got something in that garage!"

We had the garage surrounded, and we watched as the lights inside the garage kept turning on and off. At one point, Hughes walked past the front of the garage and then the rear. When he passed by the front, he could not hear anything, but when he walked past the garage at the rear, by the pedestrian door, he could hear someone working on the van. I was no mechanic, but when he explained the noise, I knew what was going on. Hughes checked the pings on Manuel's phone and found that he was the one inside the garage. Of course! Then it clicked for us: Manuel was the mechanic that dismantled the trap, and that was his only job! He must have been paid well for a few hours of work in close quarters with little light, but I was sure this wasn't his first rodeo.

I made a call to my wife and told her I might not be home for dinner and that it was going to be a long night. Danielle knew the drill because she'd grown up with two parents who were cops; she understood.

The minutes turned into hours, and next thing we knew it was 10 pm and Manuel was still working on that van and hadn't come out once. Suddenly, the garage opened, but only halfway, and Manuel appeared. He went under the door like a game of limbo. He walked out with something in his hand and continued to walk all the way to apartment 311. Arturo arrived a few minutes later, and two unknown males came down the stairs to meet with him. One of them entered Arturo's car with him, and the other went to the garage. Then they both went back up to the apartment and Arturo stayed in his Denali, waiting.

Manuel returned to the garage and closed the door firmly behind him. Mateo arrived at the complex at midnight and pulled up to the garage. The garage door rose, and Manuel was standing on the other side, holding a big ass black duffel bag that looked heavy for him. He got into the passenger seat of the silver Altima with Mateo and set the bag at his feet. That bag must have just come out of the trap in the van.

Mateo pulled away from the garage and Arturo followed behind them in tandem. The precious cargo needed a special escort, and I was sure they were armed to the teeth. Hughes gave them space but followed them out of the apartment complex and watched them turn right onto Central Pike. Back to the trap house!

Hughes observed the silver Altima pull into the house, but Arturo continued past and turned left on Chandler Road. The truck traveled on Chandler Road for a short distance then turned around in a makeshift driveway. Hughes passed by them because he knew it was just a heat lap. He did a big loop around the neighborhood and passed back by the house on Central Pike. The Denali was now parked in the driveway, and we knew they'd turned in for the night.

I stayed behind at Maple Leaf Apartments to watch the garage for the rest of the night. I didn't want to take my eyes off that load van, and I wanted to be right there when they got back to business in the morning, so I slept in my car.

I checked my phone when I woke up and saw I had missed a ping at 5 am, thirty minutes before. I sat up fast, my head spinning with adrenaline and saw the ping updates of Francisco's black Dodge moving from the stash house to the Super 8. I then looked up at the garage and couldn't help but yell to myself, "Fuck!"

Arturo's Denali and Manuel's Toyota truck were both parked right next to the garage, so they'd been on the move that morning, too. I never slept through a ping, but this morning, of all mornings I had slept through them, and I had no idea if anything had gone down.

For the next three hours, nothing else happened. No cars moved, and I had no idea if anything was happening in the garage or not, but nobody came out of it.

The team brought me coffee, which I seriously needed at this point. Hughes drove an old SUV the Task Force owned to the complex and parked it facing the garage. They'd rigged a camera to the mirror, but it didn't have a power source so we couldn't rely on its footage all the time.

Thomas brought Hughes back to the office for his car, and then the team took up positions at both the garage and at the Central Pike house five minutes away. Manuel was still pinging in at the Super 8, so it looked like it would be a day of waiting around for something to happen.

Around 10 am, the wire room touched base with us to let us know Shawn had made a call. He had been practically MIA for over a week, which had us guessing he wasn't dealing as much or he was using yet another new number. He had spent multiple nights at his favorite bar until the early morning hours, which we had picked up from his pings. We had gotten used to his low profile, but now that he had set up a deal with his regular buyer, Ayden McClain, we made a plan to watch the action that afternoon.

Meanwhile, Manuel, who was wearing the same clothes from the previous day, was the only guy of the team who seemed to be awake. He was just going in and out of his motel room smoking cigarettes like a freight train. Eventually, he walked to the gas station across the street and got some snacks and a couple beers.

Diesel reported that Mateo's Altima was leaving the residence at Central Pike. He followed Mateo to Old Hickory Boulevard where he turned into a Mexican restaurant. Mateo ordered and used his wait time to make a call, but we didn't have that phone tapped. Once he got his food, he just returned to his house on Central Pike.

Around 1 pm, the GPS tracking device on Shawn's car showed that he was in Madison near Ayden's house. It was around this time the wire room let us know Shawn tried calling Arturo. It was clear that Arturo was not ready and certainly not awake after his late night. Arturo was testy on the phone, but he agreed to meet Shawn later that afternoon.

An hour later, Edwin texted Shawn and said "Bro, I changed the pace of that marathon last night. Ready to run another one."

Shawn responded, "Lol okay."

No one was running a damn marathon. Sounded like Edwin was using code for how fast the cocaine was moving on the streets. Around that same time, Arturo hit up Shawn, asking if he had a "new one" yet. We couldn't figure out what he meant, but Shawn replied no. We hoped it didn't mean a "new" phone number.

Shawn headed to his storage unit and then got the text from Arturo that he was ready to meet. Ayden was still waiting, but Shawn told him it'd be a bit longer; Arturo always came first. Shawn headed to Hermitage to the Central Pike house and Hughes watched as Arturo came marching out and met Shawn at the trunk. Shawn grabbed a white bag from his trunk and the two walked to the back of the house. It was a quick one, and before Hughes could call it out over the radio, Shawn was back out on the road and headed towards the interstate.

A bit later, I checked the camera on the Central Pike house and saw the white Ford F-350 pulling into the driveway. I headed that way to see what was going down and said to Hughes, "You still watching Central Pike?"

"I'm on Shawn. What's up?"

"Check camera three."

The F-350 was just in the garage when I arrived on the scene.

Once he had been able to check the camera Hughes said, "Shit, that's the same truck from two weeks ago. I didn't know it had moved."

"Yep. Two possible load vehicles in two garages."

"We've got to stick on them. Something is going down for sure!"

When I turned around and drove by the house again, the garage door was closed and there was no visibility. The dates were running together in my head, but if Arturo had gotten a load two weeks ago from this truck and now he was getting another one, plus he was also dealing with the white van at Maple Leaf, then we needed to go ahead and wrap this baby up soon. This was too much to miss!

Arturo called Shawn to check in and he sounded panicked. Shawn had forgotten to text Arturo when he got home from making the deal with Ayden and running errands. It was always funny to hear the dealers caring about each other, or at least caring about their product. Once Shawn was home and the cocaine to its rightful owners, both could sit back and chill, at least for now.

One person who wasn't just sitting back to chill was me. I had been up the majority of the previous night, slept in my car watching that damn garage at the apartment complex, and then I'd rolled right into a new day chasing these guys all over town. I went ahead and asked for another volunteer to sleep in their car that night. Diesel was quick to respond, and I was relieved to go home for a few hours of sleep.

39

The following morning I called my dad on my drive out to Hermitage. Technically, because wiretaps were very secretive with the sensitive information, it was a criminal offense to divulge any of the intercepted conversations, which was how the leak issue had started in the first place. But I always talked to my dad about what was going on and I needed his advice.

"How's it going, son?"

"I'm fucking tired, Dad. Is this month over yet?"

Dad sighed. "It's only March 9th."

"You know, I knew this career path wasn't going to be easy, and I'm okay with that for the most part. But, Jesus, I just want to bring these guys in and be done with it!"

"Did you get sleep last night?"

"Yes! But not the night before."

Dad half-laughed and then coughed hard into the phone.

"Whoa, Dad, easy there."

He took a second to answer and I felt fear creep up the back of my neck. His throat cancer had been kicked for over a year, but it was never a guarantee.

"Sorry about that," Dad said. "Just swallowed wrong."

"You sure?"

He waited a little too long to answer. "Yeah. So, what's going on now with the case?"

"Dad . . ."

"Okay. It's really nothing to be worried about, but I'm just having some lung pain. I'm thinking it's just allergies, but I did make another appointment to make sure."

"Shit."

"No, don't do what you do and go to the worst case scenario now. It's not so bad, but it trips me up, especially in the morning. Probably because of laying down all night and then these damn allergies."

"When's the appointment?"

"Tomorrow. Results would come back next week. I'll keep you posted on it, so don't worry about it right now. You hear me?"

"I'll try not to."

"Good. You've got enough on your plate. So, what's got you stressed this morning?"

I tried to put out his lung pain out of my mind. The last thing Dad ever wanted was people unnecessarily worrying about him. I was extra glad I had thought to call him this morning, though. I thought I was going to lose him a couple years ago, and that feeling never really goes away. Every phone call with him was important because I would always know what was going on with him, and he could always know what was going on with me.

I told him about the two load vehicles but about how difficult it was to prove anything was being moved or when it was happening. I also updated him on how Phillips and Davis had been interviewed by OPA but nothing else had happened from that, yet.

"Have you heard from James again?"

"Not since his first day in the bubble."

"Poor guy. Next time you talk to him, you let him know I'm proud of him for mouthing off to the administration. I would have done the same thing."

I laughed. "Will do, Dad."

"And you just keep working hard. Fuck them. All that matters is this work and you've got it in the bag! Just be patient and wait for the right moment. You and Hughes will take those suckers down before too long and you'll be heroes."

I smiled. "Thanks, Dad. It is easier to wake up at 5 am when I know soon I'll be taking these punks down. I just hope we catch them sooner rather than later."

"You will. I got a feeling. Take a nap when you can. Take care of yourself, son."

"You too, Dad. I'll talk to you later."

I had just pulled up beside Diesel who looked as bright-eyed as he had the night before. Then I noticed he had a giant cup of steaming coffee. He grinned at me and radioed, "Hughes is just the best, ain't he?"

I laughed as Hughes came over the radio and said, "Aw, shucks. Get back to work and keep your eyes on that garage."

Titus came over the radio from the Super 8 and said Manuel was pacing the lot, circling the building, and looking extra shifty. Hughes radioed that he was heading that way. For the next hour, we watched our cameras and the garage but nothing happened other than Manuel really working on getting his steps in for the day.

Around 9 am, Francisco drove his Dodge Ram from the Central Pike house to the Super 8. Titus snapped pictures as Manuel came out carrying an almost-empty white, plastic sack. He got in the truck and they headed back to the Central Pike house with us on their tail. For the next two hours we all sat in our cars, just staring at all the cameras, trackers, and pings.

"This shit's way too calm," Collins said over the radio.

Hughes said, "Like the calm before a storm."

As if this was the magic word, things started to pick up. Like a strategic game of Tetris, the Dodge Ram pulled out into the street, making room for Mateo's Altima to pull out first. Then Francisco followed the Altima so closely it seemed like their bumpers were touching

Manuel was with Mateo as the two cars headed over to Maple Leaf. Collins and I followed both cars through the complex as they pulled up to the garage where the van was stored.

Manuel and Mateo both got out of the Altima and grabbed bags out of the back seat while Francisco circled the parking lot. Manuel took Mateo's bags and quickly headed for the garage. This had to be part of the load.

Francisco and Mateo talked for a moment before Francisco headed back to Central Pike. Mateo headed up to apartment 311.

A few hours later around 2 pm, Hughes saw Manuel come out of the backside of the garage through the pedestrian door and he headed to the breezeway. As if on cue, Mateo came down from 311 and met him in the parking lot. They then opened both passenger side doors of Mateo's Altima and leaned to the floorboards.

"I'm going to try and see what they're doing," I said as I pulled out and headed towards them. I was worried they were looking for the tracker on the underside of the car, but it looked like they were trying to hide something in the floorboards. Then Mateo stood up straight and stared right at me. I kept on going and drove out of the complex.

Titus said, "Man, if glares could kill, you'd be dead, Bobby."

"Shit," I said as I headed to the Central Pike house. I'd basically been burned so I'd need to keep a more careful distance for a bit.

Hughes then said, "Mateo's going back inside, and Manuel's heading back to the garage. I got an idea. I have a dog leash and I'm going to try and get a closer look or at least try to hear something."

"What'll you say if they catch you?" Titus asked.

"I'll say I lost my shih tzu puppy."

I said, "Well, you are the king of bullshitting. Go for it."

Hughes made a pass through the parking lot and reported back that he could hear loud banging of metal tools inside. It was just a matter of waiting, so we settled in.

At almost 4 pm, Manuel exited the garage looking dirty and completely exhausted. He walked up to apartment 311 and went in. After being inside several minutes, Manuel and Mateo appeared in the breezeway. They walked to Mateo's Altima, both got in and left.

"Damnit, they're leaving again and that van's still there." Titus said.

"Don't follow." Hughes said. "They'll be coming back."

Sure enough, twenty minutes later the Altima returned with another guy, someone we hadn't yet seen or identified. He was a big guy, bigger than even Diesel.

Titus laughed, "Their group's got a 'Swole,' too!"

Hughes said, "Indeed. Looks like they're putting a spare tire on the back-passenger side of the Dodge minivan."

An hour later, Mateo came out of the garage carrying tools and put them inside the trunk of his Altima. Manuel came out, too, and got in the car with Mateo.

Finally, after hours and hours of waiting, the white Dodge minivan with a Texas temp tag started up and began to pull out of the detached garage at the Maple Leaf Apartments.

"Action time!" Titus yelled.

"Thank God!" I said in return.

I was so excited! We had already made the decision that if the van started heading west, we were going to take it off. The van made its way through the complex to the front and it was being driven by the unknown male Hispanic. They headed towards the interstate, so the team followed and coordinated our positions to pull it over.

"Shit," Hughes said. "They're stopping at the Super 8."

The van turned into the motel so the team spread out in the area to wait and avoid getting burned.

"Would this van just get going already?" I asked. The whole team was on edge, but no one was as ready and amped up as I was. I was ready to take them down and be done with this!

The Altima came out solo just a few minutes later. We had to put at least one guy on it to see where it was going, so Titus followed it back to the Maple Leaf Apartments. Of course.

Manuel got out of the passenger seat, jumped in his silver Toyota pickup truck and left. Mateo also left. No need to follow Manuel; that truck had a tracker. So, we made sure Mateo headed back to the Central Pike house, which he did, and the whole team met back around the Super 8.

Hughes was able to find a small opening between some trees and had an eye on the van. The unknown male Hispanic was only inside briefly before coming out of room 325. He wasn't carrying much, just a plastic bag and an orange soda, so if he was about to drive to Texas he was going to need more food. We followed him out of the Super 8 towards the interstate, our radio chatter growing.

Hughes said, "Alright guys, pay attention."

I added, "We got this!"

Director Davis said, "Let's not heat him up too early."

Titus asked, "Did y'all call interdiction yet?"

"Already done it," Hughes replied.

Davis said, "Okay, if you got the eye, then you got the air!"

"Wait, does this dumbass not know the interstate is to the right?" I asked. He had his left turn signal on.

Titus tried to encourage him like training a dog, "Come on, dude, look to your right, it's 200 yards away, don't fuck this up, come on, buddy."

"Well, not hitting the interstate clearly," Hughes said. "Keep on him."

The van turned left on Old Hickory Boulevard and then turned left onto Lebanon Road. It then pulled into the San Juan Tire Shop.

"Apparently the guys didn't fix the tire earlier and need some professional help," Hughes said.

I said, "If this is just about a tire, it seems a little risky if this van is loaded down with money."

Davis said, "We'll have to wait and see. If it is a bad tire, he wouldn't make it far on the interstate anyway."

Twenty minutes later the van pulled out of the bay with a new tire. The unknown male Hispanic took the same route back towards the interstate rather than hop on at the closer entrance ramp. He got on the interstate headed in the right direction: west towards Texas.

He stuck to 62 mph in the 70 mph zone, but he was on the bumper of a Chevy truck. Interdiction Officer Spencer Boone was locked in right behind the van and activated his emergency equipment. I think our whole team held our breath, waiting to see if this dude would lead us on a high-speed chase.

Thankfully, the unknown male Hispanic pulled to the shoulder of the interstate very slowly. Officer Boone walked to the passenger side window and asked the driver for identification. The driver, identified as Guadalupe Valdez, handed over a Texas identification card. He knew what was going down, and Officer Boone didn't waste any time. He had Guadalupe go ahead and step out of the van.

"I stopped you because you were following that truck too closely."

"Okay."

"Do you have any illegal drugs or large amounts of currency in the van?"

"No. No understand good English."

"If there's nothing in the van then can I search it?"

"Huh?"

Office Boone surprised Guadalupe by then saying, "Puedo buscar su vehículo?"

"Oh, si, si."

"Okay. Parate aqui." He told Guadulpe to stop and wait, and then he said he was getting his dog to search.

Officer Boone deployed his drug sniffing K-9 named Koda on the van. That dog went crazy! Scratched the shit out of the passenger and the driver sides of the van. Officer Boone wanted to take a quick look to see if he could find something before we took it back to the Drug Task Force warehouse, and it didn't take him long. He peeled the dashboard back and saw some square objects that were taped up. He knew that shit wasn't normal.

Officer Boone took custody of Guadalupe and transported him to the Homeland Security office. Hughes and SA Jones followed to interview Guadalupe. He wasn't going to be able to play that game where he claimed to not know or understand English because SA Jones was fluent in Spanish.

Thomas jumped in the van and drove it back to the office with the rest of our team in tow.

I hadn't eaten all day, so I grabbed some pizzas and took them to the office so everyone could eat before we searched the van. We had as many hands in that van as we could, searching every inch of it. We pulled four kilograms of cocaine, lumpy ones at that, and $197,400 cash from the dashboard. It was all wedged in there, not sparing a single inch. The money was wrapped in bundles, vacuum sealed and taped up. We were using box cutters to open the packages and we accidentally sliced through a stack of money. Nothing a little tape couldn't fix!

Chapter 39

As Hughes and SA Jones tried to interview Guadalupe, we kept sending pictures of what we were finding. SA Jones went at Guadalupe hard, but he stuck with the same lame ass story. He was just a regular guy, a hard worker who buys and sells cars. We released Guadalupe and gave him the seizure paperwork. Guadalupe managed to speak very clear English when he requested his seizure paperwork. He knew that if he didn't have something to show for the seizure then it was his ass on the line with the cartel, maybe even his family's asses too! After interviewing Guadalupe, he was transported to the bus station. Bet that was a long ride back to Texas empty handed!

Even though $197k was a shit ton of money, something still wasn't right. Hughes made it back to the office and we were talking about the money to kilo ratio. Officer Boone and the interdiction unit were getting ready to drive the van out of the warehouse when I stopped them.

"Where y'all taking the van?"

Boone said, "We're taking it to SID to use it as a training aid with the other interdiction guys."

"Can you just leave it for the night?"

"We took the whole damn thing apart." Boone laughed, looking at the van.

"I know. We need some better pictures, though. Can I give you a shout tomorrow when we are done with it and you can come get it?"

Boone shrugged. "Sure."

"Thanks. Also, you did a great job tonight! Thank you for your support."

"Anytime, man! That was pretty badass."

He grinned and we shook hands. He headed out and I talked to Hughes about searching the van again the next day. We told Director Davis and then locked up. It was midnight and it had been a long few days, but at least we had something big to show for it. The only thing to worry about now, though, was how long until Arturo and his boys figured out what had happened.

The next morning, Milliken had gone downstairs to look over the van, and we heard him shout, "I found it!"

I almost busted my ass as I sprinted down those metal warehouse stairs.

He was still yelling and pointing inside the rear of the van. He'd ripped out a side panel and deep within the cavity was the edge of a package. The team met up with us and we looked at each other. There *was* more in the van. We ripped out all the panels and gathered up another $120,000 in cash. That was $317,200 in total from this one van.

Hughes laughed and put his hand on my shoulder, "Good call on not letting Boone take it last night. There was more, and we found it."

"I knew it. Manuel was in that garage way too long. There had to be more."

Titus said, "Can you imagine if this van had been sold at auction? Some random dude would be riding around with $120k in his back seat!"

40

It had been several days, and we hadn't heard anything from Milliken's TGI Fridays boys. We weren't sure if Arturo knew we took his shit, but they were laying low. Quiet was good for us, though, because we needed to complete all the paperwork including the forfeiture warrants.

Taking this whole operation down was now the immediate goal, and we felt like it was the perfect time. We had branched off with Giani Bell and made a TF-1422 "C" entry in the case book, but we learned pretty quick that Arturo was his only source of supply. The only way to go up the chain from where we already were was to start tapping phones in Mexico and start hitting doors down there, something slightly out of our jurisdiction. I loved my job, but the thought of getting tortured and disappearing in Mexico was not my idea of fun.

Late one night, after everyone was home, the wire room intercepted a call between Arturo and Daryl, the guy I had successfully identified only two weeks before in his car after a deal.

Daryl said, "I tried to call you a couple times to see if I could come get some breakfast."

"That's cool. What time?"

"About 8ish."

"Can't. I got a school play I'm going to at 8:00. But, they all pretty this time and ready to go." Arturo was quite the family man.

"Okay, I'm in. I'm gonna swing right back."

When Daryl called back, they set up for a deal at 7 am, but the wire room supervisor didn't catch the call and the lingo. They thought the two were really talking about having breakfast together, so they didn't alert us of the deal going down. It was hard not to get mad at these contract Assistant DAs for missing key deals. Since DA Ball had sabotaged the case by pulling all the Davidson County Assistant DAs early on, we were relying on ones from other counties who didn't have much, if any, experience with wiretaps. We were grateful to have their assistance at all, though, because it left more time for us to follow these guys around town or get the rare much-needed sleep.

After seeing we'd missed the deal, the wire room intercepted a call Arturo made to Daryl.

Daryl said, "Was just fixing to call you and let you know that I was good. I'm safe. May try another one in a little bit, but I will still get another one of them." I couldn't tell what he was talking about, but Arturo clarified it for me.

"This one is fixing to run out of minutes." Shit. More phones. Hopefully we'd get to take these guys down before we had to figure out this guy's new number. We were so close!

Diesel turned to camera three's surveillance and rewound the footage. We saw Daryl pull into the house on Central Pike and stay there fifteen minutes. Thank god for these cameras or we would have had no evidence on this deal.

Given that Arturo was doing business as usual, it either meant he didn't know we got Guadalupe, or he did and just didn't give a shit.

I called my dad on the way to the Central Pike house to do surveillance. I wanted to check in because he should have heard back from the doctor by this point.

"Hey, Dad."

"Morning. How's it going?"

"Good. Just wondering if this case is going to finish in time to make it to the lake this summer."

"You think it'll wrap up in time?"

"It depends. I mean, we're determined to get the biggest load, even if that means waiting several more months. But, man, it took up almost all of last summer and I only got to go to the lake once before I joined this team. I don't want to miss it this year."

"Well, I don't want you to, either, but be careful what you wish for. This case has gotta be done right. You don't want to rush it."

"I know. And we will do it right. But, I want to have lake time with everyone."

"Me too." Dad sounded down, and I started to feel nervous.

"So, did you hear back from the doctor?"

He sighed. "It's still not for sure, but they saw something in the CAT scan."

"Shit."

Dad said, "But, even if it is something, which it may not be, it very well could be benign. Doc said there's even a chance it's just a scan error."

I nodded and started feeling a welling-up of all the fears and stress from years' back when Dad got his first diagnosis. It was just a "something" in a scan then, too, and it ended up being throat cancer.

"Also, not to start your morning off on the wrong foot, but Ashley fell again."

"Really?"

"She's at the doctor this morning. Text her later if you think of it. She acts strong because she's a momma, but I'm sure she's worried."

"Yeah, I'll check in. She didn't hurt herself did she?"

"No. It happened when she was getting out of bed and she was able to lean back enough to fall on the mattress."

"That's good." I tried to swallow down the stress. I wanted to ask Dad more questions about his stuff, but I also knew Dad probably didn't want to talk about it. Not yet, not until he knew what was causing the pain in his lungs. I was also thrown off by worry for Ashley. All I knew was the last time she saw the doctor nothing had been determined. They told her to keep taking it easy.

Dad filled the silence and said, "Where you headed this morning?"

I answered automatically, "Central Pike."

"Deals going down?"

"Yeah, we missed one, but Diesel saw they were already moving on the camera, so we're headed there."

"That's good, son. You've almost got them, just keep it up and take care of yourself, okay? Your momma's just brought me breakfast, and I'm going to eat it while it's hot."

Chapter 40

"All right. Enjoy, Dad. Talk to you later."

We hung up right as I pulled into my spot near the Central Pike house. I turned up my radio as Thomas said, "I followed Francisco's truck to Maple Leaf. He just dropped a bag in the dumpster."

I radioed in, "Heading your way."

Dumpster diving was the perfect distraction. When I arrived, Thomas had hauled the bag out of the dumpster before the system could compact everything down. We took pictures of our findings: rubber gloves, rubber bands, plastic wrapping, and boxes of vacuum seal bags. It was a lot of rubber. It wasn't the fifty kilos-worth of wrappers that we wanted, but this would do. It was all part of the case.

We let the truck go on its merry way because we had to shift our focus back to Giani who had been in touch with Arturo.

Giani said, "Yo what's up big homie?"

"Not shit."

"How them cars looking?"

"They pretty. How many you want?" Arturo was not in the mood to play along with Giani this morning.

"My boy wants to swap one out. I'm going to need two, and I'm gonna drive both cars."

"Come around 6:00."

"Bet."

Arturo didn't give a shit about all the lingo and he wasn't amused. He was all business and just wanted to know how many kilos of coke Giani was getting.

We planned to be at Giani's a little after 5 pm since he lived north of town, and I was glad we went early. I wasn't there too long before I saw Giani come out of the front door with a white bag. Giani placed it in the trunk and took off. I knew he was going to be on time. Hell, Giani even accounted for traffic hour. He did not want to fuck with Arturo. If Arturo cut you off, then you could kiss your income goodbye.

Giani was early and pulled down the driveway of the Central Pike house. He went inside and stayed a long time. After thirty minutes passed, we began to get worried. Giani was usually only there sixty seconds and he was out. Maybe he was short money and pissed Arturo off enough that he just finished him? I wasn't sure what we would do if he never came out. Drug dealers get killed all the time but not usually while someone was watching.

In the meantime, I texted Ashley to check in. She replied she got a doctor at Vanderbilt who wanted to run a few tests. She said she would have to do at least one more round of tests in a week or so before they could make a diagnosis. I told her to keep me posted and wished her luck on the tests.

Lucky for our team, or maybe lucky for Giani, he did emerge with what looked to be two kilos and headed back to North Nashville a bit before 7 pm. We headed home after making sure he got home safe, and I got a few decent hours of sleep despite my family worries. Medical stuff was always about waiting around for bad news, which I realized was a lot like my job where we were just waiting around for what was probably going to be bad news from OPA. I still held on tightly to my hope that all the medical stuff would turn out okay and that OPA would be reasonable and not take anyone else down from our team. We were feeling the effects of not having James' help already and couldn't afford to lose someone else for a bullshit reason.

The next morning, I didn't have to wait long for bad news. A local news story reported that a person found a bomb under their car. It turned out it wasn't a bomb, but it still hadn't been identified. The newscaster urged citizens to be wary of mysterious devices as they could be criminals tracking those they hope to rob.

Even though it was just a brief morning segment, it turned out our dealers had tuned in. We were set up watching the Central Pike house when Arturo arrived in his Denali at 8:30 am.

"Man, he's up early." Thomas said.

"Dealing knows no hours," Collins piped in wisely. We laughed and I turned on the surveillance camera footage to see what Arturo was up to.

"Oh God," I radioed. "He's on his hands and knees looking under his car!"

"Shit!" Collins and Thomas said together.

I just kept praying, Please don't find it, don't find it, please don't. Then I got an alert notification on my phone. The alert said, "Device Removed."

"Fuck!" I yelled. I then radioed to the team, "He got it! Shit!"

This was a huge problem. Once they found the trackers, all their phones would go down, they might buy different cars, move addresses, destroy evidence, hide drugs . . . this could turn the entire case upside down. I couldn't help but remember Dad saying, *Be careful what you wish for.* I then prayed that my own selfish prayer hadn't just royally fucked up the case.

Hughes said, "Damnit! This is not good. Come back to the office. We need to make a plan to take these guys down right now."

An emergency meeting took place at the office as we watched Arturo, Mateo, and Francisco walk to the other three cars in the driveway and get on their hands and knees. Francisco was too fat to get all the way under his truck, so he didn't find that one. Mateo was skinny, but we didn't have a tracker on his Altima. What Arturo did next was unthinkable, and just plain stupid.

Arturo gave the tracker from his Denali to Mateo, they talked for a bit, and then Mateo got in his car and drove away. Not a whole lot we could do, just watch the tracker to see where Mateo destroyed it. Mateo jumped on I-40 toward Nashville, so I mentally thanked God he was at least heading away from the lake. He continued on to I-65 south and we could not figure out where he was going.

We spent the day scrambling, running around the office calling everyone in the area who could possibly help with executing search warrants. We had thirty-one warrants that we had to get approved and assigned, and we spent the whole day planning for an early morning takedown the next day. Thankfully, we'd worked on the search warrants for the target locations for months, so other than organizing personnel we were relatively on top of things.

A small part of me was happy because I knew we were about to take this case down, but this was not the way I saw it happening. We had plenty of evidence, we just had no idea what we would get, especially if the dealers started hiding their shit or moving it to new places. Twenty four hours was a long time for a dealer to disappear or make things disappear if he wanted to.

While we made plans at the office, Mateo drove all the way to Huntsville, Alabama where he stopped at a strip mall. Google street maps told us exactly where he was headed. The tracker went right in the front door of an electronics store, actually a "spy" shop. Nothing we could do but laugh at that point.

We watched as Mateo drove back to Nashville. He didn't throw the tracker out the window or into the lake or stomp it under his foot. He didn't do anything at all to it as he returned to the house on Central Pike. He just left the tracker on the passenger seat of his car.

Arturo had left the Central Pike house and our camera showed he returned to his trailer and stayed there all day. We had no idea if he knew what was up. Maybe he switched cars or had someone pick him up down the street? Maybe he was busy burying his money and destroying his dope? He could have been doing all those things; there was no way for us to know. We were so focused on organizing and assigning the numerous search warrants to be executed bright and early the following morning.

Four of the warrants would be easy since they were just storage units. Director Davis called the necessary personnel for a quick briefing that afternoon. Hughes, Diesel, Price, Thomas, Collins, Milliken, and I were busting our asses to finish up a few things, fine tuning the search warrants and the packets. We were glad it was a Wednesday and not a Friday or the weekend because we would have been screwed.

41

At 5 am on March 19, 2015, I briefed my team behind a church on Central Pike. It was dark and freezing ass cold, but I was sweating with nerves. I knew that all the cars were where they were supposed to be at the Central Pike house, but I didn't know if the people would be sound asleep still or not.

As much as I wanted to be the one blasting that door open and yelling, "Get on the fucking ground!" I chose not to. I was overseeing the execution and search team, which meant I was the odd man out. I'd been on a ton of dope busts, but I'd always been one of the men breaking in the door. This time, as the leader, I volunteered to cover the back, waiting in the woods behind the house before the cavalry rolled in the driveway. It wasn't a long driveway, but it was gravel and it wasn't very wide. Only one car could come down the driveway at a time, so the street would get clogged soon enough.

I provided the Tennessee Bureau of Investigation and Homeland Security agents photos of Francisco and Mateo, and then one of the agents dropped me off several houses down at 5:30 am. I jumped out of the car with my AR-15 slung over my back and began walking. There was a vacant farmhouse next door, so I knew I could use the house as cover and then circle around to come up behind the target house. If Mateo or Francisco came running out the back, it was on me to take care of business. Knowing that these kilo dealers were directly connected to a cartel meant there was no margin for error. If they chose to shoot it out with police, then I would have a tough, split-second decision to make. I was top gun, but I also knew that missing would leave a rifle round traveling a very long way, and once the bullet was out of the barrel, there was no controlling its destination. I'd be responsible for every single bullet

I shot, and if anyone was caught in the cross-fire, that victim would be on my hands.

At 6 am TBI and HSI agents barreled down the drive and filled the street. I was fifty feet from the house and crouched with my gun aimed at the back door. As I heard my team approach the front door, I watched a TBI agent approach the side door with a huge metal ram in his hand. I knew what that feeling was like: when the ram was in my hand and I was busting in a door, the adrenaline rush made me feel like Rocky. The agent raised the ram and with one swing, the door flew off its hinges into the house with a loud boom. The front door was knocked down a second later.

As the agents began yelling and entering the house, I felt sweat drip down my forehead as I continued my stare at the back door.

For a few seconds, nothing happened, and I feared the targets must have caught on to our plan and were long gone. I listened to the radio at the same time because I knew thirty other search warrants were also just beginning. When I heard our location number and the sweet phrase, "Targets in custody!" my body deflated with relief.

I stood and headed to where the side-door used to be, adrenaline mixing with the feelings of success. In the kitchen, Mateo Vargas and Francisco Hernandez were standing against a wall with their hands cuffed.

I greeted them like old friends from TGI Fridays, "Hola!" I'd known these guys for so long, living parallel to their lives and never taking my mind off them, but they looked at me in horror. For a second I had almost forgotten that they'd never seen me in their lives.

I advised Mateo and Francisco of their Miranda rights, and they claimed they didn't speak English. I almost laughed. They didn't know we'd been listening to their calls for six months and knew perfectly well they spoke English. They nodded their heads about understanding their rights, but just kept saying, "No hablo English."

HSI and TBI began tearing up the house. Agents found stacks of cash in the drawers of Francisco's rooms, and several ounces of cocaine and a semi-automatic pistol in Mateo's room. HSI was finished searching in thirty minutes and they stood in the living room with their hands in their pockets. That was all I got from the Feds, thirty minutes of work and they'd given up. TBI agents searched a little longer before they called it quits, too.

I knew there was more in this house than a wad of cash and a few ounces of coke, but I also wondered if these guys had destroyed what they could after the previous day's tracker scare. I walked around the house and looked over the good stuff that the agents had gathered and photographed: a money counter, buckets of grease, vacuum sealers, big electronic scales, and weapons. We even found the "bomb" or tracker in the back of Mateo's Altima, but something was still missing. Where was all the dope and cash? Where was all the kilos of cocaine that Shawn, Giani, and Daryl were getting from this house? HSI agents decided that they were done, and they left. There were plenty of search warrants in their schedules, so they had to get to the next one.

I called for a transport car, and an MNPD officer showed up to take Mateo and Francisco to booking. The officer was young, just a rookie, so I asked him if he had ever seen a stash house before. He hadn't, so I took him around the house, showing him the packing materials and other evidence we had found. I knew something like this was exciting when you were new, especially since only a handful of officers would ever work on a case like this. Mateo and Francisco asked for coats because it was cold with the front and side doors gone. I let them put their hoodies on and then had them go with the officer. For some reason, both of them had this little smirk on their face as they walked out the front door, so I knew we were missing something big.

I called the TBI agents together in the kitchen. It was like we were in the last game of the World Series, and I was trying to orchestrate a winning run in the last inning of the game.

"Look guys, I know there is some shit in here. This is the main stash house and we just haven't found the right spot, yet. Let's keep looking. I'm going to call interdiction and see if they can bring a dog over here."

They entertained my request and the seven split up to search the house again. I heard knocking and banging as they tested furniture, the floors, and the walls. After only a couple minutes, I heard yelling from the far side of the house in the garage, which usually meant a motherload was found. I ran to the detached garage and saw several agents leaning over that same ole white Ford F-350 truck, staring at the bed.

One of the agents had wrenched the hydraulic truck bed up and removed it completely. That's when they discovered that the entire bottom was a false compartment.

Someone pointed at the ropes coming out of each side of the compartment and asked, "What's with the ropes?"

I explained that wood was attached to the other side, and how I'd seen numerous hidden compartments like this where they placed a wooden block with rope attached to it into the farthest areas of the trap. They would then pack the kilos into the cars in front of the block and pull on the rope to drag everything in the compartment out when they got to their drop spot.

I started pulling on the rope, it was really long, and finally the block of wood came out and hit the ground, thump! No kilos of coke. I shone my light into the compartment and saw it was completely empty.

I hoped for the other compartment as I began pulling that rope out slowly for dramatic effect. When the block came out with no drugs, it was like being kicked in the stomach.

"Damn." I said. "Well, this truck was clearly used at one point, but not now. Several of us went back inside. I was feeling low. We'd only gotten a few thousand dollars and not even a quarter key of coke and suddenly it was just over. That was just how it worked out sometimes, and I needed to just hope all the other locations produced something big.

When I got to the living room, one agent was cracking jokes near the entertainment center that featured a huge flat screen television. As he tried to straighten up when I entered, he stumbled and broke a piece off the top of the entertainment center. He looked at his hand in surprise. "Oops."

He then looked at me and we both realized at the same time that pieces of an entertainment center do not usually chip off so easily. He leaned to peer into the hole he'd just created and then yelled, "Hell yes!"

I breathed a sigh of relief. Finally!

Instead of having thick, wooden supports, the whole center was made out of very thin plywood sheets. As the agent easily pulled off the front panel of the top section, bundles and bundles of cash fell out. I'd never seen anything like it in real life! This was the kind of shit that happened on episodes of *Narcos* or *Breaking Bad*, but it was live and in front of my own eyes!

I walked over and kicked the bottom part of the entertainment center. The thin facade fell to the ground and a brick of cocaine poked out amidst more bundles of cash. We moved the flat screen to the floor and then disassembled the entire entertainment center piece by piece.

I radioed the rookie officer who had Mateo and Francisco and asked if he was still driving to the station. He said he was, so I told him to turn around and bring them back.

While we waited for them to return, we decided to have some fun. We took pictures of the glory spilling out of the center, the cash alone amounting to more than $500,000 from what I estimated, and then the team quickly reassembled the cheap plywood and snapped it all into place.

I told the officer to bring the guys through the front door. When Mateo and Francisco came back to their house, they were looking at me like, "What?"

I started bullshitting with them. I told them we were going to decide which items to seize and which to just leave. I began asking which property belonged to which person. I started with some clothing, then a ladder, then the couch, and the flat screen. For each item, they decided who owned what. When I pointed to the entertainment center, they remained silent.

I shrugged as if I couldn't care less. "Well, if no one is going to claim the entertainment center then we'll just dump this. We have to get it out of here because we are seizing the house, so we can just set it out by the road."

Francisco's eyes got huge, but Mateo stayed looking down at the hardwood floors.

Chapter 41

I then leaned against the frame and said, "Well we're done here, so we'll throw this out." I put my weight into it and the whole side piece broke off and fell to the ground. Cash and bricks tumbled out of the side of the center.

I grinned. "Mucho dinero!"

Then I kicked and pulled off the other pieces hiding the stash, and then stood back to take in the view. Francisco and Mateo stared at the entertainment center as the money and drugs covered the floor near their feet.

"So," I said after a moment, "where did all this come from?"

Mateo then said one word: "Lawyer."

"Well, what a surprise! You do speak English!"

I then let the rookie officer take a few pictures with all that money and dope to show his friends. Mateo closed his eyes, refusing to watch, but Francisco shook his head back and forth. Then I told the officer to take them on to jail.

I was supposed to go to other houses to help execute warrants and interview suspects, but we were at the Central Pike house a long time. Leaving the house on Central Pike that afternoon was like walking out of a movie. I'd already been sent pictures of Shawn's storage unit, and it alone held over fifty kilos of cocaine. I could only imagine how a hot metal locker full of coke would smell. It'd be like a chemical punch to the face.

I touched base with Hughes who had led the warrant at Shawn's house. Even though he was so serious most of the time, Hughes cracked up as he told me about showing the picture of the storage unit's finds to Shawn.

"Dude, I think he realized that he was a goner, because he literally peed on himself in fear."

I laughed too. "Shit, going back to federal prison would make me piss myself, too."

When the day was over, after all thirty-one search warrants were completed, the 20th Judicial District Drug Task Force had one hell of a seizure. We couldn't release anything to the department or the media because there were still a few loose ends that had to be tied. We were also waiting on a team of HSI agents that were sitting on a house in Dallas, Texas.

Besides Shawn pissing his pants, there was another search warrant that revealed some interesting information. At the residence of Shawn's in-laws, no one was present because they were already at work. After forcing entry, officers discovered 337 grams of cocaine, a loaded 9 mm Keltec rifle, several bundles of cash, and some paperwork. The paperwork revealed that his mother-in-law worked for the Veterans Court in the General Sessions Court of Davidson County, yet she had a bunch of cash and cocaine just lying around her house. It would be hard not to find conspiracy there.

Similarly, Shawn's wife worked at a prominent hospital in the area, but she had to know her husband's line of business. It was clearly all in the family. That afternoon when Shawn and his boys were getting settled into their cots in the gym at booking, Shawn made a call to his wife.

"Hey pretty, how are you doing?"

Rakell said, "Loving you, but we are doing good."

"Yeah."

"Just hold tight," she said. "Them people are just being nosey and just fishing. Hang in there, it's gonna be a hell of a ride, but we gonna fight."

I had to laugh. Yeah, we were just being "nosey" and finding dozens of kilos of cocaine meant they still had a chance to get out of this. Right.

The next day, I woke up to the official media release.

> *A six-month investigation into the lucrative upper echelon of a Nashville cocaine distribution network led to Thursday's seizure of more than 50 kilograms (in excess of 100 pounds) of Mexican cocaine valued at nearly $2 million. Hundreds of thousands of dollars in cash has also been seized, as well as 20 vehicles, 2 motorcycles, and 13 guns. Nine persons are jailed locally on charges of engaging in a cocaine conspiracy. They are being held in lieu of $500,000 bond each.*

Chapter 41

"The cocaine seized in this investigation posed a real and significant threat to public safety in the neighborhoods where it was to be distributed," Chief Luther Smalls said. "Drug operations such as this frequently breed violent crime, including armed robberies and gunfire, as persons try to acquire a cut of the large sums of money associated with kilo quantities of cocaine."

All totaled, this case has resulted in the seizure of 75.5 kilograms of cocaine valued in excess of $2.6 million from locations in the Nashville area and Dallas, Texas. More than 20 search warrants were executed Thursday in the local area.

"Congratulations to the Metro officers on the Drug Task Force [...] for their excellent work to keep drugs off our streets and make Nashville a safer place to live," said District Attorney General Chad Ball.

This investigation, conducted by Metro police detectives assigned to the 20th Judicial District Drug Task Force, initially focused on convicted Nashville drug felon Shawn Perry, 41, now an alleged multi-kilo distributor of cocaine to mid-level dealers. As the case advanced, detectives were able to identify Arturo Gonzalez, 33, of Smyrna, as the alleged supplier to Shawn. Arturo, originally from Mexico, is a convicted cocaine felon who received a 10-year community corrections sentence in 2011.

Arturo is alleged to have been assisted in the cocaine business by Francisco Hernandez, 30, and Mateo Vargas, 23, both originally from Mexico, but who have been residing off of Central Pike, just inside Wilson County. A search of that home Thursday led to the discovery of cocaine and stacks of cash concealed inside an entertainment console.

Fifty kilograms of cocaine were discovered Thursday inside a Brick Church Pike self-storage unit alleged to have been rented by Perry.

Arturo is alleged to have been supplying two other large-scale cocaine customers in addition to Shawn. Those two are identified as Giani Bell, 43, of Hurt Street, and Daryl Williams, 42, of Neely's Bend in Madison.

Three other persons charged are linked to Shawn's operations. Edwin Fields, 37, of Nashville, is alleged to have been a Shawn protégé in the cocaine enterprise. Damon Waters, 37, of Nashville, and Mason Rayner, 37, of Nashville, are alleged to have assisted in getting cocaine from Shawn to the streets of Nashville and Middle Tennessee.

Based on information developed by Metro detectives, U.S. Department of Homeland Security investigators executed a search warrant in Dallas, Texas, Thursday and seized eleven kilograms of cocaine, $10,000 cash and made two arrests.[2]

After reading the release, I decided to draw up totals for the whole case:

Round 1 in September 2014: Fifteen search warrants were executed and as a result 8 ounces of cocaine, 3.5 pounds of marijuana, meth, pills, 48 guns, and $10,615 cash were seized. No one was arrested at that time.

Round 2 in December 2014: Fifty-one search warrants were executed and as a result 30 kilograms of cocaine, 42 pounds of marijuana, a half ounce of heroin, 220 pills, 41 guns, 54 cars, 7 properties, and $488,000 cash were seized. Nineteen targets were arrested on takedown day and more were indicted later.

Round 3 in March 2015: Thirty-one search warrants were executed and as a result 60 kilograms of cocaine, a quarter pound of marijuana, 10 pills, 14 guns, 29 cars, 9 properties, and $985,000 cash were seized. Nine were arrested on takedown day and more were indicted later.

In TF-1422 "A" there were 41 people indicted and a total of 185 charges. In TF-1422 "B" there were 26 people indicted and a total of 115 charges. As a result of the case, there were a total of 67 persons indicted on a grand total of 300 charges. We had actually hit a record for one case!

With the "wall offs," the "whisper stops," and the assistance of HSI in Texas, the grand totals from case number TF-1422 were: 101 kilograms of cocaine, 74 pounds of marijuana, 103 guns, 83 cars, 16 properties, and $1,803,693 in cash! This did not include the value of all the cars, ATV's, motorcycles, houses, and parcels of land. Hell, Marlon had 15 motorcycles alone.

We were looking at over $3 million in revenue for the Task Force! This would pay our overtime and fees for the wiretaps for years to come, and I was so happy to have been the one to bring this case to the 20th. Going behind Sgt. Bagg's back and keeping the case quiet was the best decision I'd ever made. Nothing OPA could say or do could change the fact that we had successfully taken down two of the largest drug organizations in Nashville in the biggest case in Nashville history. I felt that I had made it to the top! Being with the 20th had been a dream come true. We could travel with statewide jurisdiction, there were always other units in other states that were willing to help us at any time, and we had the power to take down the big guns in the drug industry. In my mind, we were the best unit ever doing the best work ever.

Even though we had just made a record seizure, it just didn't feel the same without Sgt. Cox on the team. I was proud to be part of a team that removed so much cocaine from my city, but the politics of the police department had really affected this moment of celebration. The "leak" issue and Weakling's backstabbing and the department politics had taken a toll on our team both emotionally and physically. James had been in the bubble acting as a secretary for almost a month, and we still didn't have a supervisor which meant we were a man down. I wanted to really lean in to the short-term celebration of the most badass wiretap case in Nashville history, but there was so much weighing on my mind still.

We found out soon after that OPA was continuing their investigation regardless of our success because the Chief wasn't satisfied with Sgt. Cox's punishment. He still wanted to find a fall guy, a person who deserved to shoulder all the blame for the mess the leak caused. Sgt. Cox was punished for his management of the situation, but he wasn't blamed as being the leak culprit. Even though Chief Smalls had apologized to

Officer Vong and let him come back to work in January in his original position, the Chief's pride was still on the line, which meant someone's head was on the line. It was the end of March, seven months out from the leak, and we were still wondering, whose head would it be?

APRIL / MAY 2015

42

For the last couple of weeks of March, everyone on our team was focused on doing paperwork, testifying in court cases, and making trips to the bank. Hell, counting all that money at the downtown branch of the bank took an entire shift, and there were so many forfeiture warrants to complete along with the search warrant returns. We were buried in busywork. They say the hard work starts when you smash in the door, and it was the truth. I hoped soon I could be on a new case, back out on the streets doing surveillance and putting puzzle pieces together, but for now we had to clean up and organize all the records from TF-1422. It felt good to have all those guys behind bars for their crimes, but I also knew the game never stopped and there would be a whole new group of dealers rising in the ranks.

Unfortunately, we were still without a supervisor. Sgt. Cox was still in the bubble and would seemingly stay there for months, and the police department wasn't budging on appointing a new sergeant to our team. We had heard a rumor that Sgt. Bagg was going to become our new supervisor, but I knew Director Davis didn't get along with him so that was unlikely. Granted, few people got along with Sgt. Bagg other than the Chief and higher-ups, but Davis wasn't under the police department and he got to make the final decision.

Milliken let the team know he'd been called up for deployment starting the first week of April. He was grateful to have been part of the huge seizure and to see his TGI Fridays boys get their due punishment, and we were grateful for his help and the fact that he'd been key in finding the additional $120,000 hidden in the van. We threw him a going-away party at the end of March and were sad to see him go. It was like another piece of our family was leaving us.

A few days into April, we were starting to relax some with the completion of the seemingly endless paperwork. There would still be court dates and additional documents to provide if needed, but for now we were content to be riding on the high of the end of the case. Whoever had drawn the cartoon of me and Hughes in January had drawn a couple more over the past months, and the wall behind my computer was a collage of hilarious cartoons. My character looked more frazzled in each one, my Braves baseball cap changing directions and even lifting off my head. The artist was not wrong; I knew I looked like a mess when I was stressed. As we sorted and organized all the seized items and cash, the team also kept joking about how much bigger TF-1422 "B" was and how there was no chance I'd get an award for the case since I lead the "A" side. It all made me laugh because I didn't care about awards, and neither did Hughes. We were the kind of people who cared about the important parts, like doing a good job, not the recognition that would come with it.

Hughes had spent a lot of time since the bust tracking down Rhonda, Shawn's mother-in-law, at the Veterans Court Office. After the big bust when she and her husband had not been home during the search warrant, she had been very hard to track down. Hughes and Collins had been to her house several times, but no one ever came to the door, so they finally approached her at her office about the findings from her house: 337 grams of cocaine and almost $4,000 in cash.

During the lengthy interview with Hughes, Rhonda admitted that her husband smoked crack and would also sprinkle cocaine on his marijuana joints. Hughes said that the amount they had on hand wasn't a typical amount for personal use. She continued to play the denial game, downplaying and minimizing any involvement, but then Hughes divulged that her husband was caught on the wire selling large amounts of cocaine.

Rhonda became upset and said, "I see my client's families going through this, but now it's my family." Rhonda asked if she was going to lose her job and Hughes told her that he had to tell the judge that was over Mental Health Court, and they would decide. Rhonda became more upset and Hughes left. We heard later that Rhonda was unable to keep her job in the courts. It never paid to be in the drug game.

One warm afternoon in mid-April when all the loose ends of the case had been tied up, Titus, Thomas, and I were messing around after lunch, shooting rubber bands at each other and using folders as shields. After expanding the game into the whole Batcave and creating a rudimentary obstacle course, we were so distracting to Hughes and Diesel that they joined in the war. It was every man for himself, and the sting from rubber bands made us laugh and feel the same kind of adrenaline as when we were running after criminals. Between doing work on new cases and leads, it was nice to have a break and find time to just have fun, too, after all the overtime and weekend hours.

The fun ceased, though, when an interdiction sergeant arrived at the building and had to be checked in. Melissa alerted us, so we quickly righted the furniture barricades and hurried back to our offices like kids when the parents came home.

Sgt. Randy Mott strode past our office without looking in. He had a serious look on his face, and we were filled with a sense of dread. Sgt. Mott worked under Lieutenant Spine, like Sgt. Bagg and Sgt. Cox, but he had never come to our office before. He went straight to Director Davis' office and shut the door behind him.

"Maybe he's been appointed as our new sergeant?" Titus said.

I replied, looking down the hallway at the closed door, "I doubt he'd just show up if that was the case. They would have sent out a memo on it first."

Thomas added, "I have a bad feeling about this."

We sat at our desks and waited, the adrenaline from the game turning into an antsy energy as the minutes passed.

We finally heard Davis' door open and footsteps in the hall. Sgt. Mott still looked serious as he stopped at our door, but he also looked a little nervous. "TFO Wood, come to Director Davis' office."

I looked at Thomas, whose facial expression didn't change as he stood up. Before he followed Mott, he said, "I knew it. Here it comes."

Chapter 42

Titus and I didn't respond. There was nothing to say, and we now had just as bad a feeling about it as well. Thomas took a deep breath and then left the office with his shoulders back, ready to face whatever was about to happen. He'd faced OPA multiple times already and had lost his patience with them. If he was going to go down, he'd go down fighting.

I said quietly to Titus, "Probably leak bullshit again."

"It's not his fault, though."

"Yeah, but they wouldn't care about that. He mouthed off to them like Sgt. Cox did, and we saw what happened to James." I tried to focus on the papers in front of me, but it was impossible to focus while waiting for Thomas to return.

A few minutes later, we heard the door open and close. Sgt. Mott walked past our office and went straight to the front door.

"That was fast," Titus said.

I clenched my jaw and waited to hear the door open again. When it did, I stood up and Thomas walked into the office with no expression at all on his face. Director Davis had followed and said, "Bobby, will you drive Thomas home?"

I nodded. Director Davis patted Thomas on the shoulder and said, "I'm going to figure this out, Thomas. We've got your back."

Thomas nodded and started moving things around on his desk.

Davis went back to his office and we watched as Thomas stuffed some of his personal things into a plastic bag.

I had no idea what to say, but I needed to say something. "So, it was bad, huh?"

Thomas nodded and said, "Took my gun and badge."

"Fuck," I said as I sat down. He was done. In such a short meeting, Thomas' career had effectively ended. He didn't even have a car because he was using one of the 20th's cars, so that was why I'd be driving him home. How was his wife going to take it? His kid?

Titus asked, "On what grounds?"

Thomas surveyed his desk and moved to the door with his full bag of belongings. How quickly a desk could be cleaned out.

He said, "Truthfulness."

Contrary to what its label would suggest, "Truthfulness" was a fireable offense. It meant the lack of truth, or that an officer was lying, which would lead to instant decommissioning. This meant OPA had decided Thomas had lied in the interviews, even though there were all kinds of evidence to support him. If Thomas hadn't been sure about something, it was because his source, the citizen informant Chance, hadn't been clear. I knew for a fact Thomas had never once lied.

"That's bullshit," Titus said.

Thomas nodded, looking deflated and tired. "Well, I'm supposed to go home immediately, and I guess I'm ready." He held up his plastic bag with a shrug. I nodded and stood, grabbing my car keys.

Titus said, "We'll miss you, bud. I'm sorry this happened."

Thomas didn't reply as he walked towards the front door and I followed. Melissa looked from Thomas to his bag and shook her head slightly in disappointment. She knew the whole story as well as anyone, and I could tell she was thinking about how bullshit the police department seemed at that moment. The DA office and hierarchy had its own issues, but after Sgt. Cox was decommissioned, Melissa told me she just didn't understand the petty police politics and drama. Now that Thomas was leaving, she looked to be even more grateful to work for the DA instead.

Once in the car, we began our journey across town to Thomas' house on the outskirts of Davidson county. It was a long drive, and I was grateful he started to talk because it would have been painful to make that ride in silence.

"They said that they didn't have records on Chance being an officially registered CI."

"How's that possible? Chance had given information before."

"I don't know." Thomas said. "I basically said the same thing, and they said the file couldn't be located."

"Shit, that's not your fault though. We assumed Chance was registered because he'd done this before."

"Yeah, well, they decided to blame me for Chance being unauthorized and for Chance not knowing which day Eddie moved his shit. I guess Chance's faulty memory is my fault. And the decommissioning of Vong. And basically everything else. They seem to think I'm a liar and every fucking thing about the leak was my fault."

"But, it's not. They have the recording of the interview of Chance, and the Chief and Korbin are who blamed Vong just as much as we did."

"I know that. You know that. Our team knows that. But as soon as it's written on paper, it can be twisted however they want." He shook his head. "And, you know, I keep thinking about if only I hadn't cocked an attitude with them in that last interview. If I had just kept my mouth shut and complied with the questions and didn't react to them starting rumors about my marriage . . . if I had just laid down at their feet, maybe this wouldn't be happening."

I didn't know how to respond at first. He did have a point. The department wanted men to kiss rings and lay down at supervisor's feet like dogs to be tread on. The chain of command, hierarchy of power, and key political alliances made all the difference in someone's career. Weakling had played the game in such a way that got him promoted. Thomas played the game fairly, and he was being driven home without his badge.

I said, "So, what happens now?"

"Twenty days suspension. Or the green mile."

Thomas was going to the same fate as Officer Vong. While Vong had sat on the green mile until the Chief apologized and then he'd gotten reinstated to his old unit, I knew Thomas wouldn't have so bright a future. Unless something miraculous happened, Thomas would be on the green mile at the Criminal Justice Center until he couldn't take it anymore and finally quit or until he was fired. Even if he was reinstated, he'd probably be forced to accept the twenty days of suspension, and the rules on suspensions state he would have to be on patrol for two years before he could get promoted or transferred to a specialized team. The police department touted that patrol was the backbone of the department, but everyone knew that if they forced an experienced, hard-working narcotics detective back into patrolling the streets, it was not a reward. Going back to patrol was a punishment, even if it meant wasting the talent of experienced detectives. After being in the most elite drug unit for years, Thomas, like Sgt. Cox, would be back on patrol on the lowest rung, and that was a best-case scenario for him.

I said to Thomas, "Maybe I can prove it was Lazaro's niece. Maybe I can find a way to get that information in the right hands."

Thomas shook his head. "The 'right' hands are at OPA and they were already given the report. They chose not to use that information on purpose."

"I don't understand why they've done nothing with the evidence. They were so quick to decommission Vong, but if it's a sergeant's niece, even if he's a political favorite, they won't touch it."

Thomas didn't reply, so I just added, "This is just insane."

"Yes. Yes, it is." Thomas said. We were just turning on to his street. He looked out his window at his house when we pulled up and said, "They said they're releasing the interview summaries, by the way. Since they're 'closing' the investigation and your case is wrapped up, Korbin's summaries and the OPA decisions will go public." He then looked at me, "At least it's done."

"Dude, you don't deserve any of this."

He shrugged and picked up his plastic bag. He looked back at his house. "This is going to suck."

"We'll figure something out. It's not forever."

"We'll see." He then looked at me and held out his hand for me to shake. "It's been an honor working with you, Bobby."

I shook his hand and said, "It's been an honor, Thomas. Thanks for being a good friend and teammate."

He got out of the car and said, "Keep up the good fight."

As I pulled away and headed back to town, I thought about everything he said. I couldn't help but feel responsible for his fate. If I hadn't started up TF-1422 and gotten Charlie tied up with Eddie, the leak never would have happened and Chance would never have reached out to Thomas. If it weren't for my case, James would never have been decommissioned for "failure to supervise" and Karen wouldn't have come forward with her unfounded sexual harassment claims. If James hadn't helped me get on the 20th in the first place, he and Thomas might still have had their jobs. I was responsible for James being in the bubble and Thomas going to the green mile.

The weight of guilt made me drive slower than usual back to the office. What was the rush? When I got there, someone else might have been decommissioned in the last half hour because of my case. Without really thinking about it, I dialed my dad.

I told him what had happened and he sounded like his old self again as he railed against "the idiots at OPA." He agreed the whole thing was bullshit and told me it wasn't my fault for what happened to Thomas or James. I wasn't convinced.

He said, "Well, what are you going to do about it now?"

"I was driving back to the office, but I passed by the exit. I think I'm going to OPA."

"Damn, right, that's my son! Give 'em hell!"

I tried to laugh but I felt tired. "I'm not going to give them hell. I am going to ask Korbin about Lazaro's niece. They have all that information, and they've done nothing with it other than sit on it and pin the blame on Thomas instead. I need to know why."

Dad said, "I think you know why, but if you have to ask, then I say go for it. I don't know that they'll tell you the truth, but maybe he'll be a decent guy for old time's sake."

"Yeah, I'm hoping so." I was almost to OPA's building and added, "Also, no word from Ashley's doctor?"

"Not yet. Maybe Friday."

"Okay. Well, I'm here, so wish me luck."

He did and I hung up. I walked inside feeling a sense of calm fall over myself in my resolve to talk to Sgt. Korbin. If they were going to make the summaries public, I could try and have them look into Lazaro's niece first.

I waited outside Korbin's office until his secretary said he was available.

Korbin smiled in a strained way when I came in and said, "What can I do for you, TFO Young?"

I wasn't looking for a fight, so I answered, "Thanks for seeing me Sgt. Korbin. I just wanted to ask a question about the leak investigation."

He dropped his smile and said, "That's none of your business, TFO Young."

"With all due respect, it is my business, sir. My teammates are the ones getting stuck with the blame when there is clear evidence that the leak came from Sgt. Lazaro's niece. I want to know why the report we sent over was never acknowledged." I felt a surge of confidence after saying my piece. I knew what I was doing, and I was glad I was there to try and make things right.

Korbin stood and interlaced his hands behind his back. "Your report was invalid. The evidence was unfounded and based on slanderous assumptions."

I felt like I'd been slapped in the face. "But, her boyfriend has a federal record. And, the photos of her with Ken, the Vietnamese target . . ."

Korbin cut me off and raised his voice, "This has gone on too long, TFO Young. I have direct orders from the top to tell anyone attempting to dig into this matter to drop it immediately." He walked around his desk towards the door. "I warned you in the fall that this case would cause trouble for everyone, but you refused to pull the plug on it. That was your choice. Now, it's time to live with the consequences." He opened the door and gestured for me to leave.

I felt my face heat up. I could have punched him.

He said quietly, "Forget it and go back to work, Bobby. We're done here."

He stared at me until I made my way out of the room. I felt sick with anger. I didn't even want to call my dad because I was too embarrassed to say I'd just had my ass handed to me. I could have fought Korbin on the point, but where would that have landed me? There was no way he was going to budge, and I'd just be shooting myself in the foot.

I headed back to the office and tried to keep myself busy and distracted from all the bullshit. I needed to focus on my work again. It was the only thing keeping me sane.

43

On Friday morning, only two days after my tense conversation with Korbin, I went to Director Davis' office to check in before I started the day. I knocked on his door and said, "Director, do you have a minute?"

He looked up. "OPA just released the interview summaries to the public."

"Seriously?"

He nodded. "And if they are all like the one I just read, we have a serious problem."

"Shit."

The office spent the entire day reading all the released summaries. The tension rose significantly in the building as we went line-by-line through the summaries and marked both inaccuracies and straight-up false statements. Because they were now public knowledge, we cringed at all the names mentioned as being involved in the investigation, including the confidential informants' details. The police were supposed to keep certain information sealed in order to protect people like informants, but OPA was laying it all on the line for anyone to see.

Included in the documents was my own interview and the full tracking order report I'd written for Vong's vehicle. Over the course of the afternoon, I started getting almost constant emails from other officers and higher-ups critiquing the tracking order, but I couldn't easily answer any of them. The Chief had ordered us to write it, so I did and included all the information possible. If I started emailing everyone back with "This was done by order of Chief Smalls himself," I'd have an "emergency meeting" with the Chief in no time at all.

I had other things to focus on anyway, like Thomas' summaries. Korbin wrote, "Wood was the lead investigator in the investigation of

Officer Thammavong because he gathered every piece of evidence which focused on Officer Thammavong as the source of the leak." Sgt. Korbin had also noted that Thomas had the faulty memory—not his confidential informant—for when Eddie moved his guns. Korbin concluded that Thomas' failure to deliver correct information resulted in Vong's unwarranted punishment. Well, no wonder they put all the blame on him. This was such an exaggeration and misrepresentation of what had happened. All Thomas did was relay the information Chance had passed along to him, and the only evidence he looked for on Vong was ordered by the Chief himself.

James' summary stated, "It is clear Sgt. Cox focused only on Officer Thammavong as the source of the leak, even when provided solid information someone else may be responsible." I almost laughed aloud at the absurdity of the statement. James had told the captain not to decommission Vong because of the lack of evidence! At the end of James' summary, Korbin stated that all violations against Officer Vong were unfounded and Sgt. Cox had ignored all the evidence that could have cleared Vong sooner.

Among the many assumptions and inconsistencies in James' interview, one line stood out to me: "Sgt. Cox ignored TFO Phillips and TFO Weakling when they provided him with articulable reasons why Officer Thammavong was not the source of the leak."

Phillips told us, "Sgt. Cox never ignored me on that! I didn't say that. I didn't think we had enough intel on Vong to decommission him and needed to look into it more, but Sgt. Cox never disagreed with that idea."

I responded, "I think this has a lot more to do with Weakling's personal vendetta against Sgt. Cox, and you just got lumped into it." I didn't say that Phillips did tend to exaggerate and get wrapped up into drama. Maybe he had said something against Sgt. Cox in his interview and just didn't remember.

Out of everyone that was interviewed, Jimmy Weakling was the only one who did not have an interview date, which was very suspicious. There was a brief synopsis included of a statement from him, though, and it sounded exactly like a cover-up for a snitch. The first two sentences were a blatant lie about what actually occurred: "TFO Weakling was called to the Office of Professional Accountability for an impromptu interview. He was ordered to come directly to the office, and not to reveal to the staff at the 20th JDTF he was being questioned." This was horseshit. Weakling had gone to OPA on a day we needed him and couldn't reach him, and then he must have asked for protection when he got promoted.

Weakling's statement was summarized to show he was dissatisfied with our office's lack of due diligence in investigating the leak and how he was certain from the beginning that Vong was not the leak. He also made a lot of accusations against Thomas' "lack of concern" for the high stakes of the leak issue and how the team was trying to cover up the mess. I made a note on the statement that Weakling was supposed to have been in charge of the leak investigation at our office, but he conveniently had left that out in his "impromptu" secret interview. He also had left out details of his drunken phone call to Sgt. Cox, telling him he didn't want to have anything to do with the leak case work.

Reading through the summaries was sickening. Everyone was pissed about their own interviews and how anything they had said was twisted to shed the truth in a completely false light. Director Davis was right, this was a serious problem.

Davis called a team meeting at the end of the day. For the first time, I saw a different Director Davis. He looked both exhausted and furious. He didn't outright talk bad about the police department, but he did say, "Like all of you, I have some big concerns about how this investigation has gone. On the one hand, there is not much we can do to stop whatever political bullshit is going on behind the scenes, but on the other hand, now that these idiotic summaries have been released, I have a plan to try and save Thomas' job."

I couldn't help myself and let out a, "Hell yeah!"

The rest of the team agreed and it was the first time all day any of us had smiled. Director Davis continued, "Every interview OPA conducted was recorded and transcribed. Sgt. Korbin would write the summary from the actual transcriptions, so those reports exist in their records. Since the summaries are now public, we have the right to request those transcripts and compare them side-by-side with these summaries. I have already started the process, and if they don't comply quickly, I'm going to need back-up with keeping OPA accountable to their own rules of transparency. We can't hold certain people accountable for their actions, but we are going to make sure Thomas isn't fired for something he didn't do. We can save his job with the truth."

It was like an inspirational speech at the end of a movie where a baseball team is trailing by one point at the bottom of the ninth. The whole team enthusiastically agreed with Davis' plan, and he said, "I'm going to quote Sgt. Cox and just say, thank you for being the best Bat-team ever."

That was exactly what we needed to hear. All day we'd slumped lower in our seats, feeling the weight of all the madness. Now we were smiling and sitting up straight, ready to do anything to protect our team just as we were ready to protect our city every single day.

Director Davis had boosted our spirits and ended the meeting saying, "Now, stop working for a few hours and enjoy your Friday night."

I texted my wife as I headed for my car. We were back to our Friday margaritas at La Hacienda, and I was excited to relax and decompress with her. I had texted her bits and pieces of the summaries all day, so I was ready to talk it all out and give her details on Davis' plans.

We had margaritas and ate chips and tacos as I told her all about the day. Danielle updated me on her classes and job, too, and it felt good to have a normal Friday night where we could just spend time together. It was a relief to be away from the bullshit for a couple hours.

As we walked to our cars later, my phone buzzed in my pocket. I had gotten so used to all the GPS pings and wire room texts that I immediately assumed it was work, even though the wiretap was over and I hadn't gotten a ping in weeks.

When I saw it was my brother-in-law calling, I told Danielle to sit in my car with me for a second. My brother-in-law rarely called me, especially late on a Friday night, so I knew something wasn't right. I answered and put him on speaker.

"Hey, Randy."

"Hey, Bobby. How's it going?"

"Good, we're just leaving La Hacienda. What's going on?"

"I just wanted to call for Ashley. She wanted me to let people know that we got word from Vanderbilt today about her diagnosis." He paused as if almost nervous. He and my sister had been together since high school and I'd never heard his voice like this. He always was the strong provider for my sister when she'd gotten pregnant at eighteen, and I looked at Danielle who also looked worried about the way he sounded.

He finally said, "She's been diagnosed with ALS."

For a moment, my brain didn't totally understand what he was saying. I knew of ALS and how it had something to do with muscles, so it made sense why she was falling, but I realized I didn't quite know what it meant to have it. Danielle had her hand over her mouth and looked to be holding back tears.

"Shit." I said.

Randy sniffed on the other side of the phone and I felt tears come to my own eyes. He said, "Yeah. They said the worst case scenario is she might only have three to five years. Maybe longer with these treatment things, but, shit, I don't know. It could be bad." Ashley, who had just had her fourth kid the previous August and who was so strong and amazing, was diagnosed with a disease that might take her life in three years. Of all things, I thought about our childhood and how she would have me play Barbies with her whenever Angela was too cool to play with her younger siblings.

Randy sniffed again and I tried to pull myself together to answer.

"You know, we'll get through this, Randy. It's going to be hard, but she'll get through this. She's strong and she's got all of us with her. We're going to be okay. She's going to be okay."

He blew his nose and said, "Yeah, I know. I'm just still a little shocked I guess. We'll be okay. We'll get through this. We always get through everything."

"Exactly." I said, wiping tears away from my cheeks and taking breaths to steady myself. "Thank you for letting us know. If you need anything at all, please call us okay, dude?"

"All right, man. Thanks."

Chapter 43

We hung up and Danielle and I sat in the silence in the car.

Danielle was wiping her own eyes and said, "She'll be okay."

I nodded and hoped we were right. I wanted to call my dad, but it was late and I didn't know if Randy or Ashley had talked to them already or not. I needed to wait until the morning. I had planned on taking some time off over the weekend to relax, but now I knew I'd be going into the office in the morning. Work was something good to focus on, something I could control. I could do some work on the new case that we were just beginning to organize. I could work more on memorizing Korbin's summaries and finding every bit of information wrong in all of them. I could continue going through the papers and casework on Thomas' desk to get that organized. Shit, I could organize my mountain of papers on my desk and that would take a whole weekend probably. I had to focus on work.

As I pulled into our driveway, I realized I had been repeating to myself, "We'll get through this. We have to get through this."

44

The rest of April was a blur of throwing myself into work and trying to stay strong for my family. We still had our Sunday dinners, but we struggled to keep talk positive. Angela, my oldest sister, being the super detailed and organized person she was, kept wanting to talk about things we could do to help Ashley's situation. She had ideas for crowdfunding and church events and organizing food delivery. Ashley didn't say so, but it seemed like she was grateful for Angela's energy but also not ready to "do" anything about the situation, yet. We were all still just trying to grasp the implications of her diagnosis.

Her three girls seemed to understand their mom was sick but not contagious, but I knew Ashley was keeping a strong front for them so they wouldn't worry. Randy held it together, also, but I saw him sneaking glances at her.

In addition to the stress of Ashley, my dad let us know that the spot they'd found on the CAT scan was concerning enough that he was scheduled for a biopsy. The results showed the mass was cancerous. The doctor believed this little bit in his lungs may have started when they were still just treating his throat cancer. They thought it was growing slowly, which was a good sign, but it was still there, causing him pain and he'd be starting radiation again soon enough.

My brain felt like shutting down, so I spent most of my time at the office and when I called Dad I kept conversation light and short. I didn't want to face reality. I'd had about a month's rest after TF-1422, if you could call the stress of losing Sgt. Cox, Thomas, my family issues, and mountains of paperwork "rest," and I was ready to go with a new case to put all my energy into.

Diesel, Titus, and I started working on another potential wiretap case targeting a Hispanic drug trafficking organization operating in Middle

Tennessee. This group was distributing large amounts of cocaine but they weren't centered directly in Nashville like the other two groups. I had acquired a confidential informant who was "working off charges" from the TF-1422 wiretap case and they tipped me off to key players in this other drug ring. The informant wasn't one of the big guys we'd taken down, but they had connections to other counties' main dealers. I wanted to do another wiretap, so we were doing a lot of research and preliminary surveillance work to get to that point.

A few weeks after Director Davis requested the transcripts for the OPA interviews, and after multiple people on our team also put pressure on OPA to release them, we finally received a box of documents. We split them up among the team and started going line-by-line comparing them to the summaries. I took Thomas' interviews because I was determined to prove his innocence for "truthfulness." For the months of work OPA did on the leak issue, it took me almost no time at all to mark up the interview and write up a report of all the inconsistencies and twists of language. Director Davis reviewed my work, gave suggestions, and after making a final copy, he gave it his stamp of approval. It was up to him now to make sure the evidence got into the right hands to save Thomas.

Thomas was sitting on the green mile at headquarters every day, on display right out front. It pissed me off that he was probably sitting with sex offenders and other lowlifes waiting to check in with the probation office. Even though the rules said nobody was supposed to talk to punished officers on the green mile, I texted him and let him know we had found what we were looking for and were going to fight for him. He didn't respond, but I knew he was just trying to follow orders. Any small slip up would be enough for them to fire him for good at this point.

Davis set up meetings with Captain Zander and Lieutenant Spine to argue Thomas' case, and he planned on going straight to the chief if that didn't work. Director Davis made a point to stay in the room while the captain and lieutenant reviewed the transcripts, and they acknowledged there were inconsistencies. They told him they'd be in touch about commuting Thomas' sentence on the green mile. We knew it would take a long time for it to happen because that's how the department moved:

at a snail's pace. But, we celebrated our achievement of saving Thomas' career. It would be weeks before Thomas was finally put back on patrol, and only after he was forced to take twenty days suspension, but he would be reinstated. That's what mattered.

In mid-May, Director Davis, Titus, and Diesel were scheduled to fly to California. They were escorting a confidential informant from Nashville to the San Francisco area so he could assist a Drug Task Force in that area with an ongoing crystal meth case. They'd be gone a week, so the rest of us would work on our cases and hold down the fort. Things were just beginning to feel like normal again, even though we still didn't have a replacement supervisor for Sgt. Cox.

The day before Davis was scheduled to leave, there was a board meeting held in the 20th's kitchen. They never met in the conference room because the meetings were meant to be transparent and anyone from the team could attend. The minutes were shared afterwards, so I never sat in on the meetings. Plus, the tension between DA Ball and Chief Smalls had always been obvious, and it was uncomfortable to watch. Ball had tried to tell Smalls how to run the police department, and that bad blood ran deep. Because of their obvious dislike for each other, the board meetings were usually extremely brief and only covered basic financials and operations stats.

Chief Smalls and DA Chad Ball got to the office at 10 am and sat down with Davis around the small kitchen table as usual. When I reviewed the minutes from the meeting, though, it was clear this was anything but a usual board meeting. Davis brought up an inconsistency in the detailed budget. An Assistant DA whose focus was on prostitution was being paid her salary out of the 20th's bank account. Director Davis explained that the she wasn't on the 20th's payroll and didn't even do work involving drugs. It was a misappropriation of the 20th's funds.

I raised my eyebrows as I read the interaction. Davis was firm and was really calling DA Ball out on this, and Ball just replied, "I'll check on that and see what's happening." He then changed the subject to move on with the meeting.

The office was buzzing about Davis calling Ball out in a board meeting in front of Chief Smalls. I was proud of Davis for standing up for what was right.

Davis, Titus, and Diesel left the next day for California.

A few days into their trip, there was a story run by a local news station on changes within the police department and DA's office. We had heard nothing about it and were shocked to read the news story:

> *Davidson County District Attorney Chad Ball and Police Chief Luther Smalls announced Friday the realignment of Nashville's major drug investigation unit.*
>
> *Since 1988, the 20th Judicial District Drug Task Force has been headed by the District Attorney's Office and assigned to investigate major narcotics traffickers within Davidson County. Under the reorganization, all police and investigative functions of this major drug unit will be placed under the authority of the police department.*
>
> *In a press release to the media, the District Attorney's Office said it will continue to "support, assist and advise the unit in addition to pursuing vigorous prosecution of cases involving the sale of illegal narcotics."*
>
> *With advanced technology and the sophistication of the criminal element, it is best for these narcotics investigations to be under the chief of police." DA Ball said.*
>
> *The joint release said the reorganization will "provide investigators with greater access to police department resources while maintaining the mission of the unit and the personnel (and) will allow the DA's office to dedicate more resources to the prosecution of major drug cases instead of the day-to-day management of a law enforcement unit."*
>
> *The realignment becomes effective July 1, 2015.*[3]

I felt a growing dread as I read the announcement of our task force's "realignment." Instead of being under the DA, the team be under the authority of the police department. The Chief and DA had announced the change to the media before even letting us know, which meant that shady things were going on behind the scenes they didn't want us to know about. As much as they clearly disliked each other, they must have had a secret meeting as soon as Director Davis left town. Was this change because of Davis' assertion that the DA's office was misappropriating the 20th's funds? Or, did it come back to the leak issue? Or, was it about money and the millions the 20th had just taken in from my case? Was it all just the game of politics and control of power? I didn't want to believe it but the thought crossed my mind: *Did Sgt. Bagg have anything to do with this?*

His same words repeated in my head as if an answer to my question: *If I have to take it down myself, I will, and I'll make sure you go down with it . . .*

I called Director Davis immediately after reading the article. He and DA Chad Ball had never gotten along well, but they at least had a working relationship. I asked Director Davis if he had known anything about it.

He said, "This article is the first I'm hearing of it."

"So, you didn't know DA Ball wanted to transfer the task force to the police?"

"I knew he didn't like our team and the work we were doing. He told me once that police work should be done under the police department, and anyone under the DA should be support and not out in the field. He said we should do wiretaps but for other organizations, for detectives in law enforcement, and that we shouldn't be doing our own cases. But I didn't know that would mean he'd sell us out like this, especially when I'm out of town and am not even alerted of the changes. I'm on the fucking board of directors! I should have known about this!"

I couldn't imagine how he must be feeling. His boss had basically just ripped the rug out from under him.

"This is shady bullshit," I said.

"You got that right. We just take down two huge drug rings, bring in millions of dollars for our team's expenses, and now suddenly our whole business is being transferred to the police department? Something doesn't smell right about this." Director Davis had never been this frank and conversational with me, and it was a little unnerving.

"So, what do we do about it?" I asked.

He snorted and said, "What is there to do about it? Keep our eyes open. That's all we can do. I've got to go. I need to make some calls. I'll see you in the office Monday, Bobby."

"Okay, travel safe, Director."

I was shocked by Director Davis' response, but I was even more shocked that Ball and Smalls hadn't notified or consulted Davis before publicly announcing a transfer. Was that even legal to do without the whole board of directors on board?

I couldn't stop thinking about the possible transfer all weekend. I didn't know how the team was going to function under the police department. The twenty wiretap computers and technology all belonged to the DA's office, and from what Director Davis said, it sounded like the DA was going to continue offering wiretaps for outside cases. If the 20th wasn't going to have our own wiretap computers, how would we do our jobs right? I knew the police department did not have adequate facilities or equipment to allow the unit to properly function. This secretly organized "realignment" felt shifty.

At least we had until July 1st to figure out what it would mean for us and our future work. Until then, we would just hope it would all work out as long as we kept working and keeping our eyes open. As Davis said, that was really all we could do.

JUNE 2015

45

The first half of June was really quiet in the Batcave. We had heard nothing from DA Ball or Chief Smalls since the one media outlet ran the story of the realignment. Director Davis was pissed waiting to be told what would happen to our department, but all communication he sent to DA Ball was left unanswered.

Thomas was about to be released from the green mile because Captain Zander had alerted Director Davis that the motion to commute Thomas' sentence was finally approved. The paperwork just had to hit the system and Thomas would be sent back to patrol.

Our whole office was on edge in what felt like the calm before a storm. Even Hughes who always stayed positive and focused seemed distracted.

I stopped by his office one day to check in with him and learned what was causing his distraction. Since Hughes had officially been hired as a full-time agent with the 20th the previous July, he was coming up on a year out of the police force. If you were even one day over a year out of the force, you had to go back through the entire 25-week academy again. This hadn't been an issue since Hughes wanted to work for the 20th for the foreseeable future, but since our team was being transferred to the police department, Hughes didn't quite know where that left him. I tried to be supportive and positive, but, shit, I didn't know what would happen either. At some point we would have to be given more information, and that finally happened on June 15th.

At 2 pm, Chief Luther Smalls arrived at the Drug Task Force and stormed back to Director Davis' office without greeting or acknowledging any of us as he passed our offices. The whole office went silent with anticipation. Ten minutes later, the Chief left the building just as fast as he'd entered it.

Director Davis called everyone to the conference room, telling us that it was important. Once everyone got in the same room, he told us, "Okay, guys, this is it. We all knew this was coming but now it's official. DA Ball no longer wants anything to do with our Task Force, and Chief Smalls just gave me the official notice that he is taking over. He said it was going to be a 'seamless' transition, but somehow, I doubt that."

"Wait," I said, "but what will happen to you and Hughes since you're not with the police department?"

Davis said, "Well, I don't know. I bet they will want us to rejoin the department and then they will probably try to throw us back on patrol since we have been over here for so long."

I said, "That's bullshit!" at the same time Titus said, "That's crazy!"

Diesel added, "Damn! I finally made it to the best unit ever and now this shit happens."

Collins and Hughes didn't say anything at all.

Director Davis said, "I don't know who will be your supervisor or how things are going to play out, but, just as a head's up, I hear Sgt. Bagg is in the running to be your supervisor."

The phrase left a silence in my brain that was filled with the words, *If I have to take it down myself, I will, and I'll make sure you go down with it . . .*

As if flipping a switch, I set my head down on the table and instantly began to cry. All the emotions of the previous year and the built-up stress over the leak and the case, all the anxiety about my sister and my dad, all the issues over the years with Bagg that still lived in my memory, it all rushed out of me like a tidal wave. Even though my teammates were sitting around me in a painful awkward silence, I didn't feel one ounce of embarrassment as I cried.

I managed to say, "This shit's not going to work out is it? I don't want to be negative, but I'm not stupid, and I can see through this bullshit. We're going down."

Titus patted my back and said, "Dude, we're not going down."

I shook my head, still hearing Sgt. Bagg's threat.

"What's going on, man?" Diesel asked.

Where would I even start?

Titus said, "Talk to us, dude."

I knew I looked like I was overreacting, but I couldn't help the reaction to hearing Bagg might be our supervisor. A rumor was one thing, but hearing it from Director Davis made it so much more real. Everything that had weighed on me for so long was causing this, and I didn't know how to stop it. I was sad, but I was mad, too. And, I didn't want to admit it, but I was honestly a little afraid of what would happen to me. Sgt. Bagg's threat had basically come true, hadn't it? Or, it mostly had. Maybe I was being irrational. My dad would know what to say about the situation. He'd say that Dick Bagg was just a sad, lonely man who threw around empty threats because he hated himself. He'd say Dick Bagg was full of shit and he couldn't take away my worth and all the good I did in my work.

I sniffed and tried to pull myself together. "Sorry, guys. I've been having a rough time. My dad is battling cancer again, and my sister was just diagnosed with ALS."

"Shit." Titus said.

I continued, "I've just thrown myself into work to deal with it because it's what I have to do. I can control work, so that's what I focus on. But, it also feels like all the hard work just doesn't fucking matter now. Our team has changed so much, and I don't know what's going to happen to us. So, what am I even left with? This political bullshit is overshadowing everything amazing we've done this past year."

I felt someone sit down on my other side. Davis said, "That's not true. No matter what happens, the work we did was still important and it has left the city better than before."

"Yeah," Hughes said. "Who cares about the drama? No one can take away the fact that we just busted the two biggest cocaine rings in Nashville and made the biggest seizure in Nashville history. We're a bunch of badasses."

I snorted. "Do badasses cry about their personal problems at work?"

Titus patted my back and said, "Dude, even Batman cried."

We all laughed and Collins said, "Not true. Batman makes onions cry."

We then laughed harder. It was the first time in weeks we'd really laughed about anything. Ever since the rubber band war the day Thomas was decommissioned, we'd not joked or horsed around at all.

We started making more jokes about Batman being a badass who cries, and then we were on to Hulk Hogan and Dwayne Johnson, and we finally ended up just telling Chuck Norris jokes for half an hour. By the end of it, Director Davis was pretending to roundhouse kick us out of the conference room to get back to work. Titus and I headed back to our office, and I felt a lot better. Making stupid jokes was the distraction I needed, but I still had the knot in my gut telling me shit was not going to get better. For the moment, though, I could ignore that feeling, and just get back to doing the work I loved.

Before I left that night, I was alone in my office staring at the cartoons on my wall. I didn't feel like the frazzled, crazy-eyed character anymore, but I couldn't really place the empty feeling in me.

"Reminiscing?" Collins stood in the doorway with a half-smile.

I said, "The case just feels like so long ago."

I turned my chair as Collins sat in the chair by the door with a sigh. "Yeah, it does. The past couple months have just been something else."

I nodded.

He continued, "It's probably been even harder for you with your family stuff. I think things will work out, though."

"But, what if they don't, man? I mean, cancer and ALS aren't exactly colds. There's all these treatment options, but there's no guarantee they'll get better, you know? And then, on top of all that, our team is being realigned in the police department, which could mean anything."

Collins nodded and folded his hands in his lap. "All I can say about the family stuff is be there for them as much as you can. It's okay to focus on work some to deal with the stress, but don't miss out on time with them. You can't get that back."

I felt emotion well up in me so I took a deep breath to push it down. I was not going to cry twice in one day.

Collins must have noticed because he lightened the mood by saying, "And, shit, when it comes down to it this is just a job, right?"

"My dream job, though."

"Mine, too. But, it's not everything. I think I could also be happy doing security at a school. Seeing kids and protecting them, that's honest work."

"I think you'd do well at that."

He grinned. "Same. So, what do you got? I mean, worst case scenario, what would you do if you didn't have this job?"

I didn't even have to think long to say, "My oldest sister Angela is a badass business owner in town, and she thinks I could start my own PI business."

He nodded. "Is that something you'd like doing?"

"Definitely. Being a private investigator would be a lot of fun. But, I don't want things to change. I never want to leave the Batcave or this kind of work. I'm only seven years into my career, and I don't feel done, yet."

"That makes sense." He then chuckled, "If nothing else, stick it out till the ten year mark so you can get your pension when you retire."

I smiled then.

He continued, "For what it's worth, I think you'd make a badass PI, Bobby."

"Thanks, Collins."

"No problem. It's good you've got that in your back pocket. Some guys really believe there's no life outside of police work, and that shit just ain't true."

"My dad always has to remind me of that. He got screwed by his administration after thirty years as a CSX railroad policeman, so he retired and thought his life was over. But, now he's actually more relaxed just being a hotel security guard supervisor. It's just something to do and he enjoys the people."

Chapter 45

"See? Shit always works out. It's not always what you want, but it always works out." He grinned.

I nodded and said, "Thanks. I feel a little better."

"You look better. I'd rather see you looking crazy-eyed than teary-eyed any day."

We both laughed and then I got my stuff together to head home for the evening. Things with work and family still felt uncertain, but it helped to be reminded that I had options and that my team was there to support me. Collins had been a mentor-like figure to me back in 2013 when I was temporarily assigned to the 20th for the Dilaudid case. It was my second wiretap case but the first I'd led, and Collins had been a huge support. I was glad he still had my back.

A couple days later, Hughes stopped by our room and sat in the chair by the door.

He said, "So, a deputy chief reached out to me and made an offer for me to rejoin the police department before July."

The knot in my stomach tightened. Hughes was going to leave, too.

"That's a good thing, right?" Titus said.

"Yeah, I mean, if I take it I won't have to go through all the training shit. I'd have to leave the team before July in order to be rehired, though, and I'd be going back on patrol as Davis predicted. They said it wouldn't be for long, though."

"Damn," I said.

"Yeah. I don't want to leave this team, but on July 1st the 20th will shift to the police department anyway, and I'll be out of a job. I'd need to transfer, like, now."

I looked at him. He looked almost nervous, which was weird for Hughes. He seemed to know what he had to do, though, so I said, "I guess you don't really have a choice."

Hughes nodded. "I guess not. I guess I'm going to go back to a uniform."

Titus said, "That sucks, man."

He shrugged. "Better than the alternative. At least I'll still be doing the job I love, which is fighting crime."

"That's true," I said. "I support your decision, but I know that's not an easy one to make. We'll miss you on the team."

"Oh, don't get sentimental now. You'll be coming on over to the department soon, too, so we'll still be working together. Besides, I'll make my way back to the Bat-team before you know it."

I forced myself to laugh. "Yeah, it probably won't take you long with your experience and credentials. Your talent would be wasted drawing diagrams of wrecks and answering domestic calls."

"Exactly." He then made a sly face like a cartoon villain and said, "This won't be the last you see of me, Batman!"

We all three laughed together and Hughes slinked out of the room. I called after him, "You dumbass!"

Titus and I resettled in our chairs and he said, "Well, another down, huh?"

"I guess so."

He thought for a second and then said, "Man, what is happening to us?"

I didn't answer. I kept it positive with Hughes, but I wasn't being real with how I was feeling. I didn't want to fall apart in front of the team again, but the hopeless feeling from the meeting with Director Davis had stuck with me. This was my fault. My case had started all of this craziness and now the team was being transferred to the police department and Sgt. Bagg might be our new supervisor. This dream job was turning into a nightmare.

When Hughes was transferred the following Monday, it was just me, Titus, Diesel, Collins, and Director Davis left on the 20th. The office was feeling drained and emptied.

We kept ourselves occupied, though, because soon enough everything would be changing and we needed to be ready.

The first part of the changes happened when we received an email from Captain Zander on June 25th. He wrote, "Please be advised that effective July 1st what was formerly known as the 20th Judicial District Drug Task Force will become the Major Case Task Force. I am looking forward to working more closely with each of you as we move forward

Chapter 45

to investigate significant cases. As to shift hours, the below will apply as of July 1st."

As I scanned the hours for the list of names, my eyes stopped at the top name of my shift: "R. Bagg."

Fuck. It was true. Sgt. Bagg would be working over me again, and I wanted to punch a wall.

Captain Zander ended the email with, "Obviously, there will be several other issues to work out as we move forward, and I look forward to a seamless transition." His note on "other issues" felt as ominous as Dick Bagg's name at the top of the list. It meant more changes would be in the works, and clearly, judging by Bagg being lumped into our team suddenly, we wouldn't know what those changes would be until they happened. Welcome back to the police department bullshit! Your first course is a nice slap in the face!

I tried to take deep breaths and worked on convincing myself that this really was nothing to worry about, at least not right now. It was just a new supervisor, and I had spent years learning how to avoid him in the office. And, it was just a simple name change. Instead of the 20th Judicial District Drug Task Force, we were just going to be on the Major Case Task Force. I went to my email signature and simply changed my title and unit name. Chief Smalls told us that it would be a "seamless" transition. We would lose our statewide jurisdiction, but we could still investigate big drug dealers and do wiretaps, so our jobs wouldn't be changing.

As I reread the email, I realized there was one big problem: Director Davis was not on that list. I went to his office immediately and asked why he wasn't included.

"They offered me a position back if I went through the academy again."

I nodded, since this was what I expected would happen. "And?"

"I'm not going back to patrol." He said, his face serious. "I'm not going back to being a sergeant who works the graveyard shift. I'm years past that point of my life, and I don't have time for that bullshit."

"So, what are you going to do?" I asked, my chest feeling tight knowing his response before he said it.

"I was going to let the team know later today, but I guess I'll just start letting you all know now." He took a breath and looked me in the eye and said, "I'm done with the field of law enforcement. It's just not worth it anymore, so I've put in my resignation. I'll be gone when the team makes the switch on July 1st."

I nodded, understanding his rationale, but it still crushed me. I didn't blame him at all at this point, but I couldn't help but ask, "What about us?"

He smiled in the way dads do when kids ask for advice. "You all have to make your own choices. Whatever you decide, I'll always be on your team."

"Shit, Davis. You want to make me cry again?" I made myself laugh.

He grinned and then said slowly, "I'm so proud of you, son."

I stood up as he laughed. I waved him off saying, "Okay! That's enough."

I headed for the door and then looked back and added, "But, for what it's worth, I'm proud of you, too."

He nodded and I headed back to my office.

Another down.

Only four of us would be left.

One week until I would have to see Sgt. Bagg again, and this time he would be at the Batcave. The office that had felt so safe and separate from him was now going to be run by him. Director Davis was leaving and wouldn't be there to advocate for us or keep Bagg in line.

Everything was about to change—but not for the better.

JULY / AUGUST 2015
46

On Wednesday July 1st, I called my dad on the drive to the Batcave.

"Dad, this is going to suck."

"Yep. There ain't no way around it."

We had talked multiple times in the week leading up to this point. I couldn't stand the idea of being reunited with Sgt. Bagg, but there wasn't much I could do about it at this point. There were rumors of the Batcave being closed and the team moving to the SID building, but I knew there wasn't room for us there. They also didn't have the computers or equipment we'd need to do wiretaps. The four of us left on the team were hoping it was just a rumor. We hoped they were just going to change the name of the unit, assign Sgt. Bagg as our supervisor, and then let us keep working on our impactful cases.

I told Dad, "I'm still going to bust my ass no matter who my boss is because I love this work. They can't change that."

Dad didn't answer for a second and I knew he was thinking they could change that, too. But, he responded, "Just keep your head down and stay focused on what's most important. Do your best."

"Yeah."

I drove in the silence. We had circled around this issue so many times there was nothing new to add. It felt good to have Dad there with me, though, as I drove to what felt like my doom. We finally hung up and I hesitated in the parking lot before going in. I'd worked under Bagg before and I knew one of his not-so-terrible qualities was letting his team do the work they needed to do with minimal interference. I probably wouldn't have to interact with him that much other than meetings and check-ins. He would probably take Sgt. Cox's old office, which meant I wouldn't have to walk by it to get to my office, so that was also a positive. I just had to shut down my emotions and deal with him as little as possible.

What worried me was that he didn't have the whole SID office to walk around and get his daily schmoozing. The Batcave was small with only a handful of people in the building. I wouldn't have much of a buffer against him.

I finally headed in, my heart racing and stomach in knots. Melissa smiled sympathetically at me when I passed her desk. She knew how I felt about Bagg. She had been hired by the police department to stay with the team, and I was glad of it. Even if our Bat-team was changing, we still had our Alfred Pennyworth.

I managed to work all morning without having to see Sgt. Bagg, but he scheduled a team meeting before lunch. Titus had been quiet, too. He had been in a low-energy funk for the last couple months after the end of the huge case. He worked less hours and got his work done, but he didn't go out of his way to excel anymore. I didn't blame him. It took a lot of energy to try and work like nothing bad was happening.

When we got to the conference room, Sgt. Bagg was talking to Collins. Collins kept a smile on his face to match Bagg's, but Collins knew the truth about Bagg and I could tell he was faking it. He had been there when Sgt. Cox was hired, so he knew what was behind Sgt. Bagg's fake niceties.

Sgt. Bagg looked the same as months prior when he'd helped with the search warrants on my case. His polo was unbuttoned to show a bit of chest hair and he kept his chest puffed up and his hands on his hips like a wannabe superhero.

I managed to greet Sgt. Bagg politely and sat down between Titus and Diesel. Collins sat down, and it was sad to see our whole team took up less than half of the conference table. Sgt. Bagg stayed at the head of the table and went over all the information we already knew about the name change and realignment of the team. He rambled for a while about the "improved efficiency" of the police department after acquiring the team and how much more effective the team could be on specialized cases now. As I half-listened to him, I could see right through to his thoughts. In his mind, he'd righted the wrong of the year before when Sgt. Cox got hired instead of him. He thought he was in his rightful place as supervisor of this elite task force, and nothing could bring him down.

We all listened silently and politely, and then he asked us for overviews of our current cases. When he dismissed us, we all left the room promptly. It was nothing like our meetings led by Director Davis when we'd stick around to have coffee and chat for a few minutes. The tension was thick enough to cut through, but Sgt. Bagg didn't seem to mind.

The next two weeks went by in a blur. I kept my head down and stayed focused on my work, and Sgt. Bagg basically stayed out of the way. I didn't know what he did all day with his time since we weren't including him on our tasks, but I also didn't care. The less I saw him the better. I learned to deal with his presence in the building and the tense atmosphere, and I was just starting to get used to it when we received an email from Deputy Chief Timothy Cream. Cream had been the guy who told us about Sgt. Cox leaving the team and talked down to us like we were misbehaving children. Lieutenant Spine should have led that meeting, but he was spineless and chose to hide in his office instead.

Cream's email was to the entire department, and it started, "As many of you have already heard, the MNPD is forming a new unit within the Specialized Investigations Division, the Major Case Task Force (MCTF)."

I immediately shook my head at this. No mention of the 20th. He was making it sound like this was a new, innovative force the police department was forming from scratch.

His email continued:

> *This unit will concentrate on cases that call for investigative resources beyond the resources of individual precincts or divisions. The goal of the unit is to bring about a higher case resolution and increased public safety. The MCTF will operate as an initiator of stand-alone investigations or as a collaborator with multiple precincts, divisions, or law enforcement agencies within adjacent or overlapping jurisdictions. The unit will be tasked to work on a variety of crimes to include but*

> *not limited to: Narcotics trafficking, Gangs related crimes, firearms trafficking, murder, murder for hire, kidnapping, serial crimes, wire fraud, identity theft, and foreign or domestic terrorism.*
>
> *The Major Case Task Force will be led by Sergeant Richard Bagg who brings a plethora of experience to the job. He will report to Lieutenant Noah Spine in the renamed Narcotics/Major Case Section of SID.*

I could have puked. Bagg brought a plethora of bullshit everywhere he went and that's it.

The last half of the email was even worse, though.

> *To staff this new unit, we are looking for a group of self-motivated, intelligent, team-oriented, articulate, and virtuous guardians who will bring their positive attitude and invest their time, talent, and training to this assignment.*
>
> *Participation in the MCTF will require significant commitment and discipline as you will be expected to be available 24/7/365. All team members will be chosen by the MCTF chain of command based on a variety of attributes to include experience, training, attitude, discipline, and potential. If you are interested in being considered for this assignment, please send a one-page letter detailing why you would like to be chosen attached to your resume of two pages or less, to Lt. Noah Spine by Friday, July 31, 2015.*

My jaw dropped. They were opening the team up for the entire department to apply for positions, which meant Sgt. Bagg was going to have his pick to create the new team. They were picking the team from scratch, and everyone was required to apply, including me, Collins, Diesel, and Titus. Our set positions on the 20th meant nothing.

Within a few minutes of reading the email, Collins appeared in our office and sat down. He closed the door behind him.

"I'm fucking done," he said.

I tried to joke, "So, you're not going to apply for the job you should be guaranteed?"

He snorted. "This is exactly why I always worked towards getting on the 20th. These kinds of games are so petty. We shouldn't have to compete for the job we're already doing and qualified to keep."

Titus said, "Seriously. Especially since you have years of experience."

I added, "Even though we only have a year of experience, we've already proven we can not only handle the job but do a really fucking good job."

"Yeah," Collins said, "we shouldn't have to prove ourselves to these assholes. Our work shows our dedication and investment. I'm already sick of this, and it's only been two weeks of walking on eggshells around the office. It's just a sign of what's to come, and I'm not sticking around for it."

"What are you going to do?" I asked.

"I actually know of a job that just came open for a school resource officer. I know someone at the school who's already recommending me for it. I just have to apply and would have a good chance at it."

I said, "Dude, that's exactly what you wanted, so that's awesome. You've always been like a teacher here, so I think you'd be a good fit."

"I thought so, too. I mean, I wouldn't be leaving for something like that if the team was still together and normal, but it might be a nice change."

Titus mumbled to himself, "Another one down."

We three sat in the silence that followed. We'd talked a lot about the team slowly disintegrating and a long time back had even joked that it was like we were being picked off one-by-one and soon no one would be left.

Collins finally said, "I'm going to miss this work and you guys and writing thousands of wiretaps for your insane cases, Bobby . . ."

We laughed, and he continued, "But, I'll be honest, I'm not sorry to leave. Not now."

"No, I don't blame you," Titus said and smiled. "Do what you have to do. I hope you get it."

Collins nodded. "Thanks." He then set his hands on his knees and said, "Well, off to polish my resume. See you kids later." He got up and headed back to his office.

Titus and I looked at each other and he gestured to the email. "So, are you going to apply?"

I nodded slowly. "I love dope work and complex cases. I don't want to go anywhere."

He agreed. We spent the next hour cleaning up our resumes and writing our application letter. Despite my attitude and fears about Sgt. Bagg picking the team, I was probably one of the first ones to put in for a position. I shared my resume and application with Titus and Diesel, the only other two left of the 20th. They both wanted help on how to curate their own applications, but I wasn't worried about them at all. They were both shoe-ins for the open positions. My fate was the only one up in the air because of my history with Bagg.

A week later, Collins was gone. Three of us left of our original team.

Lieutenant Spine emailed us around the same time and told us to email him a detailed list of our open cases and start working on closing them out. He wanted us to start documenting what we did with every moment of every day in a report to Melissa. She would keep a log of how quickly cases were being wrapped up and report back to him and Bagg. It was like being babysat and monitored.

The end of his email read:

> *Gentlemen, to ensure that we are going to be able to transition smoothly I need some current information about the open cases. Please send me an updated list of your open cases (by close of business Wednesday is fine). Please coordinate with each other so three of you do not send me the same cases. Also put in your plan of action to complete the case and what actions need to be taken such as search warrants, seizures or arrests. If you think any of your open cases would be better to pass off to another agency that could go up on a wire, please let me know that. The goal is to close up what we can or pass off to another group. I do not anticipate anyone having time to open*

a new case or start a new project. However, if this arises please advise me or Sgt. Bagg before embarking on the project.

Also, each night before you leave, send Ms. Melissa Street a detailed narrative providing proactive actions taken during the shift and what cases it involved.

I spent the next day drafting and revising an email reply to Lieutenant Spine. Since I had applied for a position with the new team, I wanted to be prompt with my compliance. I had to do everything in my power to get a chance to stay on my cases. I sent off the following email to him on July 22nd:

Currently I am actively working on two separate cases; TF-1417 and TF-1512.

TF-1417 is a marijuana case where the target is shipping hundreds of pounds of high-grade marijuana from California to Nashville, TN through the mail. I have been working on this case since 2013. We have identified one source in CA as well as many co-conspirators in Nashville. I have a CI that is "in" with the target(s) and is continuing to provide information. My plan of action would either be: pass the case to another agency so that they can complete the case or settle with just getting the target here in Nashville by intercepting a parcel and arresting the target. If we go that route, then I will need to do several search warrants on his houses and storage units.

TF-1512 is a cocaine case where the target is a Hispanic drug trafficking organization and is distributing kilograms of cocaine in the greater Nashville area. This case I have been working since early 2015, and this is the case that I have focused most of my time on. I have a CI that is "in" with one of the targets and is continuing to provide information. My plan of action would be to pass the case to another agency. I will try to gather as much information that I can in the next month on this case so it is prepped for someone else to take over. But if I see a great opportunity to prevent large amounts of cocaine hitting the streets of Nashville then I will coordinate with my chain of command for the execution. I definitely believe this is a great case for a wire intercept. Currently I have identified more than 40 participants in this case along with 25 locations (including ones in Texas). I would love to see that this case is completed to the fullest of our abilities.

These two cases have been my main focus since the last wire case. I am still dealing with seizure hearings, bond motions, gathering evidence, etc. in that case (TF-1422).

Let me know if you need any other information.

- Bobby Young

It hurt my soul to have to write those two paragraphs for Lt. Spine. I didn't want to settle or pass my fucking cases off because I had worked so damn hard on them, and I wanted to make sure he knew they were important. But, I had the gut feeling they were just going to be taken from me. It was becoming more and more clear this was not the task force I'd known.

As time passed and I wasn't hearing back on my application, I started feeling desperate. I talked to my dad daily as usual and one day asked him, "I mean, should I be groveling more? Should I be kissing Bagg's ring and schmoozing him every chance I get?"

"Is that what you want?"

"Hell no. The thought of it makes me want to punch shit. He disgusts me and I don't know if anything would change that."

Dad said, "I think you have your answer then. Besides, even if you did grovel, it would only make you feel like shit. It might not change anything and then you'll be left without even a shred of pride."

He was right.

"You're already swallowing your pride by applying to this new team even though you should be grandfathered in. If you started playing Bagg's game now, you'd hate yourself."

"But, I might have a better chance at keeping the job."

"Would you, though?" He asked.

I thought about it. "Shit. Probably not."

"And is it worth hating yourself?"

"No."

"Well, there you go. Fuck 'em."

I laughed. Dad certainly had a way with words.

No matter what I did to try and make it right, I knew I had no control over whether Sgt. Bagg would pick me for the team. I just had to wait and see. I just had to believe my application, my work experience, and the fact that I had started and led the biggest case and seizure in the history of Nashville would speak for itself.

47

Weeks went by. Sgt. Bagg had moved back to the SID building at the end of July because I think he got the feeling he wasn't wanted at the Batcave, which was true. It made things easier not having him around the office. Even my eye twitch, which had returned with Bagg's presence in the office, had almost completely gone away again.

We had less and less to do at the office, though, as our cases got closed out or moved to other departments. We couldn't start anything new, so we felt stagnant and unmotivated. I still had one case left that I was still making progress on. It hadn't been transferred to anyone else, and it was way too big to just close it. I hated feeling like I was wasting time when I ran out of immediate work to do on the case, but there just wasn't enough to keep me busy.

So, I took off earlier some days and bought tickets to a few of Nashville's minor league baseball games. Sitting and watching a game was such a luxury compared to the previous summer when I hadn't had time to go to even one of them. The old stadium had closed the previous year, too, so I had missed the last games in the stadium I'd gone to through my whole childhood. The new stadium was really nice, though, and I still loved having a beer and watching the games even though our team wasn't high-ranking. It reminded me of when I played baseball year-round as a kid and it made me nostalgic and happy.

I invited Diesel to come with me to an early Thursday night game to have a couple beers and decompress. The previous night had been rained out, so it was a double-header against Albuquerque starting at 6 pm. Like every game I went to, I got third base side tickets as a nod to Chipper Jones. We enjoyed a beer before the game began and watched the field get prepped. There was already a crowd at the sports bar on the other side of the stadium, and families were already staking claims in the grassy section with blankets.

He asked after my dad and sister Ashley, joking that if I started feeling emotional I didn't have to share. I laughed and gave him a brief update on Dad's treatment schedule and the possible experimental treatment for Ashley's ALS.

"There's no guarantee it will work, but we have to try something. It's expensive as hell, so my oldest sister Angela is looking into organizing a fundraiser with our church. She's taking the lead on it, but my mom and dad are both helping out a lot. I think it's a good distraction from his cancer in a way."

Diesel nodded. "Being distracted isn't always a bad thing. It's good your family is sticking together through all this. That's important."

My phone buzzed in my pocket and I reached for it saying, "Yeah. Family's the most important thing in life."

Diesel was also reaching for his phone as he nodded, and it felt normal because our team all had alerts set for case details. But, we didn't really have any active cases to send us updates, and I felt my body tense up as I read the subject line of an email from Sgt. Bagg: *Re: Major Case Task Force.*

Diesel and I read the email silently at the same time.

> *Applicants,*
>
> *Thank you for expressing an interest in the newly formed Major Case Task Force. The selection process has been completed and the names are listed below. For those of you who were not selected, thank you very much for your interest and please keep in mind that this is a task force so there will be a rotation. I hope many of you will reapply in the future. There were many outstanding resumes, however we were limited to six detective positions. Lt. Spine and I appreciate your interest in the unit and the time and effort you put forth.*
>
> *I appreciate your professionalism and dedication.*

Stay safe,

Sgt. Richard Bagg

I didn't even hesitate as I scrolled down to the list. I knew in my gut what I'd see, but there was still a tiny ounce of hope left in me. It drained out as I read the names.

1. Anthony Diesel
2. Reed Walters
3. Titus Price
4. Grissom Muze
5. Morgan Terry
6. Torres Gonzalez

I looked back up to the stadium. Everything went quiet. My worst fear had just come true. I'd lost my dream job.

I suddenly had a flashback to a moment I had not thought about in years. I played baseball all through my childhood and had been on a travel team for ten years. On my sixteenth birthday, I went to the summer tryouts like usual. Even though I'd missed the previous school year's baseball tryouts and was a little out of practice, I hit every ball that came to me all the way to the fence.

After each hit, I looked towards the coach, the father of a popular classmate of mine who had never coached the travel team before. The coach was never watching when I hit the ball. I was the only one batting, but it was like the coach was intentionally looking away and distracted while I was hitting doubles one right after another. I kept hitting until it was time to rotate to a new position, and I still had not had one glance from the coach. The next kid was his son, though, and suddenly the batter was the coach's number one priority. I stood at first base, dumbfounded. I tried to give every position my all, but the coach didn't give me the time of day.

I tried to shrug it off because I knew I'd done a great job. I'd been picked every year for the past ten years, and, hell, it was my freaking sixteenth birthday.

A couple hours later, the coach taped up a piece of paper with the list of names. We rushed the list and I heard kids cheer who hadn't done well in the tryouts but who were friends with the coach's son.

I reread the list maybe three times before I realized my name just wasn't on there. A lot of my friends hadn't made the team either, even though they'd been playing just as long as I had. We weren't picked because we weren't friends with the coach's son.

It was the first time I'd been faced with unfair politics, and it really affected my love of the game. Ashley drove me home and tried to console me, but even my birthday cake that night didn't taste as good. Because the team was picked based on politics, they did terribly that season. The coach's son's friends stopped showing up to play, so my friends would go to the games and hope the coach would call them up from the bleachers to step in. I never went to a game, and I basically gave up baseball. It didn't feel right anymore.

Here I was, fifteen years later, not getting picked for a team because of politics yet again. I now had to figure out where I stood: Was I going to give up my dream job of drug busting like I'd given up on my baseball dream? That wasn't a question I could answer right away.

Diesel had been silent as I processed the email. I turned to him to congratulate him for getting a spot on the team.

He half-smiled and said, "Thanks, but you not getting a spot is bullshit, especially when me and Titus both did. You have more experience than anyone who was picked!"

"Clearly that doesn't matter."

I leaned back in my seat and took a long pull of my beer. The field crew were finishing with last-minute touches on the diamond and I could see our players start to congregate in the box on the first base side. The stands were filling up quicker now and music was playing.

The only remaining members of the 20th had gotten picked, but not me. This was intentional. This was an act specifically against me, and I knew it was Sgt. Bagg behind it. Not only was I responsible for the case that led to the 20th being disbanded and my coworkers getting punished, demoted, or leaving law enforcement altogether, but I was responsible for my own fate of losing my job. From the beginning, I had picked the route that left me on Sgt. Bagg's shit list. There was no other explanation and it was now clear as day.

Through all the bullshit I'd dealt with in my career thus far, I'd never been so pissed. I wanted to go to the Batcave and refuse to ever leave it. I wanted to punch walls and pick a fight with Korbin for twisting words and punishing my friends. I wanted to yell and stomp and roundhouse kick Sgt. Bagg in the face.

As I took another drink, I closed my eyes and tried to stop myself from spiraling into blind rage. I wanted to talk to my dad because he would yell and stomp along beside me, but he would also give me advice that would make me feel better and calm me down. He would say I wasn't responsible for any of this. The leak had planted the seed, and higher-ups had manipulated the situation to spin out of control. He would tell me the whole thing was bullshit but knowing that wouldn't change the reality of the situation. I wanted reality to be different than it was, but there was nothing I could do about anything at the moment. My team was gone. My job was gone. That's all there was to it.

I opened my eyes and said, "Diesel, for the first time in a year I'm just going to turn my brain off for a night. No work, no stress, no ranting about the unfair political bullshit and the whole dumbass system. Let's just watch and talk about baseball."

He nodded. "Okay. Sounds good, dude."

Our team lost the first game 0–6 and the second game started just before 9 pm. We'd had a dinner of nachos and a hotdog each and a couple more beers. We decided to stick it out until the second game ended at 11 pm and we won 3–2. We headed to our cars on a good note.

The next day, I updated my dad on the way to the office. Because I had suppressed the anger the night before, I listened to him rage and then smiled when he gave me the advice I expected. I thanked him for his support and help as I pulled into the office and wondered how many more times I would get to walk into the Batcave.

I got a call from my friend Grissom Muze in the late morning. He was a good narcotics detective, and I wasn't surprised he'd been selected for the new Major Case Task Force, so I genuinely congratulated him on making the team.

He said, "Thanks, man. How are you doing?"

"I'm just trying to wrap up some cases. Figure out what's next I guess."

"Well, that's actually what I'm calling you about. I just wanted you to know that Sgt. Bagg and Lt. Spine just pulled me into a closed-door meeting about something."

"Yeah?" I asked. "Everything okay?"

"Well, they told me to start working on that big case you still have."

"Do what?"

"They told me to take that Hispanic case you have been working on, but they also said not to tell you yet. They just want me to work on it and get information on it. I don't know anything about the case, but I wanted to give you a head's up about it since we're friends."

Those motherfuckers, I thought to myself. I gritted my teeth and tried to answer casually. "Well, I appreciate you letting me know. Since Sgt. Bagg didn't pick me for the new unit, it makes sense that he wants you to start with this case. You can have it; I don't care. I appreciate you calling me about it."

"No problem, man."

I hung up and sprinted to my car. All the anger I had buried deep the night before in an attempt to accept the loss of my dream job boiled up to the surface. First, Sgt. Bagg didn't pick me for the team. Now, he was poaching my last case off me, the only thing I had left of my job, without even telling me. It was the last straw. I felt I had nothing left to lose and I was going to confront those assholes.

I drove 90 mph to the SID office. Before I stormed into the building, I turned a recorder on and put it in my pocket. I'd learned that recording conversations was the only thing that could save a person after what Thomas had gone through.

When I entered the SID kitchen, it smelled like old food mixed with the faint smell of marijuana from the attached property office as usual. In the hallway, Sgt. Bagg was standing at the copier, and I said, "Sgt. Bagg, I need to talk to you right now."

Before he could answer, I had already passed him and went directly to Lt. Spine's office.

His door was open and I said, "I want to talk to you and Sgt. Bagg."

Lt. Spine looked up from a steaming frozen dinner and said, "Okay. I'm trying to eat lunch but go ahead."

Sgt. Bagg came in and shut the door behind him.

"Look," I said when they were both standing by the desk, "I know you all didn't pick me for the new unit, which is fine. I just want to know what you want me to do the next couple weeks, and I want to know where I am going." I wanted to hear it from them directly instead of any more passive aggressive emails and notifications. I needed them to stop hiding the truth from me.

Lt. Spine said, "I don't know where you are going, but you are a hard worker so I am sure you will end up on a flex team or CSU team soon."

I fumed at the word "soon." This was code for *But first, you're going back to patrol*. I wasn't surprised because I hadn't had time to apply for any other special team's openings while I was waiting on the MCTF list, but it pissed me off that Spine couldn't even be straight about this.

Sgt. Bagg looked at me with pity and said, "You know, I once was approached and told I was going back to patrol the next week."

I turned on him. I wanted to yell in his face that I didn't want to hear another of his dumb fucking stories about his glory days or how he clawed his way to the top by stepping on people. I definitely didn't want to hear him pity me because he was who had put me in this position.

I forced myself to remain as calm as possible and snapped at Bagg, "Can we just bury the hatchet? Seriously. All the back and forth over the last couple years, it's stupid. I am willing to bury the hatchet."

Sgt. Bagg looked smug. He said, "You're the hardest worker I know, Bobby." He said nothing more. The comment was a total cop-out. He had been trying to get me fired for years, and he was basically saying he was not willing to bury the hatchet. I felt my face grow hot with anger at his two-faced bullshit.

Before I could answer, Lt. Spine said. "It's just not your time. I'm sure there will be openings on the Major Case Task Force soon and you can gladly apply for it again."

Not my *time*? Gladly apply *again*? What the actual fuck? Did they think I was a complete moron who would believe this bullshit? If it wasn't my "time" then why had I been selected for the most elite drug unit that they had just made disappear? If it wasn't my "time" then how the fuck did I just wrap up the biggest cocaine case in Nashville's history? I was more than capable and qualified. I felt sick at his words. I was supposed to "apply again" only to have Sgt. Bagg smirk at me with pity when he denies me again based on some new bullshit? Were they fucking kidding? Was this real?

I felt drained. I had come to ask one thing, so I asked it slowly, "What do you want me to do with this last case I got open? You want me to pass it off to someone?"

Lt. Spine said, "Nope. Just keep plugging away on it, and we will make a decision later on."

I had given them the opportunity to be honest about *one thing*. This was when they could be decent supervisors and tell me the truth that they wanted me to go ahead and hand the case over to Detective Muze. I just wanted the truth. After not being picked for the MCTF, I deserved to have the truth about the situation. I could accept my fate if they were direct and honest about it. But, they couldn't even do that small thing for me.

They looked at me, waiting for me to ask something else.

The drained feeling grew. There was no point to this meeting anymore. They were always going to be playing their games, treating those of lower rank like disposable pawns they didn't have to respect. If I didn't just swallow it and get over it, I knew I'd do something to land myself on the green mile. They had the power to move me and change my job at any moment they wanted. They had won.

If I have to take it down myself, I will, and I'll make sure you go down with it.

Sgt. Bagg had fucking won.

I said without energy, "Diesel and I have been hitting the case pretty hard."

"Well, keep at it," Lt. Spine said with a forced smile. "I'll be in touch soon with more information about your future appointment."

I nodded.

"Is there anything else, Bobby?" Sgt. Bagg asked.

I glanced at him. I hated hearing him say my name like that. I shook my head once and headed for the door. I knew I would have to submit to them in order to maintain my job in the future, but in this one moment, it felt good to leave without giving the chain of command their due respect. I didn't even wait to be verbally dismissed. I shut the door behind me and left the building, carrying the dead weight of the 20th Judicial District Drug Task Force on my shoulders.

48

I spent the next week in a daze. I talked to Dad daily and he tried to encourage me to keep my chin up and motivate me to fight back for what I wanted. Just as Lt. Spine promised, he called me a week after my meeting with him and told me to list my top three choices of precincts to return to for patrol duty. I thanked him and held in my anger. I wanted to respond, "Gosh, that's so goddamn sweet of you to give me a choice on where I want to start my whole fucking career over!"

Thankfully, I knew going into the call that this "choice" was rigged. A friendly little birdie had reached out the day before to tell me to put my first choice as my last choice when Lt. Spine called. They said the department would purposely place me at my third choice. After so many months of things going wrong, I was grateful to be reminded I had friends throughout the department now who were looking out for me. I was no longer a new guy going to patrol. I had years of experience and loads of connections to people who supported me because I had done the same for them. Hopefully I wouldn't be on patrol for too long.

I put East A detail patrol as my third choice, and a couple days later I got the official notification that I would be transferred to East A on September 1st. A small win in my book, but I still rolled my eyes at the pettiness.

A few days before the end of August, I walked into the office to Titus packing up his desk.

"It's today, huh?"

He looked up almost sheepishly and nodded. "Yeah. Got the notice to move back to the SID building today."

I slumped into my chair and watched as he organized his box of personal items. "Diesel packing up, too?"

"Just finished," I heard over my shoulder. I turned and smiled at Diesel standing in the doorway.

I said, "Well, you're just running out of here, aren't you?"

Diesel grinned and set his box on Thomas' old desk. He sat in the chair beside the door and said, "It is what it is, man."

"I know." I said with a sigh and looked back at Titus.

Titus sat in his chair and said, "You sure you don't hate us?"

I snorted. "There's no reason to hate you. You got picked for the team and I didn't. Shit, I don't even envy you really. You're who's going to have to deal with Bagg day in and day out." I shivered, which made them laugh.

Diesel asked, "So, we're still cool then? We can still hit up some baseball games?"

"Hell yes. You two can't get rid of me that easily. Besides, I'll work my way up the ladder again."

Titus said, "Shit, Hughes was only on patrol for a week before moving up again. You could be moved out of there before even showing up for duty."

I laughed and said, "We'll see. I don't plan on being in uniform for long, that's for sure."

Titus eyed me and said, "You still fit in your uniform, Mr. Uncrustables?"

I spun in my chair, grabbed a rubber band, and shot it at him before he could stand up and fully protect himself. For the next fifteen minutes, we had one last rubber band war throughout the office. Melissa gave us the stink eye and didn't join in, but she also smiled at the game. She was also heading to the SID building and was packing up her desk. Our Alfred Pennyworth was leaving, too. A Bat-team couldn't exist without its Alfred. It was official.

By 10 am the building was eerily silent. I didn't have work to do, so I took a long lunch and walked around the mall, talking to my dad. I spent my last days cleaning off my desk, organizing all my files, and backing up all my casework. I didn't know what would happen to the 20ths' records now that it no longer existed, so I made sure to keep a copy of everything I'd done with the team for my own records. They could wipe out the 20th, but I would make sure its memory and the success of case TF-1422 would live on.

On the last day of August, as I put my desk chair and Chipper Jones jersey into my car, I looked to the side of the Batcave building at the view of downtown Nashville. For over a year I had looked at the skyline as I came and went from the office, and I felt like a completely different person on this day.

The case I had brought to the 20th locked up sixty-seven people on drug conspiracy charges and brought in millions of dollars' worth of seized cash, drugs, and assets from large-scale drug dealers. Once the properties and cars were sold at auction, the amount could even double. I wondered what would happen to all that money. Even before Director Davis left, he confided in me that he had no idea what would happen to the 20th's bank account when the team realigned to the police department. If the director of the team, who was on the board of directors with Chief Smalls and DA Ball, didn't know where the money was going, how was that not shady as hell? Would Chief Smalls and the police department gain control of the money? Would it stay with DA Ball? Would they split it in half?

None of these options were going to be made public, though. The money seized from the 20th's cases were supposed to be used exclusively for overtime hours, drug investigations, drug prosecution, drug rehabilitation, and the 20th's equipment, according to law. But if the 20th was no longer in existence and had basically disappeared in the transition, where did its millions of dollars go? Whose pockets was that money now lining?

I shook my head and started up my car. The Batcave was dark as I drove out of the lot. Our dedicated, hardworking Bat-team had been broken up and tossed around the city over the previous few months. I was the last one standing of such a badass dream team of detectives, and I still felt guilty about how things had turned out.

All of our hard work had left a mark on the city's drug activities, but the city had left its mark on us. The Major Case Task Force would never be able to do the scale of cases the 20th had done. They didn't have the ability to do multiple wiretaps and would have to contract out for wire assistance for big cases. The system was going to be both inefficient and insufficient for dealing with complicated drug rings. They would perform like SID and pick off mules and daily dealers, but the top tiers would never get touched. The city-wide and state-wide trafficking and subsequent crime would never actually be affected. The MCTF could never be like the 20th.

As I drove the now familiar route back home for the last time, I picked up my phone and dialed my dad.

SEPTEMBER 2015

EPILOGUE

I woke up on September 3, 2015 at 5:30 am as usual. I'd just come off of my new scheduled "weekend" of having Tuesdays and Wednesdays off, and I went to the closet to pull out my recently washed and no-longer-dusty uniform. I looked in the mirror and saw myself at the beginning of my career seven years prior. I was back in the patrolman's uniform, but I had years of experience under my belt including a multi-million dollar case with a team that had somehow vanished into thin air.

TF-1422 and my time with the 20th Judicial District Drug Task Force taught me a lot about people, both those I worked with and the criminals we tracked. I was young and felt that I had made it to the top. There was no better unit in my mind than the 20th. My hard work and dedication got me to that point, and that mattered to me, my wife, my family, and my teammates. I always said I would rather have a bunch of friends than some chintzy awards for cases, and I'd ended my time with the 20th with loads of friends, no awards, and a couple enemies.

Although I was only a part of the 20th for its last year in existence, it was one of the best times of my life. I never imagined that a small team of hardworking guys could turn one ounce of cocaine into a record seizure worth more than three million dollars. I was presented with many obstacles during that time, and I figured out how to jump over each one with the support of my team and family.

Politics was the only thing stopping me in my tracks. Regardless of our record-breaking work, the 28-year-old unit dissolved quietly with hardly any media coverage or questioning. If I didn't know better, I'd believe someone was trying to hide the fact that we existed at all.

My experience taught me that money is an evil tool, and a man is only as good as his word. For some, this line of work is just a power game: a chess match to see who can end up king. Some play the game fairly through hard work, and some take what they can get, even if it means stepping on people along the way. My friends and teammates were honest detectives, but we were all negatively affected by a few bad apples. In addition, the DA and Chief were two people that couldn't get along, and their fighting over power and money took a toll on our team and the entire city.

All the hard work, the late nights, going undercover, the wiretaps . . . that life was officially over for me because of outside politics. I would never walk into the Batcave ever again. I would never be a part of the same dream team. Inexplicably, I was starting back at the bottom of the barrel, but I was determined not to be there for long.

I wasn't ready to leave the police force, yet, so I resolved to get back to SID as soon as possible to continue working drug cases. No, there was probably no chance at getting on to Bagg's elite Major Case Task Force, and I wasn't going to play his petty games to get there. But, I knew that hard work and solid stats still spoke for themselves in some areas of the department. I'd quietly take the punishment of doing time on patrol, but I would come back with renewed energy to tackle bigger and more complicated cases at SID. My stats and irrefutable hard work would put Sgt. Bagg's game and the MCTF's efforts to shame. Bagg was going to regret making me pay when I made his pride pay double in return.

My new shift with the East A unit meant an early start: a 6 am departure. Before leaving the house on my first day, I kissed my sleeping wife and slung my clean Chipper Jones jersey over my shoulder. I wouldn't need it for work anymore, but, just like my chair, I had to bring it with me.

I walked out of my garage, polyester uniform and all, and stumbled to my truck in the early dawn light. As I drove down interstate 40, the same interstate used by so many of the drug traffickers I used to investigate, I blinked at the bright sunrise ahead of me. It felt like a sign that I was ready to tackle whatever came next, and my mind was quiet with resolve. I passed the Titans stadium and over the Cumberland River, and just before I pulled in to the police station my phone buzzed.

Dad texted me, "Keep your head up, son. I love you and we are so proud of you."

I nodded and took a deep breath before walking to the building. The 20th was officially behind me, but it lived on in my resolve for revenge. The political game had gotten personal, and I wasn't going to sit back and let the bullshit stop me anymore. I was just getting started.

APPENDIX

Book Key and Additional Terms

20th: The 20th Judicial District Drug Task Force.

4 and a baby: Four and a half ounces or 126 grams.

4 and a half: Four and a half ounces or 126 grams.

4 way: Four ounces or 112 grams.

A-1: Drugs of great quality.

ATF: Bureau of Alcohol, Tobacco, Firearms and Explosives.

Bands: Money, referred to in $1,000 increments.

Bird: A kilogram.

Bread: Money.

Car: A kilogram.

CBP: US Customs and Border Protection.

Cheddar: Money.

Chips: Money.

CI: Confidential Informant or Citizen Informant.

Coke: Cocaine.

CS: Confidential Source.

CSU: Crime Suppression Unit.

DEA: Drug Enforcement Administration.

DHS: Department of Homeland Security.

Diamonds: High quality of cocaine.

Dime: A small amount of drugs, typically $10 worth or could be used for anything with a "ten," such as $10,000 or 10 kilos.

DOD: Department of Defense.

Dope: Drugs.

Dope Phone: Also known as a throw-down phone; a temporary, inexpensive phone drug dealers or criminals utilize to deter detection by law enforcement. After being used for a short time, dealers will throw away the phone and change their phone number to try and stay under the radar.

FBI: Federal Bureau of Investigations.

Flex: A proactive police unit that focuses on enforcement.

Foreman Grille: A small electronic appliance, white in color, used to cook food. The color matches that of cocaine.

Glass: Crystal Methamphetamine or a reference to the good quality of cocaine.

Green: Money or marijuana.

Heat Run: A maneuver utilized by criminals to check for a tail or to see if they are being followed.

Hit: Diluting a narcotic to increase its weight, which makes it less potent.

HSI: Homeland Security Investigations.

ICE: U.S. Immigration and Customs Enforcement.

Juice: One ounce or 28 grams.

Key: A kilogram or 2.2 pounds.

Kilo: A kilogram or 2.2 pounds.

Kilo Press: A hydraulic press machine used for bricking cocaine.

Machine: Money counter.

Moons: Oxymorphone tablets or pills.

Nina: Nine ounces or 252 grams or a "quarter-key."

Nine: Nine ounces or 252 grams or a "quarter-key."

Off: Arrested.

Pandas: Oxymorphone tablets or pills.

Pans: Oxymorphone tablets or pills.

Panties: Packaging or wrappings around the drugs.

Ping: A GPS notification where a specific cell phone is located.

Plug: Source of supply or the person distributing drugs.

PO: Probation or Parole Officer.

Ram: A battering ram, used to force a door open during the execution of a search warrant.

Re-rock: The process of turning a kilogram into additional kilograms.

SOD: Special Operations Division.

SOP: Standard Operating Procedures.

SOS: Source of supply.

Stacks: Money, referred to in $1,000 increments.

Stepped On: Diluting a narcotic to increase its weight, which makes it less potent.

TBI: Tennessee Bureau of Investigation.

TFO: Task Force Officer.

Title III: Title III of the Omnibus Crime Control and Safe Street Act of 1968 (Wiretap Act).

Trap: Hidden Compartment.

Trap House: A temporary location utilized by drug dealers and users.

Trey-Six-Five: $36,500; the going street price for one kilogram of cocaine in Nashville, TN in 2014.

Two: Can reference two ounces or two kilograms. It depends on the level of dealer or user that is using the terminology.

USPIS: United States Postal Inspection Service.

Weed: Marijuana.

Whisper Stop: a traffic stop conducted by a uniformed officer who has been given a tip-off from another officer as to illegal activity in the vehicle.

Whole One: A kilogram.

Windows: Crystal Methamphetamine.

Wire Room: A secured, heavily controlled facility where electronic intercepts are conducted by law enforcement. The room contains computers and the necessary equipment to effectively wiretap a target's phone.

Wop: money.

Work: Meaning that you have narcotics available to sell.

Zip: One ounce or 28 grams.

Article Citations

1. "Cocaine Distribution Network Dismantled: 19 Persons Arrested." 12.10.2014. Nashville Government website. https://www.nashville.gov/News-Media/News-Article/ID/3557/Cocaine-Distribution-Network-Dismantled-19-Persons-Arrested
2. "MNPD Detectives Assigned to Drug Task Force Target Major Cocaine Organization" 3.20.2015. Nashville Government website. https://www.nashville.gov/News-Media/News-Article/ID/3859/MNPD-Detectives-Assigned-to-Drug-Task-Force-Target-Major-Cocaine-Organization.aspx
3. Quinones, Alex J. "Drug Task Force Now Under Metro Police." 5.22.2015. Fox 17 Nashville. https://fox17.com/news/local/drug-task-force-now-under-metro-police

Made in the USA
Columbia, SC
25 November 2024